KU-710-514

RAPE

The Misunderstood Crime

JULIE A. ALLISON
LAWRENCE S. WRIGHTSMAN

UNIVERSITY OF WINCHESTER
LIBRARY

SAGE Publications
International Educational and Professional Publisher
Newbury Park   London   New Delhi

Copyright © 1993 by Sage Publications, Inc.

All rights reserved. No part of this book may be reproduced or utilized in any form or by any means, electronic or mechanical, including photocopying, recording, or by any information storage and retrieval system, without permission in writing from the publisher.

For information address:

SAGE Publications, Inc.
2455 Teller Road
Newbury Park, California 91320
E-mail: order@sagepub.com

SAGE Publications Ltd.
6 Bonhill Street
London EC2A 4PU
United Kingdom

SAGE Publications India Pvt. Ltd.
M-32 Market
Greater Kailash I
New Delhi 110 048 India

UNIVERSITY OF WINCHESTER

Printed in the United States of America

Library of Congress Cataloging-in-Publication Data

Allison, Julie A.
  Rape : The misunderstood crime / Julie A. Allison, Lawrence S.
Wrightsman.
    p. cm.
  Includes bibliographical references and index.
  ISBN 0-8039-3706-7. — ISBN 0-8039-3707-5 (pbk.)
  1. Rape—United States. 2. Rape victims—United States.
I. Wrightsman, Lawrence S. II. Title.
HV6561.A48 1993
364.1′532′0973—dc20   93-14800

99 00 01 02 10 9 8 7 6

Contents

Preface

The 1990s promise to be interesting. The decade began with William Kennedy Smith, Mike Tyson, and Clarence Thomas. Each of these men was accused of violating the personal rights of another human being; a female human being. Smith was tried and acquitted; Tyson was tried and convicted; Thomas was not tried in a legal courtroom, but tried nonetheless, and apparently vindicated. Each of these individuals was to some extent a public figure; each of their alleged victims became a public figure.

Why is it that when an accusation of rape (or, in Thomas's case, of sexual harassment) is made, the victim becomes the focus of attention? Why is it that only an estimated 2%-5% of all rapists are ever convicted? We believe that this happens because the crime of rape is misunderstood. We also believe that knowledge can be a powerful force in combatting the prevailing myths and misconceptions concerning the crime of rape, and hope that this book will help to provide a more comprehensive understanding.

We wrote this book with a basic understanding: Violence is unacceptable. To the reader this may seem an obvious point. But as we repeatedly argue throughout this book, there is no one type of rape, no one type of rapist, and no one type of rape victim. Yet there does seem to be a prototypical conceptualization of rape in the minds of all of us—that of the madman with a weapon waiting for his victim to arrive. Some rapes are committed by those with mental disorders, but most aren't. Many rapes are committed by strangers, but most aren't. Many rapes involve weapons, but many don't. Nonetheless when one hears about accounts of rape that do not fit this stereotype, they seems somehow to become distorted into something less than rape–less violent, less serious. This book was written to provide a comprehensive understanding of rape from a psychological perspective. It does not focus on any one specific aspect of rape, nor is it driven by any specific theoretical viewpoint. Our goal is to examine the research on the topic of rape and synthesize it for the reader. Our literature search was extensive and, we believe, quite thorough. In addition, we included a variety of different sources: theoretical, empirical, journalistic, anecdotal, and material from individuals we talked with during the course of our writing. Although we believe that our use of resources was comprehensive, we do not claim that this book will provide a complete understanding of the crime of rape because we do not believe that a complete understanding of rape exists at this time. For example, throughout this book we speak of the female victim and the male rapist. The primary reason for this is because the majority of rape victims are female and the majority of rapists are male. Males are raped and females do rape; it is not yet known, however, how many victims of rape are male or how many females rape.

We hope that the 1990s is a decade in which people will better come to understand the reality of rape. There are many indications that this may occur. More and more victims of rape are coming out and telling their stories. The media are paying attention to the problem of rape. Prosecuting attorneys are prosecuting more allegations of rape. And the research on rape continues. However, more and more people are being raped. The media are still selective about which rape stories get the coverage. The conviction rate is still extremely low. And funding is a problem for researchers. We still have a long way to go, but perhaps this book will also serve to bring people one step closer to such an understanding.

Acknowledgments

The origin of this book was a chapter on rape, prepared by the second author for a textbook for psychology-and-law courses. As we expanded and updated the coverage into a book, we benefited from the availability of a number of colleagues at the University of Kansas and at Pittsburg State University. Charlene Muehlenhard has served as a model of a responsible scholar, whose highly productive research program has asked and answered relevant questions about the nature of date rape and influences upon it. Nyla Branscombe has shown us, by her work, that scholarly work and research can help us understand knotty theoretical issues while still answering questions about social problems. David Holmes provided a helpful sounding board when the writing hit obstacles. Through her enthusiasm and her concern for social issues, Cynthia Willis has served as a model colleague.

The faculty members in the Psychology and Counseling Department at Pittsburg State University provided a genuinely supportive environment for this project. David Solly, chair of the department, was always responsive to requests for assistance. David Hurford and Rozanne Sparks were always there to offer heart-warming encouragement and support when things seemed overwhelming. And the genuine concern of Rick Lindskog and Don Ward served as reminders that this endeavor was truly worthwhile.

Of course, any errors and misinterpretations in this book are the responsibility of the authors, and not of our colleagues.

We wish to acknowledge the assistance of Amy Heili and Katia Silva, whose very careful typing of this book helped its production go smoothly. Diane Adams, Dawn Finch, Dawna Finch, J. J. Hight, Adam Murphy, Krista Nelson, and Steven Valasquez each carefully reviewed chapters of this book and provided valuable suggestions.

1 Why Study Rape?

Consider these contemporary facts:

1. A recent United States Department of Justice report stated that the rate of attempted rapes in the United States *decreased* a whopping 46% from 1973 to 1987 (Associated Press, 1991).

2. *People* Magazine, in analyzing its newsstand sales, found that the worst selling issue for a recent year had a cover headline that cried out: "Raped on Campus: A Victim's Anguish" (Donahue, 1991). Similarly, *Newsweek's* worst seller during 1991 had a cover story on rape linked to the William Kennedy Smith trial (Donahue, 1992).

3. A candidate for governor of Texas in 1990, way ahead in the pre-election polls, made intemperate statements such as "Rainy weather is like a woman being raped; if it's inevitable just relax and enjoy it." He was defeated, in a surprising upset.

Each of the above factoids is subject to many interpretations. When they are considered in combination, a naive optimist might employ them to conclude that rape is of lessening concern in our society and that people are finally becoming aware of the magnitude and urgency of the problem. The highly publicized rape trials of William

Kennedy Smith and Mike Tyson seemingly made salient the nature of sexual assault in our society. But we challenge a view that the awareness of rape is at an appropriate level. The theme of this book is that rape remains largely a misunderstood crime. Incorrect information still abounds about the frequency of rape, the characteristics of rapists, and the recovery of survivors. Focus falsely remains on the victim as an instigator of most rapes. Sexual assault is still treated casually by people who should know better; the authors of the National Crime Survey have even observed that, based on their research, "rape is clearly an infrequent crime" (Kalish, 1974, p. 12, quoted by Koss, Gidycz, & Wisniewski, 1987, p. 162), and a *Newsweek* article about the Mike Tyson case suggested that the recent publicity should remind men that date rape is "imprudent."

Recent publicity about rape may—ironically—have had a deleterious effect on rape victims' coming forward. White and Sorenson (1992) cite a newspaper source stating that after the publicity regarding the April 1991 incident in Palm Beach, FL, involving William Kennedy Smith, the number of women in Palm Beach County seeking rape exams decreased by a factor of 10. As they note, "society's response to rape accusations has a direct and immediate impact on many women" (p. 188).

Equally disturbing is that the implicit message, for some, is that rape is an act within acceptable standards. The mayor of Independence, MO, a city of more than 100,000 people, is quoted in a magazine as saying that the only difference between rape and seduction is salesmanship (Campbell, 1990). A jury in Florida failed to convict an accused rapist because the woman was "asking for sex" when she appeared in public in a brief outfit. Four boys were charged with raping a high school student while in the *governor's mansion* of South Dakota (Associated Press, 1990). And the Department of Justice study with which we introduced this chapter failed to find any decrease in the incidence of *completed* rapes from 1973 to 1987, only in *attempted* rapes. (The headline on one of the articles we saw about this survey—"U.S. rapes falling, study says"—reflects society's desire to think positively about the problem of rape.)

Rape is not under control; in fact, 2 months after the publication of the Department of Justice study, the chair of the United States Senate judiciary committee said that rape was at "epidemic proportions" in the United States (quoted in L. Katz, 1991). The most recent figures, for example, report an increase in reported rapes from 1990 to 1991 of 59%.

Hence one task for this book is to review and evaluate the psychological research and knowledge about rapists and rape victims, so that social scientists are fortified as they challenge the prevalent myths and misconceptions about rape. A second goal is to inform students about the ever-increasing knowledge about the crime of rape and its effects on survivors of rape.

Why Is Rape Misunderstood?

What is the basis for our claim that rape is a misunderstood crime? One reason is that the scenario for the act is simplified in the media and hence in the minds of the public. The rapist is usually portrayed as a stranger, his motivation is entirely sexual, and the victim is always female, young, and physically desirable. Granted that the world is complex and at times overwhelming and hence we must all simplify it; yet one task of the social scientist is to remind us of the multiplexity of rape. Not all rapes are by any means alike—in the motivation of the rapist, in the act itself, and in the relationship of the attacker and the victim. Even the age of the rapist may defy expectation; recently an 8-year-old boy was convicted in Illinois of raping a girl a year before; he was tried as an adult and sentenced to a year's probation (Associated Press, 1992a).

First, consider the motivation of the rapist. For decades, rapists were portrayed as sex-starved or insane or both. In contrast, for the last 20 years, experts have emphasized that rape is usually a crime of violence, not passion. It uses the sexual act for its fulfillment, but its instigation—this view emphasizes—frequently is not sexual tension. Most rapists are not sexually deprived; they have other outlets available for their sexual needs. In fact, one survey found that many rapists are married (Melani & Fodaski, 1974).

But even this view is too simplified. Rapes may be committed by persons whom the victim does not know (stranger rapes), by an acquaintance, by a date, or by a spouse. As a result of a decade's scrutiny of date rape, experts (cf. Parrott & Bechhofer, 1991) recognize that the motivation of the date who rapes may be to achieve sexual release, although not all date rapes are similarly motivated (see Chapter 4). And as an indication of the specificity of recent analyses, one psychologist (Shotland, 1989) has argued cogently for making distinctions between men who attempt to rape a woman on their first date and men who try to rape a woman with whom they are in an established relationship (see Chapter 4, Box 4.3).

One goal of this book, then, is to document and illustrate the multiple motivations for rape. Men may rape men, although much more often the object of their attack is female. Rarely, women may rape men. Men may rape for sexual reasons or to express feelings of power, anger, aggression, or sadism (Dean & deBruyn-Kops, 1982). A sexual assault by a stranger—who in fact may or may not be sexually deprived or insane—develops as a result of different motives from those of a drunk college freshman who perceives that his date is consenting to his sexual advances. A husband who forces himself on a nonconsenting—even resisting—wife may encapsulate a complex set of motives. Make no mistake, we consider all of these to be rapes: We believe all of these rapists should be prosecuted and punished. But we argue that the act of rape would be better understood if, at the forefront, everyone recognized the multiple motivations for sexual assault. Chapters 2 through 5 amplify on this important distinction, by first examining similarities but by also allocating separate chapters to different types of rapists and rapes.

Allusion above to date rape or rape by a spouse leads us to other types of frequent misunderstanding—those of the relationship of the rapist to the victim and the nature of the victim. It is true that the Smith and the Tyson trials have recently alerted some of the public to the frequency and perniciousness of acquaintance rape and date rape. With regard to the rape by a man of his wife, the majority of states have recently made spousal rape a crime. But expectations still persist that the victim is inevitably a young woman in her late teens or twenties. Yet, as Russell (1984) notes, females of *any* age, social class, or ethnic group are vulnerable to rape. The National Women's Study survey found that more than 60% of the rape victims said they were first assaulted before they were 18 years old (Pesce & Blais, 1992). In 1989, five New Jersey teenagers, including co-captains of the high-school football team, were charged with sexually assaulting a 17-year-old mentally retarded girl, while eight of their friends looked on (Hanley, 1989). In Dallas a 6-year-old girl was kidnapped from her bed and raped so brutally that she suffered serious internal injuries (Pederson, 1989). In Georgia, a 46-year-old man was charged with raping a 4-year-old girl. While it is true that the high-risk groups are adolescents (ages 13-17) and young adults (ages 18-24), several surveys have discovered that between 10% and 12% of victims are more than 50 years of age (Katz & Mazur, 1979).

Given that the predominant stereotype holds that the rapist is a stranger, it assumes no prior relationship between the two parties. But recent estimates conclude that as many as 85% of victims knew the perpetrator (Warshaw, 1988). Thus the stereotype is wrong. There are many different motivations for rape, many different situations and settings in which it occurs, and many different kinds of rape victims, including men.

The Incidence of Rape

The report of a claimed "decline" in attempted rapes leads to another type of misunderstanding concerning the incidence of rape. The incidence rate for rape is, we grant, very hard to assess but it is almost certainly higher than the public believes it to be. First, some rapes are never reported to the police and hence never become statistics in crime reports. Psychologist Mary Koss and her colleagues (Koss, Gidycz, & Wisniewski, 1987), using results from their own surveys, estimate that the incidence rate of rape is 10 to 15 times higher than the Justice Department statistics (Freiberg, 1990). Some rapes aren't even labeled as such by the victims. Consider, for example, a husband who coerces his wife to have sexual intercourse with him, despite her protests. This act is now considered as rape in the majority of states, but many women believe they have no right to decline their husband's advances. When spousal rape occurs, the likelihood that the wife will report it as such is quite low unless physical abuse is part of the assault. Other victims are reluctant to call the police, especially when raped by a date or acquaintance. (And according to the 1991 Department of Justice survey, among women who were raped in or near their home and reported the attack, 48% said the attacker was someone they knew. Box 1.1 gives further results of the Koss survey that found even a higher percentage of victims who knew their attacker.)

The Failure to Report

This reluctance to report a crime is, of course, in direct contrast to victims' reactions to other major crimes. Whenever an attempted murder or a major robbery or arson occurs, the victim or someone

BOX 1.1

The Scope of Rape

Koss, Gidycz, and Wisniewski (1987) administered the Sexual Experiences Survey to a national sample of 6,159 women and men enrolled in 32 colleges and universities throughout the United States. Although most were single and white, the subjects represented all different religions, ethnic groups, and marital statuses.

Results indicated that since the age of 14, 27.5% of the 3,187 women reported experiencing an act that met the legal definitions of rape. (These included *attempted* rapes.) But only about a quarter of these acknowledged it as rape, and only 5% reported the act to the police. In fact, 42% never revealed their experience to anyone. Only about 1 in 20 sought counseling services. In all, 53.7% of the women revealed being recipients of some form of sexual victimization, including the following:

14.4%: sexual contact
11.9%: sexual coercion
12.1%: attempted rape
15.4%: rape

Almost 4% had been victimized in the 6 months immediately prior to the survey.

else informs the police. We can assume that the incidence rates for these crimes in the crime reports are very close to actuality. For example, in 1989, a total of 1,564,800 motor vehicles were reported stolen in the United States; we can assume that only a very small number of actual car thefts were not reported as such.

To compound the problem, the rate of nonreporting of rapes is a matter of controversy. Feminists have emphasized that only a small minority of rapes come to the attention of the police. Russell's (1984) survey found a report rate of only 9.5%. Koss et al. (in the

BOX 1.1 (Continued)

In the survey, 25% of the 2,972 men admitted involvement in some form of sexual aggression and 7.7% of the men reported perpetrating an act that met the legal definitions of rape or attempted rape. (Almost 1% of the women admitted to such acts.)

Presence of aggression or victimization did not differ as a function of the size of the city where the college or university was located, the type of school, or the extent of minority enrollment. But victimization was more likely at major universities (17%) and private colleges (14%) than at religiously affiliated colleges and universities.

These results are consistent with other surveys:

1. Kanin and his associates (Kanin, 1957; Kanin & Parcell, 1977; Kirkpatrick & Kanin, 1957), who found that 20% to 25% of the college women they surveyed reported at least one forceful attempt to obtain sexual intercourse by a date.

2. Russell's (1984) probability sample of 930 adult women in San Francisco, with 24% reporting forced intercourse.

3. A survey by Kilpatrick, Best, Veronen, Amick, Villeponteaux, and Ruff (1985) via telephone of 2,000 randomly chosen females living in Charleston County, SC, in which 14.5% disclosed one or more sexual assaults.

4. A National Women's Study survey, financed by the National Institute on Drug Abuse, concluded that more than 12 million American women—one in eight—have been raped at least once (Associated Press, 1992b).

survey described in Box 1.1) estimate that only 1 out of every 20 date rapes on campus (or 5%) is reported. In contrast, the 1991 Department of Justice survey claimed that 53% of rapes or attempted rapes are reported to the police (Associated Press, 1991). From 5% to 53%—this is a huge discrepancy in estimates.

Whatever the true report rate is has a bearing, of course, on estimates of actual numbers of attempted or completed rapes. Almost two decades ago, Russell (1975) estimated that when both the unreported and reported rapes and attempted rapes were included, more than 1,500,000 attacks occurred in the United States in one year. The Senate judiciary committee study suggests that currently almost two million rapes may go unreported annually (L. Katz, 1991). Such estimates have led to predictions that between 20% and 30% of females in the United States will experience at least one rape or attempted rape in their lifetime (Ellis, 1989; Koss & Oros, 1982; Muehlenhard & Linton, 1987).

In contrast to the above estimates of literally millions of rapes annually, the Department of Justice survey concluded that 137,509 rapes and attempted rapes occurred in 1987, down from 159,890 rapes 14 years earlier. And the FBI figure, for the year 1985, was even smaller: a total of 87,340 rapes. No wonder rape is a misunderstood crime! (Box 1.2 contains a further discussion of the problems in such estimates.)

How do we evaluate these official crime report figures? Putting aside the false precision of any survey that estimates the number of rapes in a given year down to the last digit, we mention a final problem in trying to quantify the incidence of rape in the United States. That is that the *rate* of reporting—which by all accounts is much less than complete—is doubtless increasing. That is, regardless of whether the number of rapes is getting larger or smaller each year, the percentage of rapes that survivors report to police is increasing. More and more rape victims are, in the words of Maureen Dowd (1983), "refusing to withdraw into a silent scream" (p. 27).

The increase in report rate is a positive development. Yes, reporting their attacks runs risks for survivors—further embarrassment and possible ridicule, at least subtle harassment, and possible retaliation—but it should in the long run aid victims' recovery, as well as reduce the future incidence of rape and increase public awareness. But the accelerating rate of reporting only adds to our futility as we seek to understand the magnitude of rape in the United States. In this regard, rape is a "misunderstood crime" for authorities and public alike, because the reliable data are not there to answer legitimate questions about actual incidence rates.

Another problem is that high rates of rape incidence are discounted by some U.S. citizens, who endorse the myth that many rapes are false reports, created out of an effort to obtain sympathy, protect a self-image, or wreak vengeance. The matter of false rape reports is illustrated in Box 1.3.

BOX 1.2

A Distinction Between Prevalence Rates and Incidence Rates

One reason that rape is truly a misunderstood crime comes from the difficulty in reconciling apparently conflicting "official" reports of the crime's severity. "How often do rapes occur?" would seem to be a simple question to answer, but it is not. Recent surveys have, with regard to the number of rapes in 1990, reported figures anywhere from 130,000 (Justice Department) to 683,000 (National Women's Study survey) (Pesce & Blais, 1992). To provide answers, the National Crime Survey uses incidence rates: here a woman is either a rape victim during the past 6 months or she is not a victim.

Other surveys may use prevalence rates: that is, a longer time frame and the inclusion of a cumulative number of women who have been sexually victimized. Furthermore, the National Crime Survey approach uses a screening question that requires the respondent to infer the focus of inquiry; it uses questions about rape that are embedded in a context of violent crime and assumes women will conceptualize their experience as rape. For example, the initial screening question is: "Were you or anyone in your household knifed, shot at, or attacked with some other weapon by anyone at all during the last six months?" (Bureau of Justice Statistics, 1984). Then: "Did someone try to attack you in some other way?" Only then are questions asked that use the term *rape*.

Why Is the United States So High in Rape Incidence?

Despite the assessment problems described above, experts believe that the United States has the highest incidence rate of forcible rape of any industrialized country. Even when we take into account the inaccuracy from unreported attacks (a problem in all countries), we find that the rate in the United States is 13 times that of England,

BOX 1.3

False Reports of Rape

In the spring of 1985, Americans were momentarily distracted from their usual concerns by the drama of Cathleen Crowell Webb, who recanted her testimony of 6 years before that she had been raped by a man named Gary Dotson. Despite her claims that Dotson was innocent and that no rape had occurred, the judge refused to overturn the conviction or release Mr. Dotson from prison, where he was serving a 25-50 year sentence. (Dotson's sentence was commuted by Governor Thompson of Illinois, permitting him to be released from prison while still leaving his conviction on the books. In 1989 all charges against him were dropped.) What really happened to 16-year-old Cathleen Crowell back on that evening in 1979? We are not sure.

We do know, however, that certain claims of rape are unjustified. More recently—in November 1987—a black 15-year-old named Tawana Brawley was found in a garbage bag with feces smeared on her body and racial epithets scratched in ink in her skin. She told of a Thanksgiving-weekend-long ordeal in which she was taken into the woods near Wappingers Falls, NY, and raped by four white men, one of whom had a police badge. Even though she never filed a complaint with the police, leaders of the New York City black community became zealous supporters of her cause.

For more than half a year, Tawana Brawley's story was accepted by many people, although some remained skeptical and suspicious. In mid-1988, two TV reporters claimed that she was lying (Taibbi & Sims-Phillips, 1989). The grand jury came to disbelieve her story, and after a 7-month investigation, concluded that she fabricated the story and that her condition was almost certainly "self-inflicted." (She had refused to testify before the grand jury.)

A year later Ms. Brawley reportedly told a boyfriend that she hadn't been abducted; instead, she had run away from home to prevent getting beaten by her mother's live-in lover for staying

BOX 1.3 (continued)

out too late (Hennessee, 1989). According to this report, her mother had helped her concoct the story. However, Ms. Brawley denied all of this and still has not told the story in her own words.

But a more recent book by six *New York Times* reporters even accounts for what Tawana Brawley did during the 4 days she was missing; they report that she spent the time in an apartment that her family had recently vacated (McFadden et al., 1990).

So false reports of rape do happen. But how often? Again, the frequency is difficult to assess, but one comprehensive review (Katz & Mazur, 1979) estimates that the false report rate is about 2%, the same for other major crimes.

Two points seem important to us. First, whatever the percentage of reported rapes that *are* false, it is lower than the public's estimate, for several reasons. Cases like Cathleen Crowell Webb's and Tawana Brawley's make news; virtually everybody hears of them. Most actual rapes do not receive anywhere near this much attention in the media. Furthermore, the need to believe that many reports of rape are falsifications is part of a self-protective mechanism operating on persons with the macho personality syndrome, in that it reduces guilt over their exploitation of women.

Our second point is that sometimes false claims can be distinguished from others because of the actions of the purported victim, the lack of physical evidence, or facts and evidence that conflict with a claim that a sexual assault occurred. At the time of the report by Tawana Brawley, reasons existed to be suspicious about the story of abduction and gang rape by white racists. For example, who put the cotton wads in Ms. Brawley's nose so that she would be spared the odor of excrement? As one commentator (Ellen Goodman, 1990) observes, "hardly the sensitive work of an attacker" (p. 7). No evidence of a rape or an assault was found by the examining doctor, and an eyewitness had even seen Ms. Brawley climb into a garbage bag. However, lack of physical evidence, per se, is hardly grounds to conclude that a rape did not take place.

4 times that of West Germany, 5 to 10 times that of France, and 20 times that of Japan (Kutchinski, 1988; Quinsey, 1984; Russell, 1984; Smeal, 1991).

Why is rape so frequent in a country that is looked upon by some as the model for the rest? In order to answer we must first review the anthropological classification of societies. In rape-prone societies, rape is often a ceremonial act, or it is a device by which men threaten or punish women (Sanday, 1981). In such societies violence against women may be allowed, or at least overlooked by law-enforcement officials. Especially in such societies are women devoid of power or any role in decision making.

The predominant style of men in these societies reflects what Mosher and Sirkin (1984) have labeled the "macho personality constellation" or hypermasculinity. Such men have calloused sexual attitudes toward women; they see violence as manly and desirable, and they view danger as exciting. In fact, Reiss (1986) has found that in societies with a high incidence of rape, the macho personality is more likely to be endorsed as the appropriate one for males. Box 1.4 includes some items from the attitude scale designed to measure "hypermasculinity." This will not be our last encounter with this orientation in this book; when we consider the characteristics common to rapists in the United States in Chapter 2, its salience surfaces again.

Clearly an example of a rape-prone society is the Bantu-speaking Gusii tribe, located in southwestern Kenya. LeVine (1959) estimates that the annual rate of rapes is 47.2 or more per 100,000 population. (The rate in the United States, depending on the estimate, varies from 14 to 30 per 100,000.) A Gusii proverb is "those whom we marry are those whom we fight" (Brownmiller, 1975, p. 7). In the Gusii society it is considered quite normal for sexual intercourse to cause the woman pain. "When a bride is unable to walk after her wedding night, the groom is considered by his friends to be a 'real man' and he is able to boast of his exploits, particularly if he has been able to make her cry" (Sanday, 1981, p. 10). In another rape-prone society, the Yanomamo of Venezuela, girls are married well before menarche because all women beyond the age of puberty are routinely raped if they don't have husbands (Schafran, 1991).

Of 156 subsistence societies spread throughout the world, Sanday has classified 18% as "rape-prone," 35% as possessing rape but not frequently enough to be considered rape-prone, and 47% as "free of rape." She places the United States in the middle category.

BOX 1.4

The Hypermasculinity Inventory

Hypermasculinity, or the macho personality, is a construct useful in identifying propensity to rape. As this orientation receives mention in several chapters of this book, we thought it would be useful to include some sample items from the scale.

Items from the Hypermasculinity Inventory are in a forced-choice format. One choice always reflects hypermasculinity. Sample items:

1. a. Some people have told me I take foolish risks.
   b. Some people have told me I ought to take more chances.
2. a. I hope to forget past unpleasant experiences with male aggression.
   b. I still enjoy remembering my first real fight.
3. a. When I have a drink or two I feel ready for whatever happens.
   b. When I have a drink or two I like to relax and enjoy myself.
4. a. Some women are good for only one thing.
   b. All women deserve the same respect as your mother.

Source: Mosher & Sirkin, 1984.

In the "free-of-rape" category are all cultural groups, whether tribes or nations, in which the act of rape is either very infrequent or nonexistent. Among these—note that they are almost half the total—are the Tuareg of the Sahara Desert, the Pygmies of the Ituri rain forest in Africa, and the Arapesh of New Guinea (Mead, 1935). In these rape-free societies, women are treated with considerable respect, and prestige is accorded to female reproductive roles. The second consistent characteristic emerging from Sanday's analysis is that in rape-free societies violence is minimized, and people's attitude toward the natural environment is one of reverence.

But let us now consider the other extreme. Why are some societies rape prone? Such societies embrace a configuration that includes interpersonal violence, dominance by males, and separation of the sexes. Susan Brownmiller (1975), whose views we will examine in more detail later, has classified rape as a means by which men subjugate women; she writes, "It is nothing more or less than a conscious process of intimidation by which all men keep all women in a state of fear" (p. 5).

That seems characteristic of many of these rape-prone societies. By limiting women's freedom and making them dependent on men for protection, the threat of rape provides support for a social system based on male dominance. Thus the relationship between a society treating women in a possessive, dominating, and demeaning manner and the tendency for a feminist theory of rape.

But what of the United States? As mentioned, Sanday's analysis places it in the middle category: among the 35% of societies world-wide in which rape occurs, but not so frequently as to be classified as "rape prone." Yet such a classification deserves scrutiny. Yes, the rate of rape in the United States—as far as we know—is not as high as in the Gusii tribe. Whether the macho personality is *the* one endorsed for males in the United States is a matter of debate. Reactions to the film *Thelma & Louise*—in which two women reject the ethos that makes them dependent on men for protection—are as provocative as is the message of the film itself. Certainly men strong in a macho personality orientation in the United States were threatened by a film whose message was that women can effectively reject the sexist and domineering overtures of men.

Certain aspects of American society lead toward a classification of the United States as "rape-prone." Melani and Fodaski (1974) claim that "we live in a culture that, at best, condones and, at worst, encourages women to be perennial victims, men to be continual predators, and sexual relations to be fundamentally aggressive" (p. 84). And Johnson (1980) observes: "It is difficult to believe that such widespread violence is the responsibility of a small lunatic fringe of psychopathic men. That sexual violence is so pervasive supports the view that the locus of violence against women rests squarely in the middle of what our culture defines as 'normal' interaction between men and women" (p. 146).

Just how does American culture condone rape? A decade ago television soap operas began to portray rapists as heroes. On *General Hospital,* when Luke raped Laura, not only did she refuse to report the attacker, but she eventually fell in love with him and married him (Waggett, 1989). Romance novels, highly popular in the United States, often capitalize on a rape scene. One author,

Jude Deveraux, had one manuscript returned to her by her editor because it had no such scene. "I was told that I had to have the hero rape somebody–preferably the heroine–to prove he's virile," she said (Kayle, 1989, p. 69).

So, how rape-prone is the United States as a society? Even though the reported incidence figures place it in the middle category, we would prefer to give an "it depends" answer. At the beginning of the chapter we quoted some political leaders who have made remarks that reflect an insensitivity to women. The publicity over the alleged rape by William Kennedy Smith has reminded us that for at least three generations the men in the Kennedy family–the family that some say comes the closest to royalty in the United States–have shown a sexual compulsiveness that reflects a pervasive contempt for women in our society (Carroll, 1991).

At the same time, the nature of ideology in the United States is quite differentiated and fractionated, and it operates at several levels. To most U.S. citizens, rape remains particularly abhorrent, and they live in a complex society composed of feminists of both genders alongside pockets of macho males and some hyper-feminine women who persist in subscribing to myths about rape.

The fact that the United States is also the most violent of the industrialized countries is also relevant to this question. The homicide rate in the United States (about 6 violent deaths per 100,000 people per year) is twice that of Finland, the world's second most violent industrialized nation. In a society that "equates masculinity with dominance and sex with violence . . . rape becomes a way for adolescents to prove their masculinity both to themselves and each other" (Hood, 1989, p. 23).

Theoretical Explanations

Given that rape occurs more frequently in the United States than in many agrarian societies and more than in any other industrialized society, we need to examine the motivations of individual rapists in our society. Chapter 2 examines these motives in detail; at this point we want to introduce some differing theoretical explanations.

In a book on theories of rape, Ellis (1989) identifies three explanations: the feminist theory, the social learning approach, and the evolutionary theory. These are summarized in Box 1.5. The

(text continued on page 18)

BOX 1.5

Theories of Rape

In a useful review of the literature, Lee Ellis (1989), a sociologist, has identified three contemporary perspectives on rape:

1. The Feminist Theory of Rape

Rape is considered to be "the result of long and deep-rooted social traditions in which males have dominated nearly all important political and economic activities" (Ellis, 1989, p. 10). The presence of both prostitution and pornography permit a portrayal of women in subservient and degrading ways. At the extreme, women come to be viewed as little more than property (Clark & Lewis, 1977; Dworkin, 1981). The key term is the powerlessness of women; it causes dependency and subservience to men. For example, Andrea Dworkin (1989) has written: "All men benefit from rape, because all men benefit from the fact that women are not free in this society."

The feminist approach does not consider sexual gratification to be a prime motive for rape; rather, "rape is seen as the use of sexuality to establish or maintain dominance and control of women by men" (Ellis, 1989, p. 11; see also Burt, 1980; Brownmiller, 1975; and Groth, Burgess, & Holmstrom, 1977).

2. The Social Learning Theory of Rape

Albert Bandura (1973, 1978) is credited with developing social learning theory, which proposes that "aggression is learned primarily through imitation (modeling), and thereafter sustained largely through various forms of intermittent reinforcement" (Ellis, 1989, p. 12). As applied to explaining rape, social learning theory would see it as an aggressive behavior that was learned from observing acts in real life or the mass media, especially aggressive acts that go unpunished.

Although social learning theory is similar to feminist theory in its belief that social and cultural learning is largely responsible for rape, the two differ in that social learning theory sees as underlying causes of rape those cultural traditions that are more

BOX 1.5 (Continued)

directly linked with interpersonal aggression and sexuality. Relative to the feminist approach, social learning theory is more willing to believe that rape is sexually motivated. As explored in Chapter 2, the link between pornography and rape receives a different evaluation in the two approaches.

In summary, "social learning theorists see rape as resulting from the joint influences of cultural and experiential factors mediated by attitudes, sex role scripts, and other thought processes that link physical aggression and sexuality in the minds of males" (Ellis, 1989, p. 14).

3. The Approach of Sociobiology; or, An Evolutionary
   Theory of Rape

The proponents of the evolutionary (or sociobiological) theory of rape share these common views:

Social behavior evolves because it is adaptive to propagating the species. Among mammals, males and females have evolved tendencies to allocate their time and energy in different ways with respect to the tasks of reproduction. Females care for the offspring while "males tend to emphasize securing as many sex partners as possible" (Ellis, 1989, p. 14). In fact, given the relative speed with which males can fertilize females and hence help create new offspring, copulating with many sex partners is a very productive activity for males (Quinsey, 1984).

But males are at a disadvantage, compared with females, in being able to identify their offspring once they have been born. Given this lessened initial "investment" and less certainty of their parenthood, "evolutionary theorists believe that males have a stronger tendency for evolving traits (behavioral and otherwise) that increase their chances of inseminating large numbers of females, rather than fastidiously taking care of a few offspring" (Ellis, 1989, p. 15). If so, *forced* copulation, or rape, may have been a reflection of the rules of natural selection (Gibson, Linden, & Johnson, 1980; Hagen, 1979; Symons, 1979).

(Continued)

BOX 1.5 (Continued)

It should be noted, states Ellis, that evolutionary theorists consider such aggressive copulating tactics to be an extreme response to natural selection pressures; this point is discussed in more detail in Chapter 2.

Also, if this theory is valid, females should have evolved strong tendencies to resist or avoid forced copulation, because it is in their best interests to have a sex partner who has exhibited evidence of being willing and able to make a long-term commitment to her and any offspring she may bear (Mellen, 1981).

presence of these contemporary viewpoints has the virtue of reminding us that rape cannot be easily explained away by any one label. Every one of these conceptions has some applicability but also each one is, in the words of Diana Russell, "flawed by its failure to acknowledge the possibility that men who rape strangers, for example, may be very different from husbands who rape their wives or men who rape their dates" (Ellis, 1989, p. 103).

Organization of the Book

This book seeks to provide a comprehensive up-to-date review of the crime of rape from a psychological perspective. Our emphasis is on psychological theories and research findings that are aids in understanding the motivations for rape, the effects of rape upon victims and their friends and family, and the possibilities for reduction of the incidence of rape in our society.

Chapter 2 examines the rapist. Factors that distinguish rapists from men who are not likely to rape are analyzed. Some feminist scholars have advanced the belief that exposure to pornography contributes to rape; the empirical findings are evaluated in Chapter 2.

Chapters 3, 4, and 5 deal with particular types of rapists. The stranger who rapes is described in Chapter 3. Date rape and acquaintance rape are reviewed in Chapter 4, with special emphasis on miscommunication and misperception between the genders. Chapter 5 examines the incidence and causes of marital rape, as well as its relationship to wife battering.

A shift in focus begins in Chapter 6, in which attitudes toward rape are the topic. Among the issues considered are the acceptance of rape myths in the general populace, callous attitudes toward sex, and the phenomenon of "blaming the victim." Chapter 7 continues on this theme, by examining different explanations for the prevalent negative reactions to rape victims, including norm theory, defensive attribution, and a belief in a "just world."

The topic of Chapter 8 is the reactions of rape victims themselves, including shattered assumptions, the rape trauma syndrome, and self-blame. The important issue of the treatment of rape victims by the trial courts is reviewed in Chapter 9, in which we present our own program of research.

The last section of the book returns the focus to the rapist and to the act of rape. Chapter 10 reviews the extensive recent legislation that has revolutionized the legal system's reaction to rape. Effects of reforms are evaluated. How should convicted rapists be punished? Should they also receive treatment? Chapter 11 assesses these controversial questions. The various ways of preventing rape are described in Chapter 12.

2 The Rapist

By the very fact that sexual assault is part of the rapist's repertoire, every rapist is similar to every other. But rapists also differ in innumerable ways. Consider the following three rapists and contemplate their dissimilar characteristics and actions:

1. For a very long time, Dr. John Huntington Story was a family doctor in the small town of Lovell, WY. But during this extended period he raped or otherwise sexually molested several hundred women and girls, always in the privacy of his examining room (Olsen, 1989). He chose his victims—who ranged in age from 10 to 68—carefully for their vulnerability; they were often too docile, inexperienced, or embarrassed to report him. Even when some did, they were ridiculed by their friends and the town's officials. But eventually Dr. Story was brought to trial, convicted, and—at the age of 60—sent to prison (Jones, 1989).

2. Timothy Kehoe approached a woman in a bar in Dallas, TX, had drinks with her, and persuaded her to accompany him to his apartment. Once there, he gave her a pill that relaxed her, whereupon he began to set up his videotaping equipment. When she tried to escape, he beat her; the blows were recorded on the videotape. Mr. Kehoe then proceeded to rape her, while recording it on the videotape. Only the intervention of an acquaintance permitted the

woman to escape. The 72-minute videotape was later discovered by the police during a search of Mr. Kehoe's apartment. It was introduced into evidence at his trial; the jury found him guilty of aggravated sexual assault and he was sentenced to life in prison (Taylor, 1990).

3. Daniel Oltarsh was described as a rich, handsome 6-foot-2-inch junior at Florida State University at the time he was accused of date rape (Freeman, 1990). When his date arrived at the Pi Kappa Alpha house she had already been drinking, but Mr. Oltarsh—according to the police reports—handed her a bottle of wine and left her in his room to finish it. She was dangerously inebriated and she soon passed out, but the police reports stated that her date took her to the fraternity house shower room, where he and at least two of his fraternity brothers participated in a gang rape. Police later found her in the hallway of the next-door fraternity house, where she had been abandoned, unconscious, with her skirt pulled up and her underpants around her knees (Freeman, 1990). Mr. Oltarsh later pleaded no contest to charges of felony sexual battery and was sentenced to a year minus a day plus 2 years of community service and 20 years probation.

All three of these rapists share one characteristic that is *not* typical of rapists—they were processed through the criminal justice system and were all sentenced to serve time in prison. But their differences are of equal importance. Although the variability in their backgrounds and behaviors does not prove the claim that "all men are potential rapists," the differences emphasize that rapists reflect all walks of life, occupations, and social classes.

The Diversity of Rapists

In describing the alleged rape of a Palm Beach, FL, woman by William Kennedy Smith, *Time* magazine (Carlson, 1991) referred to him as "an unlikely candidate for the rapist's role." Unfortunately, when most of us hear that a rape has occurred, the stereotypical picture of an obsessed, psychopathic madman comes to mind immediately (see Box 2.1). This is an understandable reaction. It is not, however, a justifiable one. Even among convicted serial rapists, there is heterogeneity (see Box 2.2). To many, it may seem

BOX 2.1

The Stereotype of a Rapist

Research conducted by the first author and her colleagues asked subjects to indicate the degree to which 35 various characteristics were descriptive of either a rapist, a date rapist, or a stranger rapist (Allison, Adams, Bunce, Gilkerson, & Nelson, 1992). The results showed that there is, indeed, a stereotype of a rapist; four characteristics stood out as descriptive of a rapist, no matter what type of rapist subjects were describing: aggressive, dangerous, power hungry, and manipulative. Although these four characteristics were considered similarly descriptive of all types of rapists, there were also important differences found.

For example, the date rapist was rated much more positively than the stranger rapist. In general, subjects found the date rapist to be more confident, outgoing, well mannered, clean-cut, psychologically stable, outspoken, well liked, friendly, attractive, intelligent, loving, and having higher self-esteem, compared to the stranger rapist. The date rapist was also perceived to be less shy, quiet, deprived, angry, mentally ill, and dangerous, compared to the stranger rapist.

The results of this research also suggest that when subjects are asked to describe a rapist, they are more likely to describe a stranger rapist than a date rapist. Of the 35 characteristics, 80% were found to describe both the rapist and the stranger rapist similarly, but only 54% of the 35 characteristics were described as similarly characterizing both the rapist and the date rapist.

Significant gender differences were also found. In general, females perceived that all rapists were more likely to possess more negative and less positive characteristics than did males.

unconscionable to believe that a man (or a woman) could do such a horrible thing unless the perpetrator were perverted in some way. Separating "rapists" from "normal" people allows us to continue living in what we believe to be a secure environment. But are matters so simple? Are all rapists maniacs who are easily identified and hence avoidable with appropriate caution?

Traditional Psychiatric Views

The traditional view of rape held by professional persons has contributed to this aberrant image, by taking a psychiatric perspective (Lottes, 1988). This orientation reflects several psychoanalytically based assumptions, including the following:

1. rape is the product of great psychological disturbance,
2. the act of rape is primarily sexual in nature, and
3. the behaviors associated with the act of rape are both strange and abnormal (Albin, 1977; Glueck, 1925; Karpman, 1951; Scully & Marolla, 1985).

One of the regrettable implications of this perspective is a conclusion that rape is an infrequently occurring event that is perpetuated by only atypical and unusual individuals who differ drastically from the norm. For example, Cohen (1976) argued that "every act of rape is expressive of psychopathology: of a disturbance, moderate or severe, in the developmental history of the offender and his current efforts" (quoted by Koss & Leonard, 1984, p. 217). The psychoanalytic perspective also focused often on the victim, implying that her psychology may have influenced the rape as well (see Box 2.3).

More Social Psychological Perspectives

Despite the initial popularity of the psychiatric perspective, attempts to understand rape as only an unusual and atypical act have not proven useful. Koss and Leonard (1984), after thoroughly reviewing the psychological research, concluded that the empirical evidence linking sexually aggressive men with psychopathology is inconclusive and quite weak. Attempts to demonstrate that rapists are more pathological, even in comparison with other types of criminal offenders, have also been unsuccessful.

In the past two decades, the search for understanding has turned toward more social aspects of the sexual aggressor. As noted in Box 1.5 and further in this chapter, both the feminist viewpoint and the social psychological one point toward societal and cultural factors

BOX 2.2

The Serial Rapist

In 1978, The FBI Behavioral Science Services combined efforts with law enforcement agencies all across the United States to investigate violent crimes. Part of their efforts included profiling the serial rapist. It was believed that if a profile of the serial rapist could be obtained, this could aid in the detection of the rapist. At this time, Special Agent Robert Hazelwood and several colleagues (Hazelwood & Burgess, 1987; Hazelwood, Reboussin, & Warren, 1989; Hazelwood & Warren, 1989) began their investigative research, which included many long interviews with incarcerated rapists. They limited their interviews to those rapists who were incarcerated, had committed 10 or more rapes, and who had exhausted their judicial appeals. The number of actual sexual assaults committed by the rapists, however, ranged from 10 to 78. For these reasons, their findings *cannot* be considered generalizable to the majority of rapists. However, it is perhaps their sample that best fits the stereotype of a rape: The majority of the victims were complete strangers, and the rapes were most likely to occur in the home of the victim, after the rapist had forced entry into the victim's home in order to overcome her quickly. Below are some of the findings that have come out of this line of research. Note that even among serial rapists, there are vast differences.

Of 41 serial rapists interviewed:

- The average age of the rapists at the time of their first attack was 21.8 years
  The average age of the rapists at the time of their second attack was 25.8 years
  The average age of the rapists at the time of their last attack was 29 years
- 85% of the rapists were white
  12% of the rapists were black
  2% of the rapists were Hispanic
- 54% had generally stable employment
  38% had unstable employment status
  8% were described as chronically unemployed

BOX 2.2 (Continued)

- 71% had been married at least once
  34% had been married more than once
- 51% had served in the armed forces
- 12% scored below average on formal intelligence tests
  36% scored within the average on formal intelligence tests
  27% scored "bright normal" on formal intelligence tests
  24% scored "superior" or "very superior" on formal intelligence tests
- 20% grew up in economically submarginal homes
  27% grew up in homes that were socioeconomically marginal
  37% grew up in homes that were socioeconomically average
  17% grew up in homes that were socioeconomically advantaged
- 46% had been previously institutionalized in a correctional center
  12% had been previously institutionalized in a mental facility
- 78% were living with another person at the time of both the first
  and the last rape, within a family context
  22% were living alone during the first and last rape
- 76% had been sexually abused as children
- 36% had collected pornography

Obviously, with this heterogenous sample, an exact profile of the serial rapist is hard to obtain. An investigative authority, given this information, would most likely search for a white male in his twenties or early thirties who is employed, has been married at least once, has served in the Armed Forces (although most in this sample had been of age while the draft was still active), is of above average in intelligence, was raised in an average or above-average socioeconomic environment, is currently living with another person in a family context, and was sexually abused as a child. Descriptions by the friends of these men included "average," "friendly," "a leader," and "willing to help out a friend." Hazelwood and Warren (1989) also note that the vast majority of the rapists could be described as neat and well-groomed men who took pride in their personal appearance. This may lead to a chilling conclusion that a serial rapist is no more different than the man next door. These rapists also confirmed assertions by those studying rape that there is no type of personality that renders victims likely to be raped: 98% of these rapists reported that they chose their victims because of their "availability" at the time.

BOX 2.3

Psychoanalysis and Focus on the Victim

Although it seems logical that when one is trying to explain rape, one would focus on the rapist as opposed to the victim, such is not always the case. To ask "Why was the victim raped?" instead of "Why does the rapist rape?" has a long history and is still prevalent today. This focus is partly a result of the psychoanalytic perspective.

As the originator of psychoanalysis, Sigmund Freud actually said very little about why rape occurs. However, Freud did make mention of sexual assault while discussing suicide in his writings. In a footnote Freud observed that

> After all, the case is no different from that of a sexual assault upon a woman, where the man's attack cannot be repelled by her full muscular strength because a portion of her unconscious impulses meets the attack with encouragement. It is said, as we know, that a situation of this kind paralyses a woman's strength; all we need to do is to add the reasons for the paralysis. To that extent the ingenious judgment delivered by Sancho Panza as governor of his island is psychologically unjust (Don Quixote, part 2, Chapter 45). A woman dragged a man before the judge alleging he had robbed her of her honor by violence. In compensation Sancho gave her a full purse of money which he took from the accused; but after the woman's departure he gave him permission to pursue her and snatch the purse

as among the primary influences on the behavior of the rapist (Brownmiller, 1975; Medea & Thompson, 1974; Russell, 1975). In direct contrast to the psychiatric model of rape, these perspectives consider rape not as strange and abnormal, but rather as a conforming, or even overconforming, response to cultural beliefs and standards.

Cultural beliefs standards place the acceptance of rape myths at the forefront—myths that serve to enhance male dominance and female passivity, and alternatively, to explain and perhaps justify the occurrence of rape. Various theoretical explanations of rape—introduced in Chapter 1 and employed further in this chapter—

BOX 2.3 (Continued)

back again from her. The two returned struggling, the woman priding herself on the fact that the villain had not been able to take the purse from her. Thereupon Sancho declared: "If you had defended your honor with half the determination with which you have defended this purse, the man could not have robbed you of it." (Freud, quoted in Forrester, 1986, p. 61)

Neo-Freudians later presented their own, more detailed, explanations for why rape occurs, based on the ideas of Freud. Although the psychoanalytic explanations did include an analysis of the rapist—and his irresistible impulses, or diseased mind— much of the focus of this explanation attended to aspects of the victim. This model of victim-precipitation proposed that within the mind of every woman who is attacked lies deep unresolved conflict. This conflict is between the conscious wish to repel the rapist and the unconscious desire the encourage the violence, which subverts the ability of the victim to resist. Karen Horney (1973) put it quite succinctly: "What the woman secretly desires in intercourse is rape and violence, or in the mental sphere, humiliation" (p. 22). Therefore, because of such urges, they "unwittingly cooperate with the rapist in terms of covertly making themselves available to the rapist" (Littner, 1973, p. 28). Hence, with one footnote, the seed for the myth that women secretly wish to be raped was nourished.

reinforce this point. Furthermore, Chapter 6, on attitudes toward rape, describes Burt's (1980) position that the development and adherence to a broad ideology of values and beliefs may serve to encourage the acceptance of myths about rape. We will expand on this point in this chapter.

Characteristics of Rapists

One purpose of this chapter is to identify both the similarities *and* the differences among rapists. Let us consider the similarities first, by asking if there are characteristics that rapists share and that distinguish them from persons who do not commit rapes.

Demographic Similarities

First, the obvious: Most rapists are male. All of us know this, but the present goal is to place this demographic fact in association with another fact: Rape is a crime that incorporates coercion and violence toward another person.

Gender, as a correlate of criminal behavior, is so obvious that its significance is often disregarded. But its *consistency* across societies is impressive. Throughout all the countries in which records are kept, men are arrested anywhere from 5 times to 50 times more often than women (Wilson & Herrnstein, 1985).

Similarly, physical aggressiveness is one of the few consistent sex differences that has been found to exist between males and females: Although a few studies have found no differences in the level of aggression exhibited by males and females, those studies that do find differences consistently find that men are more physically aggressive than women (Tavris & Wade, 1985).

So there is one consistent factor that promotes rape: being male. Surely things are not so simple; in rare cases, females have raped, and not all men rape. Trying to determine what factors distinguish those males that rape from those that do not has consumed the careers of many professionals. Hundreds of studies have been published in this area by these professionals. Yet, the data collected by these researchers indicates that we are still at a very early stage when it comes to explaining why men rape (Hall, 1990).

One of the primary problems with the research in the area of rape is that most research includes a few select variables to study. Rape is not caused by a few select variables; rather, it is most likely a product of many combinations of many different factors. We will discuss these factors that have been studied, but the reader should keep in mind that those factors that have been found to be associated with rape do not, by themselves, cause rape. There is no one explanation for the occurrence of rape.

Childhood Experiences

There exists a widely held belief that childhood experiences have a profound impact on later behavior. Specifically, it has been suggested that growing up in a violent home where at least one parent was violent toward the other, or either of the parents physically abused the children in the family, promotes violent behavior in these children as adults.

There is some support for this proposition. Groth (1979) found that 90% of his offender sample had been the victims of childhood sexual abuse. Scully (1990) interviewed 114 convicted rapists and found that the incidence of childhood sexual abuse was much lower than the percentage reported by Groth—only 9% of these men reported that they had been the victims of sexual abuse as children. However, 34% of the convicted rapists in Groth's sample had been the victims of child physical abuse. Although the sample in Scully's research was considerably smaller, she finds that although some convicted rapists had been victims of violence as a child, 50% reported growing up in nonviolent homes. Hence, growing up in a violent home is a related factor to sexual violence as an adult, but it is not a causal relationship.

Calloused Attitudes and Beliefs About Women

Perhaps one of the most consistent findings in the literature is the role that the existence of traditional sex roles, adversarial attitudes toward women, and the accompanying acceptance of rape myths has on the proclivity to rape (Burkhart & Fromuth, 1991). In studies that primarily involve large numbers of male college students, it has been found that men who believe in the traditional sex roles, have adversarial attitudes toward women, and who believe in rape myths have consistently been involved in sexually aggressive activity more than those males who do not adhere to these values (Koss, Leonard, Beezley, & Oros, 1985; Lisak & Roth, 1988; Malamuth, 1986; Muehlenhard & Linton, 1987; Rapaport & Burkhart, 1984). It has also been found that convicted rapists have relatively high acceptance of violence against women (Scully, 1990; Scully & Marolla, 1984). In fact, nearly half (45%) of convicted rapists in one study believe that some women like to be hit because they believe it means men care about them (Scully, 1990).

Such attitudes adhered to by those who rape serve as a justification for denying their own responsibility in the rape, or even that a rape occurred. One rapist, responding to two researchers' requests for interviews wrote the following:

Mr. Sussman, I'm not a rapist (per se) as you think, what happen six
(6) years ago I would like to forget it. But I would like to add something
to your research. Both person that was involved in my case's brought
the rape on themselves.

I was robbing this one person apartment, she came in on me, I told
her not to be afraid, to sit down, she did sit down, and the next thing
I knew she was running out of the apartment screaming for help. I
ran out after her, and caught her took her back to the apartment. If
she wouldn't have ran, that wouldn't have happen.

And in the other case, I would say I was more the victim in this
case, this person came to the door, dressed with a towel wrapped
around them. I told the person to go and get some clothes on, she
went into her bedroom to put some clothes on, but she put the clothes
on so I could see her. I was in the other room watching her more or
less so she couldn't do nothing funny, and when she started putting
on clothes, there she was right in front of my eyes.

In both case's the person's brought it on there selves, running and
screaming, and not fully dressed when answering the door. (Sussman
& Bordwell, 1981, p. 198)

Such denial by rapists is common. Their own adherence to
attitudes that denigrate women and rationalize rape through the
behavior of the woman, or the dress of the woman, or by the very
fact that the woman is physically capable of having sex all serve to
justify, in the mind of the rapist, that effectively, a rape did not
occur. Another rapist interviewed by Sussman and Bordwell (1981)
spoke of the "Law of the Rapist":

If they conduct theirself as a lady, clean-cut and what have you, they
don't have to worry about any of this. If they conduct theirself as a
hussy, then they got it coming by the law of the rapist. (p. 6)

So it is that this rapist believed that some women actually deserve
to be raped. This type of mentality serves to dichotomize women
into two groups: Some women are put on a pedestal and are to be
protected by men from other men; others are considered whores
and are viewed as deserving of rape. This man's victim, however,
was the 63-year-old wife of his boss, while she was in her home. As
Frankfurt noted while introducing the research: "So much for the
Law of the Rapist" (quoted in Sussman & Bordwell, p. 6).

Why the consistent association of such attitudes with rape? In
addition to attitudes' role in both encouraging and justifying rape,

each of these attitudes involve the creation of a power differential that gives males power over females. As one example, consider the traditional date: The male initiates the date, makes the decisions about the date, pays for the date, and drives during the date. Each of these factors places the power into the hands of the male, and rape has been found to be more likely to occur under each of these conditions (Muehlenhard & Linton, 1987). Issues of power and dominance have been found to play a motivating role for rapists.

Power and Dominance as Motives for Sex

When Groth (1979) wrote what is now a germinal book about why men rape, he identified the motive of power as the most common among rapists. As will be discussed in Chapter 3, the rapists whom Groth interviewed indicated that many offenders desired to conquer and sexually dominate their victim. Work by Malamuth (1986, 1988) studying primarily college students has also found that males who have engaged in sexual aggressive activities endorse dominance as a sexual motivator. For example, they were more likely to agree with statements such as: "I enjoy the feeling of having someone in my grasp"; or "I enjoy the conquest." It has also been found that nonconsensual sexual behavior is predicted by anger and dominance motives for sex.

These studies, and others (e.g., Burkhart & Stanton, 1988; White, 1988) suggest that sexually coercive styles may be connected to a more fundamental and distinctive orientation to sexual activity. That is, the sexual behavior of sexually aggressive males is motivationally *overdetermined*. For these men, sex comes to serve many motives: power, dominance, anger, neediness, as well as purely sexual motives (Burkhart & Fromuth, 1991). For the sexual aggressor, it may be impossible to disentangle these motives.

Social Perception and Social Skills

Yet another interesting factor that has been found to predict sexual aggression involves the social perceptions of men who engage in coercive sexual behavior. In one study, for example, males from a sample of the general population were asked to view videotapes depicting four different male/female interactions (Murphy, Coleman, & Haynes, 1986). In each scene, a male actor attempted to initiate a social interaction with a female. The female actor responded in one of four ways: she was either hostile, assertive, seductive, or friendly. Males serving as participants were then asked to identify the behavior. It was found that those men who had reported engaging in coercive sexual behavior were less able to discriminate the hostile from the assertive females, or the seductive from the friendly response of the female.

Other studies have also found that convicted rapists may be deficient in their social skills. Lipton, McDonel, and McFall (1987) found that convicted rapists, compared to males who were currently in prison for both violent and nonviolent nonsexual crimes, have social information-processing deficits that predispose them to misconstrue women's cues. Rapists have also been found to be lacking in heterosexual skills and knowledge and in need of social-skills training (Abel, Blanchard, & Becker, 1978; Becker, Abel, Blanchard, Murphy, & Coleman, 1978).

General Aggressive and Manipulative Styles

It has been recently suggested that the foundation for an explanation for sexual aggression may also be important to explaining more general violence against women (Malamuth, Sockloskie, Koss, & Tanaka, 1991). That is, those variables that may serve to predict sexual violence against women may also be useful in predicting generally violent behavior. Rape is, therefore, one means among many of expressing violence.

Generally aggressive behavior styles, as well as some characteristics of antisocial conduct, have been found to predict sexual coercion. Men with histories of sexually coercive behavior have been found to be less well socialized, to be more impulsive, and to be more involved in physical violence (Burt, 1980; Calhoun, Kelley, Amick, & Gardner, 1986; Malamuth, 1986; Rapaport & Burkhart, 1984). Finally, males who engage in coercive sexual behavior are generally more aggressive and hostile individuals.

It also appears that males who report there is some likelihood that they would force a woman to have sex if assured of not getting caught condone masculine values and advocate the general use of manipulation to obtain rewards (Allison & Branscombe, 1992).

One study that investigated manipulativeness also included other variables theoretically relevant to predicting males' self-reported likelihood of using force to obtain sex (Allison & Branscombe, 1992). This study included assessments of Machiavellianism, hypermasculinity, affect intensity, and anger. *Machiavellianism* is a construct that refers to persons who characteristically manipulate others through guile, deceit, and opportunism, and includes a component centering on a zest for dominating and controlling others (Christie & Geis, 1970). *Hypermasculinity* is an assessment of the "macho" man (Mosher & Sirkin, 1984). It consists of three related components. First, calloused sexual attitudes toward women are important. Second, a conception that violence is manly and good is present, and finally, a view of danger as exciting is involved. Studies have shown that males who score high on the hypermasculinity scale are more accepting of callous sex, whether casual or coercive (Sullivan & Mosher, 1990) and they also report a history of sexual coercion and force in dating situations (Mahoney, Shively, & Traw, 1986; Mosher & Anderson, 1986). *Affect intensity* refers to the amount of affect, or emotion, that is experienced by individuals (Larsen, 1984). It has been found that some individuals do, indeed, experience emotion—whether it is happiness, sadness, or anger—to a stronger degree than do other individuals.

In Allison and Branscombe's study, the only variable that was uniquely related to advocating the use of force to obtain sex was Machiavellianism—the more a man adhered to Machiavellian principles, the more likely he was to report that he would use force to obtain sex. Perhaps more important, however, the *combination* of these variables successfully discriminated between those who reported they would use force from those who reported they would not. Those males that would use force were more Machiavellian, more hypermasculine, *and* were likely to experience emotion, particularly anger, to a stronger degree. Here again is evidence that a multivariate approach is needed before one can begin to understand the complexities underlying sexual coercion and rape.

Toward a Multivariate Approach

The above research that has examined the psychological factors related to sexual aggression does support the contention that, although not necessarily pathological in nature, there are individual differences that are associated with sexual aggression (for other reviews, see Burkhart & Fromuth, 1991; Hall, 1990). However, the recent call for a multidimensional approach to understanding sexual aggression is loud and clear. The underlying explanation for sexual aggression is complex, and no single variable has been found to be a very powerful predictor of sexual aggression (Burkhart & Fromuth, 1991; Hall, 1990; Malamuth, 1986). For some rapes, all of the above mentioned factors will be present; for others, only one or a few may be present.

Some researchers have begun to answer the call. Malamuth (1988) contends that aggression against women may be influenced by common underlying factors that include attitudes that accept or condone violence against women, dominance motives, antisocial personality characteristics, and sexual arousal to aggression. Although nearly all of these factors were found to be related to sexual aggression, a combination of these factors did a much better job of predicting sexual aggression. Malamuth, Sockloskie, Koss, and Tanaka (1991) developed and supported a model that argues that a hostile home environment may lay the foundation for the potential to be aggressive toward women, sexually or physically, through two paths: (1) hostile attitudes and personality characteristics, and (2) a high level of sexual promiscuity that may combine with hostility to lead to sexual aggression. They note the importance of model building to our understanding of aggression, and suggest that such models could be used to explain both sexual and nonsexual aggression. (See Box 2.4 for a similar development.)

Differing Theoretical Perspectives

As we have mentioned, no "profile of the propensity to rape" will ever be able to predict every rapist because motivations, circumstances, and relationships differ. Chapter 1 introduced the theme that contrasting theories of rape have been developed. At this point we seek to relate two of these theories to the more specific factors that were found to be related to coercive sexual behavior.

Biological Theories of Rape

The suggestion that a man rapes because of some biological or genetic tendency for him to do so is both compelling and frightening; furthermore, it supports the suggestion of some feminists that all men are potential rapists. Susan Brownmiller's (1975) influential book has articulated the latter position:

BOX 2.4

Why, Specifically, Does a Rape Occur?

The multicausal theory of Finkelhor (1984) for explaining the occurrence of child sexual abuse can also be applied to the occurrence of rape, as suggested by Russell (1988).
Four conditions must be met:

1. First, someone must want to rape or assault women sexually.
2. The person's internal inhibitions against acting out this desire have to be undermined.
3. This person's social inhibitions against acting out this desire (for example, fear of being caught and punished) have to be undermined.
4. The would-be perpetrator has to undermine or overcome his or her chosen victim's capacity to avoid or resist sexual abuse.

Man's structural capacity to rape and women's corresponding structural vulnerability are as basic as the primal act itself. Had it not been for this accident of biology, an accommodation requiring the locking together of two separate parts, penis into vagina, there would be neither copulation nor rape as we know it. . . . Man's discovery that his genitals could serve as a weapon to generate fear must rank as one of the most important discoveries of prehistoric times. (pp. 4-5)

Another biological viewpoint, however, argues that there may be a genetic component involved in rape. Sociobiologists propose that their evolutionary approach cannot be dismissed when attempting to explain rape, if one is to understand fully the dynamics of rape (cf. Thornhill, Thornhill, & Dizinno, 1986).

Sociobiologists study the biological basis of social behavior in various species, including humans. They rely on evolutionary theory and genetic inheritance to explain social behavior. Their major premise—an extension of Darwinian theory of the survival of the fittest—assumes that it is the *fittest genes,* rather than the fittest individuals, that nature selects to survive. Social behaviors evolve, according to the sociobiologists, because they are genetically adaptive and serve to produce offspring.

To apply this theory to the behavior of the rapist, sociobiologists argue that rape occurs because it is a form of behavior conducive to creating offspring. In some basic way, all of humankind is motivated to create offspring; this is the basis for having sexual intercourse, both consensual and nonconsensual. According to Donald Symons (1979), a proponent of the biological deterministic theory, the process of natural selection predisposes males to "copulate with fertile females whenever this potential can be realized" (p. 101).

This controversial perspective does not subscribe to the proposition that all men will rape. To the contrary, those who do rape do so only because they are unable to pass on their genes and produce offspring in other, more socially acceptable, ways, such as through marriage. This conception reflects a quite traditional view of cultural values, in noting that in order to attract a mate, a male must have both resources and status. Without such assets, females will not be interested, as this goes against the survival of their genes, and the male will have no chance to reproduce. This inability to find a mate produces the desperate alternative of rape, an act of last resort.

Although the theory is not explicitly about rape myths, the development of such myths is congenial with the theory because these myths provide a justification for otherwise unsatisfied men to rape. Several other hypotheses stem from the sociobiological explanation. For example, men who are sexually active would not be expected to rape. Those who are poor and without female sexual partners would be considered more likely to resort to rape.

Predictions can also be made concerning the choice of the victim. Women in their more fertile years should more often be the victims of these men in despair (for further discussion on the derived hypotheses, see, e.g., Thornhill et al., 1986). It is not acknowledged, however, that women unable to find mates will take this type of recourse. The theory relies almost exclusively on men competing for women.

Little evidence has accumulated to support this sociobiological perspective. Although young women in their fertile years are most susceptible to rape, many individuals who are not fertile, including children, postmenopausal women, and men, are also raped. And though rare, this perspective cannot account for why some rapists kill their victims. Finally, a significant number of rapists experience sexual problems during the act of rape itself; some are unable to achieve erections, or do not ejaculate during the rape (Groth, 1979). This evidence is inconsistent with the proposition that rape is the result of a need to perpetuate the species.

Psychological Theories of Rape

A second general approach to explaining rape emphasizes personality, attitudinal, and cognitive qualities within each rapist; we thus use the term *psychological theories* to label this category. To refer to a theory as simply "psychological," however, may not be specific enough. Psychological theories of crime are numerous and can take on quite different approaches (see Box 1.5). All share in common, however, the basic assumption that "crime is the result of some personality attribute uniquely possessed, or possessed to a special degree, by the potential criminal" (Nietzel, 1979, p. 52). If used in the context of rape, a potential rapist must possess within himself some type of quality that produces a propensity to rape—for example, a deep sense of anger or hostility toward women. We have seen some of these psychological qualities supported in the research discussed earlier. Further examination of the psychological approach is to be found in Chapter 3, in Groth's typology of rapists.

Pornography: Does It Affect Rape?

One hypothesis derived from the above analysis is that those societies and individuals reflecting attitudes that degrade women, including pornography, contribute to the incidence of rape. It is true that rapists show relatively high levels of sexual arousal when they are exposed to depictions of rape. One rapist told an interviewer:

> I went to a porno bookstore, put a quarter in the slot, and saw this porn movie. It was just a guy coming up from behind a girl and attacking her and raping her. That's when I started having rape fantasies. When I seen that movie, it was like somebody lit a fuse from my childhood on up . . . I just went for it, went out and raped. (Beneke, 1982, pp. 73-74)

In contrast, men who are not rapists, at least in most studies (cf. Barbaree, Marshall, & Lanthier, 1979), show no signs of sexual excitation when shown scenes of rape. Is this a reliable difference? If so, why does it occur? In this section the empirical work of the past decade on the effects of pornography, especially violence-laden pornography, are examined within the previously identified determinants of sexual coerciveness.

First, some distinctions. Pornography is often separated from other erotic material because its content is manifestly degrading and abusive (Longino, 1980). Pornography usually involves the fusion of sexuality and violent behavior. Erotic material, as opposed to pornography, may have a goal of sexual arousal without illustrating or advocating violence, victimization, or depersonalization. However, what is degrading and abusive is often subject to many different interpretations. As Supreme Court Justice Potter Stewart wrote: "I can't define it, but I know it when I see it" (Longino, 1980, p. 26).

During the past two decades, pornographic material combining sexual behavior and violent acts has become so easily available that people can rent videotapes reflecting this combination of themes at their neighborhood store. Some feminists and others note that with the increased availability has occurred an intensification of the brutal treatment of female victims in at least some of the films. For example, Slade (1984), in a content analysis of hard-core films, found that since 1970 violence has become more graphic and brutal when it occurs, although only the minority (10% or less) of such films portray violent acts. Is it coincidental, then, that since 1980 the rape rate in the United States has consistently increased?

Some feminists have criticized pornography for its degrading and humiliating treatment of women. In 1984, the National Organization for Women passed the following resolution:

> NOW finds that pornography is a factor in creating and maintaining sex as a basis for discrimination. Pornography, as distinct from erotica, is a systematic practice of exploitation and subordination based on sex which differentially harms women and children.

The Program of Research by Donnerstein, Linz, and Colleagues

A few paragraphs earlier we quoted one rapist's explanation for the causes of his own behavior. When we ask if this is a legitimate and generalized cause, one answer comes from the research program of Edward Donnerstein and his colleagues (Donnerstein, 1982; Linz, Donnerstein, & Penrod, 1984, 1987b, 1988; Malamuth & Donnerstein, 1982). These studies and similar ones by Feshbach and Malamuth (1978) *consistently* show that men who are exposed to violent pornographic materials (in either a printed or a pictorial medium) develop calloused attitudes toward women, and are more likely to be more aggressive toward women in subsequent interactions than those who do not view such materials.

An early, prototypical study was done by Donnerstein and Berkowitz (1981). Male college students were led to believe that they were participating in an experiment on the effects of stress on learning. They were told that they would be paired with either a male or a female student. During the early portion of the experiment, the supposed partner gave the subject a high number of electrical shocks, communicating that the partner didn't think much of the essay that the subject had written. In the next part of the experiment, the subject was exposed to one of four films: a neutral talk-show interview, an erotic film depicting sexual intercourse with no violent content, or one of two pornographic films that combined aggression and sexual behavior depicting a woman being slapped and sexually assaulted.

One of these pornographic films had a final scene in which the woman was smiling at her attackers; in the other version, the woman was clearly suffering at the end of the film. After watching one of these four films, the subject was given a chance to be aggressive toward his partner by administering electric shocks. When his partner was a female who had just angered the subject (by administering the shock), both of the pornographic films increased the subject's level of aggression, but neither film did when the subject thought his partner was male.

More recently, research in this program has attempted to determine the *separate* effects of the aggressive and sexual components of violent pornography. The authors summarize the results of two studies (Donnerstein, Berkowitz, & Linz, 1986):

> In the first study, male college students were angered by either a male or a female confederate and were then shown one of four different films. The first film was similar to the aggressive pornography used in studies discussed earlier. The second was X-rated but contained no aggression or sexual coercion. Subjects rated the second film just as

UNIVERSITY OF WINCHESTER
LIBRARY

sexually and physiologically arousing as the first film. The third film contained scenes of aggression against women but without any sexual content. Subjects rated it as less sexually and physiologically arousing than the previous two films. The final film was of neutral content.

After viewing the films, the men were given the opportunity to aggress against male or female confederates of the experiment. The results showed that the men who viewed the film that was both aggressive and pornographic displayed the highest level of aggression against the woman, but the aggression-only film produced more aggression against the woman than did the sexually explicit film that contained no violence or coercion. In fact, there were no differences in aggression against the female target for subjects in the sex-only film condition and the neutral film condition. In the second study, subjects who viewed the combination of sex and violence displayed higher levels of aggressive behavior than subjects in the sex-only group, and subjects exposed to the violence-only depiction also exhibited higher levels of aggression than the sex-only group. (Linz, Penrod, & Donnerstein, 1987, p. 720)

The claim by some feminists and others that pornography—whether violent or not—leads to a treatment of women as sexual objects receives some empirical support from a study by McKenzie-Mohr and Zanna (1990), although the effect is found in only certain types of men. Men who were masculine sex-typed, as measured by the Bem Sex Role Inventory, behaved differently from men who were androgynous (i.e., describing themselves with about as many feminine characteristics as masculine characteristics).

Subjects in McKenzie-Mohr and Zanna's study first watched a 15-minute videotape, either an innocuous film about the House of Commons or a film of a heterosexual couple engaging in non-violent sexual intercourse and oral sex. Subjects in the latter condition were told, prior to the film, that it dealt with a prostitute having sex with her client.

After completing a questionnaire, each subject was then individually interviewed by a female; the interview questions did not deal with the films, but instead was oriented to adjustments to college life. The female interviewer was not aware which film the subject had watched, or his Sex Role Inventory score.

For only those male subjects who were masculine in their self-description and who had watched the film of sexual intercourse, the female experimenter gave ratings as more sexually motivated.

Also, these subjects positioned themselves closer to her during the interview, and they had greater recall and faster recall times when questioned about her physical appearance. In contrast, they recalled less about the contents of the survey that the female was conducting. The authors conclude: "this group of males treated our female experimenter, who was interacting with them in a professional setting, in a manner that was both cognitively and behaviorally sexist" (McKenzie-Mohr & Zanna, 1990, p. 305). They note, as do others (e.g., Abbey, 1982), that males often misperceive females' friendliness as sexual intent (and, as we have discussed earlier, rapists accentuate this misperception).

Applications of Research Findings

Research findings such as these are being used as support for proposals in several communities to restrict the availability of certain kinds of obscene and pornographic materials. For example, in 1984 the city of Indianapolis adopted an ordinance viewing pornography as central in promoting rape, child abuse, and prostitution. (This law outlawing pornography was later ruled unconstitutional on First Amendment grounds.) Also, in Dallas an ordinance approved in 1986 requires licenses for "sexually oriented businesses," including adult bookstores and theaters, and states that applicants can be rejected if they have prior convictions for sex crimes, obscenity, or prostitution.

Another example of the use of these findings may be found in the report of the Attorney General's Commission (or "Meese Commission"), published in July 1986; it singled out pornography as a causal factor in aggression. Unfortunately, this widely publicized report did not adequately distinguish between the effects of violent and nonviolent sexually arousing stimuli. Likewise, the short-term and long-term effects were not separated; the laboratory studies do not permit a test of whether sexually violent material leads to assaultive behavior outside the laboratory (Malamuth & Ceniti, 1986).

The commission also assumed that a direct relationship exists between pornography that is degrading to women and viewers' acts of sexual aggression. No controlled study has found such a relationship (Malamuth & Briere, 1986).

Criticisms of the Meese Commission's report by Linz, Donnerstein, & Penrod (1987a) that it exaggerated and misrepresented available research on the harmful effects of pornography reflect what we believe would be the majority opinion among psychologists. But they have not gone unchallenged by some psychologists and social scientists. Stewart Page (1989), for example, notes that several studies find that the effects of nonpornographic violent material are not as strong as those of violently pornographic depictions. It may be that either erotic or violent material removes inhibitions against taboo behavior like rape (see also Box 2.5).

But when erotic and violent material are combined, everyone agrees that the result is exceedingly damaging. Former U.S. Surgeon General C. Everett Koop (1987), in reporting on a workshop, stated that all participants agreed that "pornography that portrays sexual aggression as pleasurable for the victim increases the acceptance of coercion in sexual relations" (p. 945).

Ted Bundy and the Purported Effects of Pornography

Shortly before he was executed in January 1989, serial rapist and murderer Ted Bundy claimed that exposure to sexual violence in the media while he was a child influenced his later development. In a widely seen interview with California evangelist James Dobson, Bundy said: "Those of use who are . . . so much influenced by violence in the media, in particular pornographic violence, are not some kind of inherent monsters. We are your husbands, and we grew up in regular families" (Lamar, 1989, p. 34). Bundy claimed that he spent his formative years with a grandfather who had an insatiable craving for pornography.

Bundy told Dr. Dobson, "People will accuse me of being self-serving but I am just telling you how I feel. Through God's help, I have been able to come to the point where I, much too late, but better late than never, feel the hurt and the pain that I am responsible for" (Kleinberg, 1989, p. 5A).

The tape of Bundy's last interview, produced by Dobson and titled "Fatal Addiction," has been widely disseminated, especially by those who seek to eliminate all pornography. (Dr. Dobson served on the Meese Commission.) But Bundy's claims that pornography was the "fuel for his fantasies" has been received skeptically by others, who saw it as one last manipulative or Machiavellian ploy to gain further time. Even his mother stated that no evidence existed in her son's first 28 years (before he became a rape-and-murder

BOX 2.5

A Feminist Social Scientist's View on the Effects of Pornography

Diana E. H. Russell (1988), a sociologist and respected researcher on rape, challenges a conclusion that nonviolent pornography has no detrimental effects or causes no harm for women. She states: "My reading of the research conducted on pornography in the last decade is that for the most part it strongly supports the causative link between pornography and violence against women" (1988, p. 42). First, she notes that "in many instances the actual *making* of pornography involves or even requires violence and sexual assault" (p. 42).

Pornography may predispose some men to want to rape if, for example, arousing portrayals of female nudity are associated with rape. Also, Russell notes testimony that some men decided they would like to try certain sex acts after seeing pornography portraying the same acts performed on women.

Furthermore, she finds that pornography undermines some men's internal inhibitions by objectifying women, and that this tendency is as common in nonviolent pornography as it is in violent pornography. Internal inhibitions are also weakened by portrayals that increase acceptance of violence.

Social inhibitions—for example, fear of disapproval by one's peers—are undermined by pornography that produces overestimates by men of uncommon sexual practices such as anal intercourse, sadomasochism, bestiality, and group sex. Furthermore, heavy consumption of common forms of pornography "fosters an appetite for stronger materials" (p. 71).

Russell's analysis of the research literature contrasts with the conclusions of Linz, Donnerstein, and their associates about the effects of nonviolent pornography.

suspect for the first time) that hinted at any aberrant behavior (Nordheimer, 1989).

In none of his previous interviews, including extensive conversa-tions in 1986 with Dorothy Lewis, a psychiatrist he had come to trust, did he ever cite "a pornographic preamble to his grotesquer-ies" (Nobile, 1989, p. 41). Bundy had decided at that time that he needed psychiatric testimony in order to escape the electric chair—that is, by being diagnosed as not competent to stand trial because he was supposedly too confused and irrational to assist in his own murder defense. Despite Dr. Lewis's testimony in 1986, the judge would not declare Bundy incompetent. Thus perhaps at that time he decided to portray himself as a normal youth who had been corrupted by pornography (Nobile, 1989).

The Researchers Respond

Political conservatives who dominated the Meese Commission, some feminists, and serial rapist-murderer Ted Bundy are all in agreement about the detrimental effects of pornography (see Box 2.4 for another example). But proposals to censor or curtail such material remain quite controversial (Page, 1989; Wilcox, 1987). The researchers on whose work restrictive proposals are based are quite reluctant to see censorship decisions based only on their research (Linz, Donnerstein, & Penrod, 1987a). They propose that research studies in nonlaboratory settings and longer time frames are needed. They resist the conclusion that "this type of pornography is at the root of much of the rape that occurs today" (Malamuth, 1989, p. 580).

Specifically, although they conclude that several of the Commis-sion's "findings" are sound extrapolations from the empirical re-search results, "many of its recommendations are incongruent with the research findings" (Linz, Penrod, & Donnerstein, 1987, p. 713).

Two reasons that the conclusions are seen as incongruent are:

1. "It is sexually *violent* material, rather than sexually *explicit* material, that results in harmful effects" (Linz, Penrod, & Donnerstein, 1987, p. 713).
2. Methodological limitations resulting from research in laboratory set-tings and use of "artificial" measures of aggression "prohibit direct extrapolation of experimental findings to situations outside the labor-atory" (Linz, Penrod, & Donnerstein, 1987, p. 714).

Summary

No two rapists are exactly alike. Researchers investigating the motivations of rapists, however, have discovered some general commonalities among some rapists some of the time. Most rapists are male. Many were physically or sexually abused—or both—as young boys, and have negative views about women. Such negative views may serve to perpetuate stereotypical images in their minds, and hence help them to justify their own behavior. Many rapists have strong needs for power and dominance over others, especially women, and are generally aggressive across situations. In addition, their ability to perceive social situations accurately, and their competence in social interactions may be impaired. Finally, many rapists are likely to use and enjoy pornographic material, although the debate rages on about whether pornography causes rape. Although possessing one or two of these characteristics may not be adequate in causing rape, current research is focusing on combinations of these variables, which appears more promising for predicting why rape occurs.

3 Stranger Rape

In support of its title that rape is a misunderstood crime, this book so far has emphasized the theme of the diversity of rapes, rapists, and their relationships to their victims. A truck driver's rape of a hitchhiker differs from a father's forcing himself on his daughter or a minister coercing several of his parishioners.

Rape is misunderstood partly because the relationship between the two persons is often assumed to be one of strangers. Although rape by strangers is the topic of this chapter, we need to understand that the relationship between the rapist and the victim can reflect any possible degree of previous contact, including spouses, family members, roommates, dates, co-workers, and acquaintances, as well as strangers. Rapes that reflect some of these other relationships are analyzed in Chapters 4 and 5. Furthermore, the rapist and the victim can be of the same sex (see Box 3.1).

The Variety of Stranger Rapes

Even within the category of rapes by strangers, variability exists. The sexual assault can be carried out by one person or a multitude. Although our emphasis in this chapter is on the solitary stranger, gang rape should not be ignored; Groth (1979), in interviewing men convicted of sexual assault, found that almost 10% had participated in rapes involving more than one assailant.

Gang rape perpetrated by college students, particularly within some fraternity systems, is also being identified as a problem that can no longer be ignored (see also Chapter 4).

Gang Rape

On a spring evening in 1989, a 28-year-old investment banker was jogging through Central Park in New York City when she was grabbed, assaulted, and raped by seven Harlem teenagers. According to one account, "they hit her with a pipe, hacked her skull and thighs with a knife, pounded her face with a brick, and bound her hands beneath her chin with her bloody sweatshirt, which also served as a gag" (Will, 1989, p. A-11).

She lay undiscovered for almost 4 hours and lost three quarters of her blood. Remarkably, she survived the attack, and after a long period of recuperation, she was able to return to work. However, she still has no memory of the attack.

The Harlem teenagers were charged with attempted murder, rape, sodomy, sexual abuse, assault, and rioting. Along with two other young men, they were also charged with attacking two male joggers during a 2-hour rampage in the park. All eventually plea-bargained or were found guilty at trial of at least some of the above charges (even though, remarkably, lawyers for two of the young men questioned whether the young woman-victim had ever been raped [Glaberson, 1990b]).

This so-called "wilding" incident attracted national attention and shocked our collective consciousness. Explanations for this attack were not made any easier by the fact that the young males—ages 13 to 17—mostly came from stable middle-class or working-class families in which a certain amount of discipline was enforced (Kaul, 1989). Four of them lived in buildings that had doormen; several sang in a church choir; none had a record of similar crimes. The descriptions of these boys certainly seem inconsistent with the stereotypical rapist.

The New Bedford, Massachusetts, Case

Although gang rape is especially prominent among adolescents (Groth, 1979, p. 116), adults also are perpetrators. Several years

BOX 3.1

Intragender Rapes

It is difficult to determine the incidence of intragender rape of males; few articles in the professional literature on sexual assault deal with male victims (Struckman-Johnson, 1991). Incredibly, the FBI's *Uniform Crime Report* (1988) does not include figures for rapes involving male victims because, by its definition, the victims of forcible rape are always female. But another government agency, the Bureau of Justice Statistics (U.S. Department of Justice, 1988) does report estimates of the number of victims of personal crime each year. The 1988 report estimated that one per 1,000 men, or about 9,400 men in the U.S. population, are victims of rape or attempted rape each year. Most experts, however, believe the true incidence rate is much higher (Calderwood, 1987; Groth & Burgess, 1980). Waterman, Dawson, and Bologna (1989) surveyed 36 women and 34 men who were in gay and lesbian relationships and found that 12% of the men and 31% of the women reported being victims of forced sex by either their current or most recent partner. Hence, intragender rape is a problem that deserves more attention than it is currently receiving. There is particularly little known about females who are sexually assaulted by other females.

Struckman-Johnson (1991) has investigated the psychodynamics of male rape victims and asks that with thousands of men sexually assaulted each year, why is so little known about the problem? Myths about the nature of rape impede awareness and recognition; many people assume that male-to-male rape occurs only among homosexual persons or heterosexual men who are incarcerated and have no other sexual outlet (Struckman-

before the Central Park "wilding," in 1983, a 21-year-old mother claimed that she had been raped for 2 hours by as many as 15 men in a New Bedford, MA, bar, while a dozen more watched and cheered. The response to the reports of this gang rape in the community was one of outrage. *Newsweek* magazine described the

BOX 3.1 (Continued)

Johnson, 1991). In actuality, like female victims, most male victims are assaulted by an acquaintance (Myers, 1989; Sorenson, Stein, Siegel, Golding, & Burnam, 1987). Furthermore, neither the perpetrator nor the victim is necessarily homosexual.

Most male victims do not report their assault to police, physicians, friends, or family; they are humiliated and often blame themselves for not being strong enough to resist successfully (Groth & Burgess, 1980). Perhaps the most frequent reason for the failure to report, according to Struckman-Johnson (1991), is the fear of being labeled homosexual. And the laws of some states discriminate in a unique way against rape victims who are males; if homosexual sodomy is a crime (which it still is in about half the states) the victim could be arrested for participating in "unnatural acts" (Groth & Burgess, 1980).

What motivates men to assault other men sexually is not well understood, but Groth and Burgess (1980) have proposed that unresolved or conflicting sexual identity may sometimes be the cause. Groth (1979) observes:

> Such offenders seem caught in a bind: unable, on the one hand, to admit interests in sexual encounters with other males and unable, on the other hand, to abandon pursuing some such encounter. . . . Such an offender is conflicted over and fearful of his homosexual urges, and he projects these feelings onto his victim, perceiving him as a provocative seducer. (p. 129)

But same-sex rape may also reflect a kind of group ritual. For example, "a group of men may gang rape an outsider male in order to establish the group's dominance, strengthen membership bonds, or create status for participating members" (Struckman-Johnson, 1991, p. 202).

frenzied reaction: "The local women's center reported calls from hundreds of people who were outraged over the incident—and a candlelight vigil was scheduled at New Bedford's City hall this week to protest not only the vicious gang rape but the callousness of those who witnessed it" ("The Tavern Rape," *Newsweek*, 1983, p. 25).

A year later, at the trial, details of the incident were clarified. The victim reported that only two of the defendants had raped her, two had forced her to engage in oral sex, and two shouted encouragement (Beck & Zabarsky, 1984). She testified that she had gone into the bar for cigarettes, had a quick drink, and was on her way out when she was grabbed and thrown to the floor. The men stripped her clothes off and then raped her on a pool table (Bayles, 1984).

Under a legal doctrine known as joint enterprise, all six defendants were charged with aggravated rape. The four defendants who were physically involved in the rape were convicted, but the two bystanders were acquitted. Interestingly, however, the same community that had been outraged at the incident one year previously now was apparently bitter about the convictions: "She had no business being in the bar," an elderly woman said; "she should have been home with her kids instead of destroying men's lives," said another (Beck & Zabarsky, 1984, p. 39). The horror of the incident seemed to pull the community apart; many of the women in New Bedford of Portuguese descent, like the women quoted here, displaced negative feelings toward the Portuguese woman who had been raped (Chancer, 1987). They also participated in a group of 6,000 to 8,000, protesting not the rape, but the conviction of four of their fellow Portuguese Americans. Three-and-one-half years later, the victim of the New Bedford group rape died in a Miami, FL, automobile accident.

Stranger Rape: Myth and Reality

Because of the recent heightened publicity and awareness of date rape, relatively speaking at least, the media have given less attention to rape by strangers. The magnitude of the problem remains, however. This section attempts to separate myths from facts regarding four aspects of rape by strangers: its incidence, the use of weapons, the racial background of rapists and victims, and the motivations of rapists.

Incidence of Stranger Rape

The authors of the prestigious report of the National Commission on the Causes and Prevention of Violence (Mulvehill, Tumin, & Curtis, 1969) concluded that as many as 53% of reported rapes were by strangers. The Commission reported that 29% of rapes were by an acquaintance, 7% by a family member (other than a husband), 3% by a neighbor, 3% by a close friend or lover, and the remaining 5% by some other category of person, or of an unknown relationship (Mulvehill et al., 1969, Vol.11, p. 217). But that was *in 1969*.

A decade later Katz and Mazur (1979) summarized 18 different studies, reporting percentages of stranger rape from 27% to 91%. They concluded that the extreme variation was a result of the fact that victims were less likely to report the rape when the perpetrator was a relative, lover, date, or friend. Russell's (1984) San Francisco survey of victims concluded that whereas 55% of all rapes reported to the police were stranger rapes, attacks by an unknown assailant accounted for only 17% of the total number of rapes, including those not reported to the police.

Since then, agreement has emerged that rape or attempted rape by strangers accounts for a minority of rapes—probably about 15%. Russell's random-sample survey of 930 women concluded that

> when rape and attempted rape are combined, acquaintances become the most prevalent type of rapist: 14% of the 930 women were victims of rape or attempted rape by acquaintances, 12% by dates, 11% by strangers, 8% by husbands or ex-husbands, 6% by friends of respondents, 3% by boyfriends, 3% by relatives other than husbands, 2% by friends of the family. (Russell, 1984, p. 59)

Russell's 11% reflects the percentage of *victims—16%* of the *incidents* reported in the survey were committed by strangers. But 16% is a far different figure from the percentages reported earlier. And the most recent surveys produce similar estimates; a study of rape on 32 college campuses conducted by *Ms.* magazine and Mary Koss reported that 84% of college-aged victims knew their attacker (Warshaw, 1988).

Even a figure of 15% reflects a sizable number of rapes by strangers, despite its being far from the most frequent type. And the importance of stranger rape is magnified by the use of a weapon, the next issue to be assessed.

Use of a Weapon or Threats

Our stereotype of stranger rape pictures the assailant lurking behind the bushes, brandishing a knife or threatening with a gun.

But the U.S. Department of Justice concludes that a weapon is used in only about 30% of rapes (Gelman, 1990). Note, however, that this is based on *reported* rapes; given that more violent rapes are more likely to be reported to the police, the actual percentage of rapes in which a weapon is used is likely to be even lower.

Despite the relatively low frequency with which weapons are used to rape, it does appear that stranger rapists are more likely to utilize a weapon than those who rape acquaintances. Scully (1990) found that 62%—well over half—of the 26 convicted stranger rapists she sampled had utilized a weapon, and in an additional two cases, a weapon was faked. The most frequent type of weapon used by these stranger rapists was a knife. Results reported by Mary Koss and her colleagues (Koss, Dinero, Seibel, & Cox, 1988; Koss, Gidycz, & Wisniewski, 1987) compare the experiences of victims raped by strangers with those raped by acquaintances are consistent with this notion: stranger rapes were more likely to involve a weapon than acquaintance rapes, and a knife was used almost twice as often in a rape as a handgun. Furthermore, compared to acquaintance rapes, stranger rapes were more likely to involve threats of bodily harm, hitting, and slapping. Of these stranger rapes, 54% also included verbal threats of bodily harm to the victim.

As suggested above, surveys of victims do find that the greater the amount of physical violence used by the rapist, the more likely the attacker was to succeed and the more likely the rape was reported to the authorities. In Russell's (1984) survey, 38% of the victims who were beaten or slugged during the assault reported their attack to the police. This percentage in reporting dropped as the accompanying physical violence from the rapist dropped: 18% of those who were hit or slapped reported the incident, and only 5% of those who were pushed or pinned reported the attack to the police.

Similarly, if a weapon was used in the rape, prosecutors considered the rape more credible; 58% used this factor in their decision to prosecute (Law Enforcement Assistance Administration, 1977).

Racial Background of Rapists

In the American South of the 19th and early 20th centuries a number of black men were lynched because of their alleged rape of white women. Between 1930 and 1967, 89% of all convicted rapists who were executed for their crime were black (Estrich, 1987).

Although the death penalty for rape is no longer a legal option, black men who are convicted of raping white women still receive the harshest penalties. The race of the rapist continues to be a salient part of the stereotype of the stranger rapist. As Susan Brownmiller notes: "No single event ticks off America's political schizophrenia with greater certainty than the case of a black man accused of raping a white woman" (1975, p. 230).

In a survey of *arrests* for rape in Philadelphia, Amir (1971) found that 82.5% of the rapists were black, as were 80.5% of the victims. The National Commission on the Causes and Prevention of Violence concluded that most stranger rapists came from urban areas and were "disproportionately from the ghetto slum where most Negroes live" (Mulvehill et al., 1969, Vol. 11, p. 217); their figure was 70%. We believe the more accurate statistics come from the FBI's *Uniform Crime Reports,* which cites a lower ratio—generally around 48% black, 51% white, and 1% other (Russell, 1984, p. 91). Statistics that indicate that the majority of rapists are blacks seem just another example of racism, which promises that blacks who do rape are more likely to be convicted and sentenced severely for their crime.

Regardless of the percentage, the expectation that the crime is committed by a black man raping a white woman is *not* confirmed. Bureau of Justice statistics report that the chances that a white victim was raped by a white are 78%; that a black victim was raped by a black was 70% (Gelman, 1990). But these reports recognize the need for rejoinders to the prevalent stereotypes; the National Commission noted that:

> Racial fears underlie much of the public concern over violence, so one of our most striking and relevant general conclusions is that serious 'assaultive' violence—criminal homicide, aggravated assault and forcible rape—is predominately *intra*-racial in nature. (Mulvehill et al., 1969, Vol. 11, p. 208, italics in the original)

To the point, the government survey found that, of the rapes in their study:

> 60% involved black offenders and black victims;
>
> 30% involved white offenders and white victims;
>
> 11% involved black offenders and white victims; and
>
> 0.3% involved white offenders and black victims (percentages total more than 100% because of group rapes).

In Russell's (1984) survey, 64% of the rapists were white, 22% were black, 8% were Hispanic, 3% were Asian, and 3% were "other," but black rapists were overrepresented in the stranger rape category. In those instances when the victim was white and the attacker was black, however, the rapist was more likely to be charged with a felony, sentenced for a longer term, and to be incarcerated in the penitentiary (LaFree, 1980).

Socioeconomic status of stranger-rapists seems to be a stronger determinant than race per se. Every survey reports a disproportionate percentage of stranger rapists among the poor. This finding is influential in the theory of the causes of rape proposed by Schwendinger and Schwendinger (1983), who concluded that "the impoverishment of the working class and the widening of the gap between rich and poor, which is the bottom line of current federal policies, will lead to worse living conditions for the poor and continued high incidence of sexual violence" (1983, p. 220).

The Motivations of the Stranger Rapist

Is rape an act of sex or of violence? If forced to choose, experts—partly motivated to counteract the public's view of rape as a sexual crime—have emphasized its aggressive nature. More recently, a more compound view has emerged. Psychologist Nicholas Groth, whose influential typology of rapists will be described subsequently, sees rape as a "pseudo-sexual act" and states, "We look at rape as the sexual expression of aggression, rather that the aggressive expression of sexuality" (Gelman, 1990, p. 47). Different types of rapes may have different combinations of motivation; whereas the rapist who preys upon a stranger may premeditate the rape, the rapist who assaults someone he knows is more likely to have premeditated sex (Bechhofer & Parrot, 1991).

Motivations for stranger rape would seem to be the easiest to characterize because, compared to the other types, no prior relationship exists between the rapist and the victim to complicate the motivations of the perpetrator. But even here, several possible motivations exist.

One of the most comprehensive studies of rapists using a psychological perspective was done by Nicholas Groth (1979), who—over a period of 10 years—extensively interviewed and collected data on more than 500 convicted rapists. Based on these findings, Groth developed a tripartite typology of the motivations of the rapist.

According to Groth, for all cases of stranger rape elements of power, anger, and sexuality are present. And though each exists in the mind of the rapist, rapes may be classified according to which of the elements is most powerful for any given rapist. The *anger rape* is motivated by extreme rage within the rapist, which ultimately explodes and results in rape. *Power rape,* on the other hand, is motivated by a strong need to control others and exert power over them. The last type, *sadistic rape,* is the least common, but the most violent type. In sadistic rape, sexuality and aggression become fused and culminate in rape.

Anger Rape

Anger rapes are the result of pent-up hostilities within the rapist that at some point erupt. The explosion of rage is usually due to some identifiable external event that has recently occurred (e.g., an argument with a woman friend or spouse). Through rape, the anger is released—at least temporarily. Sex becomes a weapon. Groth notes that because this type of rape serves to release anger, the rapist strikes sporadically and infrequently. The anger must build up again before another rape can occur. As one rapist put it:

> I was enraged when I started out. I lost control and struck out with violence. After the assault I felt relieved. I felt I had gotten even. There was no sexual satisfaction; in fact, I felt a little disgusted. I felt relieved of the tension and anger for a while, but then it would start to build up again, little things, but I couldn't shake them off. (Groth, 1979, p. 15)

The anger rape may be characterized by force and brutality, in fact much more force than is necessary to overcome the victim. The goal of the anger rapist is to hurt and humiliate the victim—and what better way to humiliate than to invade the most personal aspect of the self? As one anger rapist pointed out, "I wanted to knock the woman off her pedestal, and I felt that rape was the worst thing I could do to her" (Groth, 1979, p. 14). Victims of anger rape are often forced to perform sexual acts that the rapist believes to be especially demeaning, such as oral or anal sex. And though anger rapes may be violent, their duration is relatively short.

Power Rape

The power rape was the most common form of rape in Groth's sample. For these men, the act of rape serves to compensate for feelings of insecurity and inadequacy and often reflects needs to express strength, control, authority, and power. The power-motivated rapist considers the rape a sexual conquest, a way of demonstrating his manhood and masculinity. One told Groth:

> All my life I felt I was being controlled, particularly by my parents, that people used me without any regard for my feelings, for my needs, and in my rapes the important part was not the sexual part, but putting someone else in the position in which they were totally helpless. I bound and gagged and tied up my victims and made them do something they didn't want to do, which was exactly the way I felt in my life. I felt helpless, very helpless in that I couldn't do anything about the satisfaction I wanted. Well, I decided, I'm going to put them in a position where they can't do anything about what I want to do. They can't refuse me. They can't reject me. They're going to have no say in the matter. I'm in charge now. (Groth, 1979, p. 30)

The rapist motivated by a need for power uses only as much force as necessary to overcome his victim. The goal is not to harm the victim physically but to possess her sexually. The means by which this is achieved may include verbal threats, intimidation with a weapon, or physical force if necessary.

Sometimes power and anger equally combine as the motives. One rapist told Groth:

> My feelings were a mixture of sex and anger. I wanted pleasure, but I had to prove something, that I could dominate a woman. I felt exhilarated during the rape. It was so intense that it took away from the sex itself. The sex part wasn't very good at all. (1979, p. 95)

Often, the power rapist may even deny that the sexual encounter was forced upon the victim. He may come to believe that the victim actually desired him sexually, or at least, came to enjoy the experience. As one of the rapists noted:

> She wanted it; she was asking for it. She just said "no" so I wouldn't think she was easy. The only reason she yelled rape was she got home

late and her husband knew she hadn't been out with her girlfriend. (Groth, 1979, p. 30)

To come to believe that the victim somehow wanted to be raped or enjoyed it validates the power rapist's belief in his sexual competency. He needs to believe this: He may inquire about his sexual skills during the rape by asking whether she is enjoying having sex with him. Some may express a desire to see the victim again, perhaps even asking her for a date! One rapist later called his victim and asked her for a date in exchange for return of the jewelry he had stolen from her. His audacity led to his capture and conviction.

Although the power rape may be less physically brutal than either the anger rape or the sadistic rape, its duration may be relatively long. The victim may be held captive and subjected to repeated assaults over a long period of time. Because the victim may survive the rape with relatively few signs of physical injury, she may be particularly likely to encounter suspicion, or even disbelief, from others. As Groth notes, "Participation is misinterpreted as provocation and cooperation as consent" (1979, p. 43).

Sadistic Rape

Although the sadistic rapist is by far the least common of all the types categorized by Groth, this type is also the most brutal and frightening. Because the sadistic rapist eroticizes aggression, he actually finds gratification in tormenting his victim and observing her suffering and anguish. For the sadistic rapist, the whole experience is very exciting. This type of assault may involve bondage and torture, and may eventuate into murder. The assault is premeditated and very deliberate.

Despite the fact that sadistic rape is the least common type of stranger rape, it receives massive attention from the media and hence serves to perpetuate the myth that the rapist is a "madman." In fact, Groth found that often these rapists are quite personable; like Ted Bundy, they may demonstrate an ability to hide their darker impulses from others.

Furthermore, research by Heilbrun and his colleagues (Heilbrun & Loftus, 1986; Heilbrun & Seif, 1988) suggests the presence of a sadistic component to normal male sexuality. These studies found that in normal college men, viewing depictions of women *in distress* in sexual situations led to increased arousal. As they note,

"Many college males appear capable of arousal to sadistic cues, but greater antisociality may be found only in those who actively breach the social restrictions on sexual aggression" (Heilbrun & Seif, 1988, p. 56).

Although Groth does distinguish among these three types of rapists, he notes similarities across the categories. Based on his study of convicted rapists, he argues that all stranger rapists have serious psychological difficulties. He notes that the most prominent feature of all rapists is their inability to establish any kind of close relationship, or to express feelings of warmth, trust, or genuine empathy. Groth identifies two other patterns that cross the boundaries of the typology: a very high recidivism rate (with the average number of rapes per rapist being 13) and an increased use of force and aggression over time.

Conclusions

Surveys (e.g., Koss et al., 1988) conclude that, compared to rapes in which the perpetrator is known by the victim, stranger rapes:

1. are more likely to involve aggression by the offender (threats of bodily harm, hitting, slapping, and use of a weapon);
2. lead to victim reporting more fear;
3. lead to victim attributing more responsibility to the attacker; and
4. cause victims to scream for help more often.

There were no differences in avoidance strategies used by victims, except for screaming. Both types of victims reported similar amounts of reasoning or pleading, crying or sobbing, running away, or struggling to escape. Likewise, there were no differences in how angry or depressed victims of stranger-attacks were versus victims of acquaintance-attacks, or how much self-responsibility they felt.

The work of Groth provides a significant contribution to understanding the psychodynamics of the stranger rapist. But the sample of rapists that Groth used may limit generalizations. Although his sample was large, it was limited to only those rapes that were reported, and it only included the most dangerous offenders who were tried, convicted, and committed to a special treatment center.

The problem with generalizing Groth's conclusions to all rapists— or even to all stranger rapists—stems from two known facts about rape. First, only an estimated 2% to 5% of all rapists are ever convicted of rape, and second, as discussed in Chapter 1, only a small percentage of rapes are ever reported. Groth, to his credit, acknowledges that his sample may not constitute a random sample of all men who rape. He also notes that some of his specific findings may not be representative of most rapes that occur (see Chapter 4 for amplification). For example, Groth believes—and we agree—that of all the rapes that occur, the power motive may be much more prevalent than he found in his sample.

Summary

The stranger rape is most closely associated with the stereotypical rape, and is among the most feared of all crimes. When they think of rape, many people visualize a sex-starved madman waiting with a weapon for his prey. Despite the consistency in the stereotype, characterizing the stranger rape requires diversity. There is no one type of stranger rapist just as there is no one type of stranger rape victim. There do seem to be consistent motivational themes underlying the stranger rapist, including power, anger, and sadism. Although one of these motives usually serves as the primary motivation for the stranger rapist, all three are important in understand why stranger rape occurs.

4 Date Rape and Acquaintance Rape

Almost everyone is aware of the encounter between Jessica Hahn and television evangelist Jim Bakker. Although each portrays their sexual interaction somewhat differently, they both acknowledge that it did happen and that their assignation had been arranged by a mutual acquaintance. Ms. Hahn describes herself as naive when it happened; an ever-trusting follower of the evangelical minister, she was overcome by Jim Bakker's approach when they met for the first time in a motel room reserved for her in Florida.

And although everyone is aware of what happened, to call it *acquaintance rape* may be a surprise to some. But if we accept Ms. Hahn's description of the details of the meeting, that is just what it was. Ms. Hahn knew of Mr. Bakker; she had watched his program and contributed money to his cause. In that sense they were not strangers. And according to her account, he forced himself upon her; she tried to resist but succumbed. The result was a rape. Furthermore, it was, she reports, her first sexual encounter; "I will never in my life know what it's like to make love for the first time with a man I love" (Goodman, 1987, p. 5A).

The Incidence of Date Rape
and Acquaintance Rape

Chapter 2 described the act of rape as it is perceived to be. Chapter 3 pointed out that what most people fail to realize is that most rapes involve people who are acquainted with each other. It happens off campus as well as on; the victim could be a 50-year-old woman who asked the man next door to repair her toaster, or a single 35-year-old office worker who got a ride home with a colleague (Lewin, 1991). Such types of rape—known as acquaintance rape or date rape, depending on the circumstances—have been around for a long time; the Old Testament (2 Sam. 13:1-15) describes an acquaintance rape committed by Amnon, son of King David. But only recently have they come to receive attention by both the mass media and researchers in the social sciences. (The term *date rape* was apparently first used in a September, 1982, article in *Ms.* magazine.)

To be raped by someone you know—someone who knows he is known and recognized—is not an irrational abstraction or a figment of a woman's imagination. It happens, and the fact that the rapist is familiar to the victim makes it no less ugly or repugnant. The fact that some victims of such assaults had taken drugs or had one drink too many likewise does not mitigate the seriousness of the act. A rape is a rape and its consequences cannot be trivialized just because of some prior expectations by the woman or prior relationship with the assailant. Yet some date rapists—and sometimes society in general—may treat it as a different phenomenon. For example, Richardson and Campbell (1982) found that a rapist was blamed less for an assault when he was intoxicated than when he was sober. Also see Box 4.1.

It is difficult to estimate how many date rapes and acquaintance rapes occur. Many, if not most, of the rapes of this type are never reported to any governmental or social agency; Koss (1985) found that only 5% of victims reported the assault to the police. Even estimating the incidence has its problems; to do so, researchers are forced to rely on questionnaires that ask women about their experiences with sexual aggression, and women sometimes do not label themselves as "rape victims" when the instigator is an acquaintance (Koss, 1985). Despite these limitations, Koss found that 15% of the college women she surveyed described experiences that would fulfill legal definitions of rape. Andrea Parrot's survey of two

BOX 4.1

Date Rape: An Extreme View

Despite the recent publicity about date rape, dissenters and dis-
believers still exist. A letter to Ann Landers:

Dear Ann: If I read one more letter in your column from a
woman who says she was date raped I may cancel my subscrip-
tion to the paper.

Date rape is 20-20 hindsight fiction, invented by easy sluts
posing as hard-to-get and "virtuous."

Any girl whose vocal chords are intact can scream her head
off while kicking, scratching, squirming, and seeking a way to
escape.

Before you believe her claim of date rape, ask if all four of
her limbs were immobilized, her mouth gagged and her hips
held in a vise-like grip?

Also ask her why she didn't kick him in the most vulnerable
spot, which would have been easy to do if she had wanted to.

If you get a believable answer, please share it with your readers instead of insulting their intelligence by printing such clap-
trap.—Proud to be a Pig. (Landers, 1988, p. 5A; permission
granted by Ann Landers and Creators Syndicate)

campuses concluded that 20% of the women had been forced into
sex (Leo, 1987), and Muehlenhard and Cook's (1988) survey reported 11% of college women had engaged in unwanted sexual
intercourse because the other person got them drunk and took
advantage of the situation.

Many women, thinking back on their sexual experiences, will
respond affirmatively when asked the question "Have you ever had
sex with a man when you didn't want to, because he used physical
force against you?" but at the same time offer a firm "no" when asked
"Have you ever been raped?" In one study, in every incidence of this
combination, the woman knew the rapist (Muehlenhard, 1988).
However, even though victims may not label the experience as
rape per se, they suffer similar psychological and physical conse-

quences as those self-acknowledged rape victims. Koss (1988a) has reported, for example, that measures were taken 2 years before the year of the rape and 2 years following that year (5 years total). Victims were seeking general medical treatment (not directly related to the rape) up to 2 years following the year that the rape occurred.

Several explanations exist concerning why these women refuse to acknowledge that they have been raped, even though the act and the circumstance qualify it for a legal definition of rape. Some women simply may not believe that they were raped. How can you be raped, they may ask themselves, by someone you know and trust? As one woman who was raped by a "friend" explains in a letter she wrote to Ann Landers, "It took several days before I realized I was raped. Things get muddled and emotions get scrambled" (Landers, 1987). In addition, admitting to yourself that you have been raped necessarily means conceding the fact that you have been a "victim"— a very vulnerable place to find yourself. (This aspect is treated in detail in Chapter 6.)

Researchers sometimes have taken this latter aspect into consideration by administering questions that deal with rape as it is legally defined without actually including the dreaded word. As recently as 5 years ago the best estimates suggested that about one half of all rapes occurred between acquaintances or dates. But more recent estimates suggest that in *most* rapes the victim and her assailant were familiar to each other. One of the most comprehensive and representative studies to date (Koss et al., 1988) administered the Sexual Experiences Survey (Koss & Oros, 1982) to a national sample of more than 3,000 women. Of these women, 15% or around 200 reported having been raped as adults at least one time in their life. An impressive portion of these victims—85%—knew their assailant.

Some women may not label the assault a rape because they blame themselves for contributing to its occurrence—either through being naive or having placed themselves, through excessive drinking, for example, in an unsafe situation. A woman from Nevada told a *New York Times* reporter (Gross, 1991) that she did not call what happened to her "rape" until many years later. In contemplating what happened she:

1. Figured she had made a stupid mistake by agreeing to drive a fellow college student home from a party.
2. Wondered if she had led him on by going into his house.

3. Asked herself if she could have fought back more vigorously when he threw her on the bed and forced her to have sexual intercourse.
4. Felt embarrassed rather than angry after the attack was over, and apologized for "not wanting sex."

"Blaming the victim," including self-blame, is described further in Chapter 6.

Date Rape: A Special Case

We may think of "date rape" as a specific type of acquaintance rape, in the sense that a more defined relationship exists between the two parties than in the case of two routine acquaintances (Bechhofer & Parrot, 1991). And even though the mass media have recently alerted the public to the fact that date rape does exist, misunderstandings about it still prevail.

Contrary to popular opinion, date rape does not just occur on first dates. Skelton (1982) found that 36% occurred on a first date or by an acquaintance, 26% by an occasional date, and 31% by a regular suitor. Thus, any level of familiarity is possible—the couple may be on a blind date, or they may be intimate partners involved in a long-term relationship. Mary Koss and her colleagues reported in 1988 that of those victims of acquaintance rape, 35% were attacked by men they had been dating steadily. Another 29% of the sample were raped by men they knew such as a co-worker, a neighbor, or a friend with whom they were not romantically involved. One fourth of the victims had dated their assailant casually, and 11% were violated by either their husband or a family member. (Chapter 5 specifically deals with spousal rape.) Note that of these victims—all of them victims of acquaintance rape—almost 70% were raped by men with whom they were romantically involved, or at least were dating. Another study (Muehlenhard, 1987) discovered that those dates that led to sexual aggression usually occurred in couples who had known each other almost a year.

Acquaintance rape and date rape are not rare occurrences. Do they possess qualities other than the relationship that distinguish them from rapes by strangers?

Characteristics of the Acquaintance Rape

Only recently have researchers begun to examine in detail exactly what acquaintance rape is like. Some researchers have further identified important differences in the causes of date rape as a function of the type of dating relationship (see Box 4.2). When compared with rapes committed by strangers, a few important differences emerge. These include characteristics of the rape itself, reactions of the rape victim, and the perceptions of outside observers regarding the rape.

Unique Qualities of Acquaintance Rape

Compared to rapes by strangers, acquaintance rapes possess several unique characteristics. For example, the type of coercion displayed by the rapist is usually different. Although rapes by strangers more often employ verbal threats, physical violence, and weapons, rapes by acquaintances usually reflect more subtle types of coercion (Muehlenhard & Schrag, 1991) (see Box 4.3).

Koss et al. (1988) found that the most common type of strategy used by the latter type of rapists was holding the victim down or twisting her arm. Although about one third of acquaintance rapes do, indeed, involve verbal abuse, according to Koss's survey, this percentage is perceptibly lower than the 54% of rapes by strangers that include verbal threats. Many times the kind of verbal threats used in acquaintance rapes and date rapes are different from those by strangers; they more likely capitalize on verbal "manipulation." For example, one investigation (Mosher & Anderson, 1986) discovered that 44% of the date rapists in their sample admitted telling the woman that a refusal to have sex with him would change the way he felt about her; 34% of the men in this sample threatened to end the relationship. It seems that another common strategy used by date rapists is to "just do it," even after the woman protests, essentially ignoring her pleas (Muehlenhard, 1987; Rapaport & Burkhart, 1984).

Acquaintance rapes often occur at different times from rapes by strangers. Date rapes, in particular, are more likely to occur on weekends, between the hours of 10 p.m. and 1 a.m. They are also more likely to occur at isolated locations, in a car, or at the home of the assailant (Harney & Muehlenhard, 1991). They may last much longer—sometimes 4 hours or more (Seligmann, 1984). These factors may contribute to another difference found between rapes by acquaintances and those by strangers—the number of offenses. Although date rapes and acquaintance rapes usually involve only

(text continued on page 68)

BOX 4.2

Three Types of Date Relationships

R. Lance Shotland (1989) has proposed that different processes may lead to a rape at different points in a relationship's
development. In doing so, he offered an explanation for the inconsistencies in explanations for the causes of date rape—for
example, the contrast between an explanation focusing on the
psychopathology of violent behavior and one that emphasizes
traditional processes in courtship.

Shotland proposes that "date rape can be separated along
three different but not independent causal pathways . . . each
causal sequence is *likely* to occur at different temporal points
in the relationship" (pp. 250-251, italics in original). The following listings are summaries of points in his theory:

1. Beginning date rape
    a. Occurs in the first few dates at the beginning of a relationship.
    b. Given that most college students do not expect to have sexual
       intercourse during the first date, when rape does occur, the
       male may have dated the woman with the intention of raping
       her, realizing that such an action is less likely to be labeled as
       rape than would the action of a stranger-rapist.
    c. Beginning date rapists may also have a need for more, and for
       more varied, sexual experiences (Kanin, 1967).
    d. Women who date or have sex with a large number different
       males increase their chances of exposure to a sexually aggres-
       sive male who commits a beginning date rape.
2. Early date rape
    a. Occurs early in the relationship.
    b. Couple are still establishing the rules of their relationship.
    c. Males view the world in a more sexualized manner than do fe-
       males; hence a man may perceive sexual intent when the
       woman felt she communicated none.
    d. Such males want more sexual contact, and they assume that their
       dates have similar desires but disguise them and feign disinterest.
    e. If misconceptions were all that were involved, however, and
       the woman made it clear that she was misunderstood, most

BOX 4.2 (Continued)

males would probably cease and desist. But men who engage in date rape at this stage may be poorer in coping with sexual frustration and impulse control. Foreplay has led to sexual arousal, which is mixed with emotions of surprise, anger, and embarrassment over being denied consensual sexual intercourse. Under these circumstances, the sexually aggressive male may have reduced impulse control. Their belief systems (see Chapter 6) encourage them to take what they want. They rape.

   f. Women who are socially anxious may be more vulnerable to early rape, because they are hesitant to signal their displeasure early enough to inhibit the man from rape. Expressions of pain and pleading may only heighten the man's sexual arousal.

3. Relational date rape

   a. Couple has been dating for some time.

   b. They believe they know what to expect from each other.

   c. The motivation to date this woman by this man was not solely to have sexual intercourse with her.

   d. Exchange and social comparison processes are likely the causal factors. Some males who have been exclusively dating and showing affection toward a woman for a period of time may begin to feel shortchanged if intercourse does not occur.

   e. Most people who have been dating for a long period of time expect their relationship to develop toward marriage. One sign of movement, at least for the male, is sexual intercourse. In fact, for both genders, relationships in which sex did not occur are judged to be less serious (Peplau, Rubin, & Hill, 1977).

   f. If consensual sexual intercourse does not occur over the long term, the male may feel the situation is inequitable but may be unwilling to end the relationship because of his investment of time, energy, or resources.

   g. Social comparison processes may contribute, also. The male assumes that other men in similar relationships are sexually involved with their partners. The male may even compare himself with the woman's prior partners.

   h. Because of a desire to give the relationship momentum, sometime during the couple's usual "petting," the male will force sexual intercourse.

   i. The woman who abstains in a long-term relationship is likely to have conservative sexual values. But she may waver and give mixed messages.

BOX 4.3

The Profile of the Date Rape

Which seems more likely?

The victimizer:

1. is more sexually active than other males.
2. treats a woman as if she's his property, and gets angry when another man pays attention to her.
3. has a history of antisocial behavior; displays a lot of anger toward women.
4. subscribes to rape myths' acceptance of violence and similar attitudes, such as "Real men don't listen to 'no.' "
5. misperceives the actions of others, interprets passivity as permission.
6. denies that he has engaged in rape (in one study, cited by Goleman, 1989, only 17 of 1,152 male college students admitted to using physical force to have sexual intercourse when the woman didn't want to).
7. may have been drinking heavily (Norris, 1989); "The degree of intoxication of the man is the single most important factor in determining whether acquaintance rape will occur" (Bechhofer & Parrot, 1991, p. 23).

The victim:

1. is in a new environment, without friends.
2. may lack self-esteem (Skelton, 1982) or have poor social adjustment (Rogers, 1984).
3. is not good at asserting herself; does not communicate limits of acceptable behavior; may give mixed messages; does not fight back (Charlene Muehlenhard found in her study that the most powerful tactic is the statement: "This is rape and I'm calling the cops.").
4. may be drunk, fostering an assumption that further sexual activity is consensual (Norris, 1989).

one perpetrator, the rapist is more likely to commit a number of rapes over a period of time (Koss, 1988b). But the incidence of "party rape"—the gang rape of a woman by several acquaintances—

has only recently been recognized as prevalent, at colleges as well as elsewhere. Ehrhart and Sandler (1985) describe the cruel rape of a young college woman:

> It was her first fraternity party. The beer flowed freely and she had much more to drink than she had planned. It was hot and crowded and the party spread out all over the house, so that when three men asked her to go upstairs, she went with them. They took her into the bedroom, locked the door and began to undress her. Groggy with alcohol, her feeble protests were ignored as the three men raped her. When they finished, they put her in the hallway, naked, locking her clothes in the bedroom. (1985, p. 2)

In studying such incidents, Ehrhart and Sandler's interviewers were told by some campus officials that "it happens almost every week." Sanday (1990) reports that this type of gang rape is often referred to as "training" and is part of the campus party culture. Because many—if not most—of the victims end up dropping out of college shortly after being victimized and few such gang rapes are ever officially reported, the inclusion of these rapes is likely to be missed in most surveys.

Reactions of the Rape Victim

Victims of rapes by dates or acquaintances report high levels of anger and depression, just as victims of rapes by strangers do (Koss, 1988b). But partly as a result of experiencing less violence from the rapist, they also report they weren't quite as scared as were recipients of attacks by strangers. It seems fruitless to us to speculate as to which is worse. As B. Katz (1991) notes, the survivor of a stranger rape may have an easier time seeing her own victimization as a more random and less personal event. In contrast, the date-rape victim may have her identity as a social being brought into question—is she competent to function in relationships?

Interestingly, victims of date rapes did not differ from those of rapes by strangers with respect to their use of so-called passive forms of resistance (for example, using reasoning or pleading, crying or sobbing, or turning cold toward the other). Koss discovered that a large percentage of all victims reported resorting to such behaviors. Another common strategy used by both types of victims involved physically struggling to get away. Although the victims of stranger rapes were more likely to use the more active types of resistance such as screaming or trying to run away, neither type of victim used active resistance procedures very often. This is unfortunate. As elaborated in Chapter 12, these active forms of resistance may be the most effective ways to avoid a rape (Bart & O'Brien, 1984; Levine-MacCombie & Koss, 1986).

Of course, one reason why victims of acquaintance rapes may be less inclined to resist actively is a direct function of the characteristics of the rape. Before a rape can be resisted, the danger must be identified. Many women find sharing their company with a male on a Friday or Saturday night a common occurrence, in fact nothing out of the ordinary. If the situation is not perceived to be dangerous at first, the act of resistance is altered. Initial reactions to intrusions on one's limits may be that such intrusions are harmless (Rozée, Bateman, & Gilmore, 1991). Unfortunately, victims who wait too long before protesting are viewed as both desiring sex and sharing the blame for the rape (Shotland & Goodstein, 1983).

Impact on Victims

As implied earlier, the impact of the rape upon the victim's life is somewhat different when the rapist is an acquaintance rather than a stranger. Victims of the latter type of rapes are more likely to seek support from others to help them deal with the experience. Although three fourths of the women raped by someone totally unknown to them later discussed the experience with some other person, only about one half of those raped by an acquaintance did so (Koss, 1988b). This difference is important, because talking about the ordeal may be the single most important therapeutic behavior that a victim can do afterward (Davis & Friedman, 1985; Koss, 1988b). And although victims of rapes by strangers are more likely to seek professional help from a rape crisis center or the police, neither of the two types of victims are likely to do so very often. In Koss's study, of all the victims willing to talk about their experiences, approximately one fourth of the victims of stranger rape sought this type of help, but only 3% of victims involved with acquaintance rape sought such help, even though 62% of the stranger rape victims and 38% of the acquaintance rape victims felt they should obtain some type of therapy to help them deal with their trauma.

Once more, in these differences, we see the possibility that victims of acquaintance rape, by remaining silent, are reflecting heightened feelings of guilt and self-blame (Jenkins & Dambrot, 1987). Even though their physical suffering may be less, the psychological costs may be greater than those of stranger-rape victims, whose open discussion of their experience alleviates some of the psychological symptoms.

General Reactions to the Date Rape

"You can't be raped by someone you know." This is a common belief, but many women can testify to its inaccuracy. Most were shocked that their "friend" could do such a thing. Not only may such rape victims begin to question seriously their ability to judge others, but people aware of the rape may also generate doubts of their own. Unfortunately, many of the characteristics of the interaction contribute to some observers even justifying the rape by diminishing the blame to the rapist. For example, in one survey of high-school students, 43% of males and 32% of females believe that it is acceptable for a man to force a woman to have sex if they have dated for a long time (Giarrusso, Johnson, Goodchilds, & Zellman, 1979). More than half the males in the above survey also believed rape to be at least somewhat justifiable if the woman was "leading the man on." Other aspects that may lead some individuals to justify a sexual assault are the use of alcohol by either the man or the woman and the man's spending a lot of money on the woman. Given these circumstances, some people are willing to dismiss the sexual interaction as something less than a rape.

Blaming the victim—discussed in more detail in Chapter 6—is a robust phenomenon. Especially when the two people are a dating couple, people often believe that the woman—somehow, some way—should have known the man's intentions. As will be shown, women and men may differ in their reactions to different types of rape, as reflected in a study by Tetreault and Barnett (1987). In this study, undergraduate students were given scenarios depicting a sexual encounter. Half of the subjects received a description of an acquaintance rape, while the other half read about a woman victimized by a total stranger. After all of the students had read the scenario, they watched the same videotape of a rape victim (actually portrayed by an actress) in order to add authenticity to the study. Finally, they were asked to give their opinions about the encounter.

Results of the study were quite intriguing. Females who were exposed to the stranger rape were more likely to believe that the situation they had read about was more serious, and was, indeed, rape more than females who were exposed to the acquaintance rape. Females viewing the acquaintance rape also reported blaming the victim more and liking her less. Males, on the other hand, reacted in just the opposite way. They felt like the acquaintance rape was the more serious crime, and definitely rape. They tended to blame the victim of the stranger rape more, and to like her less. The men's attributions were apparently influenced by a greater devaluation of the stranger rape victim (Calhoun & Townsley, 1991).

In another study that examined differing levels of men's sexual arousal to depictions of rape, it was found that men show just as much arousal to depictions of acquaintance rape as they do to portrayals of consenting sex (Check & Malamuth, 1983). It seems clear that two very different processes are working here. How can such results be explained?

Check and Malamuth (1983) cite societal standards as the culprit, an aspect to which we will return later in the chapter. Because standards for how men and women should act are different, responses to such personal violations may be very different. Women are taught that they are supposed to be caring and sensitive without becoming too "available." They are also taught to expect the man to test the boundaries of their "availability." Women confronted with other women who have been raped by an acquaintance, therefore, may view her as somehow breaking the rules. Men, on the other hand, may believe that it's all right for a women to be sexually involved—as long as she is in a legitimate relationship. Inevitably, having sexual relations with a stranger (presumably no matter the conditions) is breaking the rules to men. Either way, everyone loses.

In several other investigations that looked at differences between men and women in how they view a rape between acquaintances (Jenkins & Dambrot, 1987; Weir, 1991), sex differences were found. It seems that, in general, men are less likely to perceive a situation in which a man forces his date to have sex as rape and are more likely to perceive that the woman desired sexual intercourse. Perhaps date rape is more serious, therefore, because they believe the woman is acting in a way that may be harmful to the man.

Whose Fault Is It?

Especially in Western society, people may become consumed with the idea that everything happens for a reason, that there has to be an answer to the question "Why?" When one is raped by an acquaintance or date, attributing blame to someone seems unavoidable, both by those involved and by outside observers.

Unfortunately, the someone who is blamed is often the victim. A writer for *Time* magazine, John Leo (1987), illustrates the subtle bias against the victim. He states that, "Like many victims, Susan was unwary and alone too soon with a man she barely knew" (p. 77). Was Susan in a car on a deserted highway? No. She was 19 years old, in summer school at a college where she met a man in the dorm cafeteria and went to his dorm room that evening to watch the news on TV and get acquainted.

Even the esteemed Ann Landers, at least back in 1985, expressed a conventional "woman at risk" view when she wrote in response: "And now, at the risk of sounding hilariously square, I'd like to suggest that the woman who 'repairs to some private place for a few drinks and a little shared affection' had, by her acceptance of such a cozy invitation, given the man reason to believe she is a candidate for whatever he might have in mind" (1985, p. 5).

Rather than communicating a message that women shouldn't take risks, society should examine the standards it uses in courtship and dating. These provide some explanations for the emergence of date rape.

Traditional Dating Norms

By the time a person reaches adolescence, the rules of how to behave when interacting with a member of the other sex are nicely ingrained. The rules are different for boys and girls, as well as for different types of situations—how one should act on a first date may differ drastically from the appropriate behavior to display while working on class project with others. This process is called *gender-role socialization,* and offers nearly impermeable stereotypes about what the roles for each gender should be.

In psychological research, the term *script* refers to a conceptual representation of stereotyped event sequences—what one is supposed to do in a given situation. For example, almost all of us retain in our minds an idea of what you do when you enter a restaurant. Once you have entered and are seated, you are handed a menu and decide what you want to eat. After you have told the waiter or waitress what you would like to order, you wait a few minutes for your meal. After you are finished with your meal, you receive the check, pay for your food, and leave. The order of a script is very resistant to change—you do not usually eat before you are seated in a restaurant. The script for dating a potential romantic partner is conceptually similar to that of walking into a restaurant. Despite the fact that we are living in a presumably "liberated" era, and the traditional courtship patterns are supposedly disappearing, most conceptions of women's and men's roles in dating remain (Rose & Frieze, 1985). This can be illustrated by reviewing the advice for adolescents about dating behavior that has been published by various prominent sources such as advice columns in magazines read by teenagers.

Research shows that appropriate behavior associated with a first date has changed very little over the past 30 years (Rose & Frieze, 1985). The male is advised to take on the more dominant role in the interaction; it is his responsibility to initiate the date and plan the evening, by choosing an activity that he is capable of paying for. Women, on the other hand, are supposed to be as pleasant and attractive as possible. Especially in adolescence the pressure to conform to such gender stereotypes is high, and both males and females believe that they are expected to live up to such standards by the other sex (Braito, Dean, Powers, & Bruton, 1981; Scher, 1984). Unfortunately, it may be that these norms that men and women feel compelled to adhere to are the very same norms that are conducive to date rape. One reason for this is that following the traditional norms automatically puts the man in charge. The next section of this chapter analyzes the implications of this power differential.

Power and Rape

As we have previously pointed out, dating norms most often dictate that it is the male's responsibility to initiate the date, to plan what the couple will do on a date, to drive on the date, and to pay for the date (Check & Malamuth, 1983). Women who initiate contact with a man are viewed less positively, whether they are attempting to start a conversation or initiate a dinner date (Green & Sandos, 1983). All of these types of behaviors related to the dating process are associated with higher levels of power, both symbolically and practically (Peplau & Campbell, 1989). Thus, in most dating situations, the male implicitly has more power.

The power differential in relationships is also alive and well in today's society. Despite the fact that *attitudes* may be changing, in that most people report that equality in relationships is preferred (Herzog, Bachman, & Johnston, 1983), this ideal is not reality (Basow, 1986). More than half of all couples surveyed in one study reported inequality within the relationship, with men overwhelmingly enjoying most of the control (Peplau, Rubin, & Hill, 1976).

These types of power may explicitly be related to rape. Brownmiller (1975) argues that rape is the direct consequence of the power differential between men and women. Exactly how is such disparity in power conducive to rape?

In an important study, Muehlenhard and Linton (1987) addressed this very question. They looked at four different factors related to the power differential in dating: who initiated the date, who paid for the date, who drove, and how well the couple had known each other. Note that the first three of these factors deal directly with behaviors that males are expected to take responsibility for. In this study, responses were obtained from more than 600 men and women at a large southwestern university. Not only were students asked to describe their experiences, if any, with sexual aggression (any type of unwanted sexual activity, including rape), but they were also asked for descriptions of their most recent date. Using this type of methodology allows valuable comparisons and enables researchers to find out what types of dates are *most* at risk for sexual aggression. For example, if Sheila has reported experiencing sexual aggression before on a date where the couple went to a local club for a few drinks, and also reports that on her most recent date these same events occurred but there was no sexual aggression, this information does not provide clues as to what factors may be conducive to rape. It is important that in Muehlenhard and Linton's analyses, no significant differences were found in the general dating patterns of those who had experienced sexual aggression versus those who had not had such unfortunate experiences. This suggests that unique characteristics cannot be attributed to women who are sexually victimized by their dates—they were *not* asking for their fate. As Muehlenhard and Linton predicted, all of the behaviors that the dating script mandates were conducive to rape. When the female reported experiencing sexual aggression, it was more likely to occur when the male was in command. That is, when the male had initiated the date, had paid for the date, and had driven on the date. How can such power factors contribute to the incidence of rape?

Male as Initiator

Whoever initiates a potential date is automatically put in an active role, whereas the one who is asked out on a date receives the passive role (Muehlenhard, 1988). It is usually the initiator who plans the date, and the decision about what to do and where to do it could contribute to the likelihood of a rape occurring. For example, a rape is not likely to occur inside a movie theater, but if it is decided that the couple will go to a secluded area to have a picnic in the evening, the chances for sexual aggression are much higher (Amick & Calhoun, 1987).

Who Pays

Unfortunately, in the American dating system, it's often the implicit assumption that money and sex will be exchanged (Korman & Leslie, 1982). Furthermore, the *more* money spent by a male on a date, the *more* he feels entitled to sexual intimacy. As Korman and Leslie (1982) note, "When the female does not desire to exchange in this manner, the obligation to reciprocate may create a situation of interactional tension in which the male actively seeks repayment for the benefits he has furnished, perhaps intensifying a scene in which the female may become offended" (pp. 117-118). Adherence to such social exchange norms begins early. In one survey of high school students, 12% of the girls and 39%—almost half—of the males said that it was at least somewhat acceptable for a boy to force a girl to have sex if he had spent a lot of money on her (Giarrusso et al., 1979).

Who Drives

The social implications of who drives may be similar to that of who pays. If the male drives, he is providing a "service" that he may feel must be compensated. Symbolically, he may feel entitled to sex with his date (Muehlenhard & Linton, 1987). The fact that the person who drives is in the more powerful position also has practical significance. The woman who finds herself the passenger in a car driven by her date and headed in a direction with which she feels uncomfortable (e.g., a country road or secluded area) is extremely vulnerable. If she remains a passenger, she may be in danger; if she gets out to walk home alone, she may also be in danger. In fact, because women are taught to fear being alone with no man to protect them (Stanko, 1988), they "may perceive the option to walk home alone at night as equally or more dangerous than remaining with their date" (Harney & Muehlenhard, 1991, p. 165).

It is a sad irony that women are taught to accept the passive role in dating when this role puts them at risk to be raped.

Dating and Sexuality:
The Double Standard

The dating script to which most people ascribe is closely related to males' and females' sexual activity. Despite the fact that *attitudes* toward sexuality appear to be advocating more permissive and egalitarian values, a study by Peplau et al. (1977) suggests that the sexual role playing by males and females still follows the traditional rules. Males still take it upon themselves to encourage intercourse, testing the limits of intimacy to see "how far they can get." Such sexual advances force many women into a situation that they feel compelled to refuse. Failure to refuse sexual advances puts women at risk of obtaining a reputation as "easy" or "loose" (Korman & Leslie, 1982). As Peplau et al. describe, "The woman's role as limit-setter is consistent with her presumed lesser interest in sex and her greater stake in preserving a good reputation and avoiding pregnancy" (1977, p. 87).

Unfortunately, the situation, following these scripts, could easily get out of hand. For example, if it is the woman's "job" to say no to sexual advances, then her refusal may not be taken seriously. It is not hard to imagine how a man being told "no" by his date may mistake her defiance as just following the rules, believing that in actuality she really wants it. Research supports the fact that some men really do believe that women want sex even though they say no (Muehlenhard & Felts, 1987; Shotland & Goodstein, 1983). One male college student and fraternity brother who participated in "party sex" commented: "Sometimes a woman has to resist your advances to show how sincere she is. And so, sometimes you've gotta help them along. You know she means no the first time, but the third time she could say no all night and you know she doesn't mean it" (Sanday, 1990, p. 113). Consequently, a male's persistence may increase because he may really believe that she is only engaging in "token" resistance. Consistent with this notion is the fact that the most common strategy used by sexually coercive men involves merely ignoring the woman's pleas (Muehlenhard, 1987; Rapaport & Burkhart, 1984). In one study, more than 25% of university men reported that they had engaged in aggressive sexual activity with a woman even after she had responded to their attempts with either fighting, crying, screaming, or pleading (Kanin, 1967). Another study by the same researcher (Kanin, 1984)—using as subjects self-disclosed date rapists—found that two thirds of them felt the fault of the incident rested with the woman (Warshaw & Parrot, 1991).

Such sexual role-playing suggests that women are actually encouraged to engage in token resistance, defined as "a woman's indicating that she did not want to have sex even though she had every intention to and was willing to engage in sexual intercourse" (Muehlenhard & Hollabaugh, 1988, p. 5). It is a common belief that many women do offer token resistance to sexual advances, and it is quite typical for scenarios of token resistance to be portrayed in the media. In such situations, a woman is usually shown initially saying "no," and eventually coming around and actually enjoying sexual intimacy, a problematic paradigm that perpetuates the myth that a woman who is raped actually wanted sexual intercourse. It is a complicated and potentially dangerous game that society advocates we play. Do some women actually engage in such behaviors?

Do Women Say "No"
When They Really Mean "Yes"?

Muehlenhard and Hollabaugh (1988) sought to answer this question; to see if some women do say no when they really mean yes—and, if so, what their reasons for doing so are. They asked more than 600 female students at Texas A&M University if they had ever engaged in such token resistance, and found that 39% of the women responded affirmatively, admitting that they had indeed told a man "no" when they did have every intention of having sexual intercourse with him. Of these women, 32.5% reported engaging in this type of resistance only once, 45.6% said they had done it 2-5 times, 11.2% reported 6 to 10 times, 7.8% reported 11-20 times, and 2.9% reported using token resistance more than 20 times. Muehlenhard and Hollabaugh even argued that "given society's sexual double standard, token resistance may be a rational behavior" (1988, p. 872). But as Abbey (1991) observes: "Unfortunately, token resistance perpetuates miscommunication between the sexes and encourages date rape. It is easy to see how a man who has previously turned a 'no' into a 'yes' might force sexual intercourse on a date who says 'no' and means it" (pp. 104-105).

The study by Muehlenhard and Hollabaugh revealed quite interesting results regarding why women may offer token resistance. With respect to level of tradition, it was found that women who have offered token resistance scored in the middle of the scale, as compared with other women. Contrary to the idea that it is the *most* traditional women who would engage in such behaviors, Muehlenhard and Hollabaugh found that those who scored highest on the scale were sexually inactive women who both meant "no" and said "no" (though women who engage in the later type of behavior are *not* only sexually inactive women). The token resisters were also more traditional than those women who were willing participants in sexual intimacy, saying "yes" and meaning "yes." In addition, the women who engaged in token resistance were also more likely to believe falsely that this was common behavior among their peers, that *everyone* follows the sexual scripts dictated by society.

In addition to level of tradition, several other factors were found to be related to token resistance. First of all, these women were found to report high levels of agreement with statements indicating an adversarial relationship between dating partners. Adherence to these types of statements indicates a belief that sexual relationships are fundamentally exploitative and manipulative; that a member of the opposite sex is not to be trusted. They also were more likely to believe that it is acceptable for men to use physical force in male-female relationships, and that women enjoy it when men use force in sexual relationships!

It seems clear that some preexisting attitudes may play a large part in determining whether a woman will engage in token resistance or not. Some of these reflect the sexual double standard; if a woman appears not to want sex but is talked into it or coerced, it may seem more acceptable to her (Muehlenhard & Hollabaugh, 1988). In addition to these preexisting attitudes, women also cited several other types of reasons explaining their behavior. These include inhibition-related reasons, manipulative reasons, and practical reasons.

Inhibition-related reasons (e.g., "I was afraid it would hurt" or "It was against my religious beliefs"). Inhibition-related reasons include emotional, religious, and moral reasons; fear of physical discomfort; and embarrassment about one's body. It appears that these women are afraid of openly expressing their sexuality and that this fear is based on their belief that sexual intimacy is explicitly wrong. Furthermore, women who cited these reasons also reported higher levels of erotophobia, or a tendency to respond to sexual cues with negative emotions. These types of reasons were reported as important by 19% of the token resisters.

Manipulative reasons (e.g., "I wanted him to beg" or "I was angry at him"). Approximately 23% of the women who engaged in token resistance offered manipulative reasons for their behavior. This includes game-playing, anger with the partner, and the desire to be in control. Interestingly, women who reported using these reasons also reported more erotophilia (a tendency to respond to sexual cues with positive emotions) and more agreement with the belief that women like it when men use force during sex. Based on the subjects' answers to the other scales, Muehlenhard and Hollabaugh (1988) concluded that although these women adhered to more egalitarian values, and did not believe in male dominance in general, they did accept male dominance specifically in sexual situations and related this type of dominance to sexual arousal.

At this point perhaps the distinction between *seduction* and *rape* should be discussed. Those are two different scripts. Furthermore, Mosher and Anderson (1986) have found that when women are induced to imagine being raped, they are repulsed and disgusted. However, when they are asked to imagine that this is only a fantasy over which they have control, it is not perceived so negatively. The key issue here is control, which is clearly not present in rape.

Practical reasons (e.g., "I was afraid I might get pregnant" or "Parents might come home"). Practical reasons are most closely related to the pressures of the sexual role-playing double standards. Such practical reasons include fear of appearing promiscuous, situational problems, concern about the nature of the relationship, uncertainty about their partner's feelings, and fear of sexually transmitted diseases. It is such practical reasons that are most closely related to the belief that all women engage in such behavior. These women seem to be acknowledging their emotional and sexual feelings, but are afraid of the consequences if they respond to such feelings. Muehlenhard and Hollabaugh suggest that token resistance may be a rational response to this perceived problem: that if she appears to be reluctant and has to be "talked into it," her behavior may seem more acceptable. For these women, it was not their own attitudes that were important in determining their behavior, but their perceptions of the attitudes held by the culture in general; 23% of women reported engaging in token resistance for such practical reasons.

Although Muehlenhard and Hollabaugh do suggest that token resistance is a rational response to the double standard, they do not advocate such behavior. The consequences of such behavior may be drastic, at both the individual and the societal level. In the first place, it's dishonest, and honest communication is essential to relationships. It perpetuates negative stereotypes of women as manipulative, and encourages the viewpoint that men may proceed even though a woman says no—that her refusal is not to be taken seriously. For those women who say "no" and mean "no" the consequences may very well be rape. Though Muehlenhard and Hollabaugh have documented that token resistance is, unfortunately, a real phenomenon, they also note that "When a woman says no, chances are she means it. . . . Regardless of the incidence of token resistance, if the woman means no and the man persists, it is rape" (1988, p. 12).

Hunter and Shotland (1990) report difficulty in reconciling the behavior of these women with the reasons they have provided. They conclude that if the reasons are manipulative ones, token resistance makes logical sense, given the woman's goals. But practical reasons and inhibition-related reasons seem inconsistent with the woman's achievement of her goals. Hunter and Shotland propose that the latter types of women may change their intent during the sexual episode. Early on, when considering these practical or inhibition-related concerns, they may *mean* "no," but "as the episode progresses, they begin to change their intent to 'yes,' perhaps without ever changing their verbal responses" (Hunter & Shotland, 1990, p. 4). That is, token resistance, rather than an attempt to mislead their dates, may be "a sign of a woman's confusion resulting from a process of changing sexual intent" (p. 4).

We have seen how the dating script advocates that men be put in the more powerful position, and the adverse effects that this may have on the woman—that is, following such scripts puts the woman at risk of being a victim of sexual aggression and rape. The script associated with acceptable sexual behavior may also force women into dangerous situations—a woman's resistance is often not taken seriously. When a woman is honestly trying to resist a man's sexual advances, yet he believes she actually wants him to pursue the advances, it is the direct result of miscommunication and of perceiving the situation inaccurately. Such illusory communications and misperceptions made by men contribute to the incidence of rape.

However, misperceiving a woman's refusal of her date's sexual advances is not the only type of behavior that men may find "suggestive." Indeed, men tend to find most any type of behavior a woman engages in to be more seductive, sexy, and flirtatious than the woman herself or female observers of the interaction believe she is being. Such misunderstandings, or "oversexualizations," are extremely common (Johnson, Freshnock, & Saal, in press).

Miscommunication and Misperceptions

Imagine the following scenario: One day after class a student approaches her professor, hoping to get an extension on an assignment. She had already put a lot of work into the project, and he acknowledges her effort. Though he does not usually accept late work, he promises to consider breaking his policy on course deadlines in her case (used in Johnson et al., in press). What is going on here? Does this female student only want an extension on her paper, or is she really just taking advantage of an opportunity to flirt with her professor? What about the professor? Is he really just interested in her class project, or does he see a potential relationship in the making? This is just what Johnson et al. (in press) attempted to find out when they presented a videotape of this very interaction to

200 students at a large midwestern university. Results showed that males consistently found the female student—as well as the male professor—to be more seductive, sexy, and flirtatious than the female observers did. Men were also more likely to perceive that the two were attracted to each other. Women, on the other hand, viewed this same interaction as professional and merely friendly. In another study done by the same researchers the scenario involved a male store manager training a female cashier. Again, men rated the woman as more sexual and friendly than women who viewed the same videotape.

According to Antonia Abbey (1982, 1987, 1991), men may be socialized to view *any* form of friendly behavior from a woman as an indication that she is interested in sexual intimacy. In Abbey's (1982) study, two students, one male and one female, were participants in a "get acquainted" conversation with each other. In addition, two other students (again, one male and one female) observed the conversation. After only 5 minutes of conversation, all students were separated and asked to fill out questionnaires concerning the two subjects who had conversed. The results of this study revealed that men consistently interpreted the woman's behavior as seductive, but both the woman who had engaged in the conversation and the woman who had viewed the interaction considered their behavior as only friendly; they were not intending to be seductive or flirtatious. Interestingly, it was not just the female's friendliness that was interpreted as seductive. Male participants consistently found their own behavior as more flirtatious and seductive than the female participants rated them. Male observers also found the man to be more flirtatious and seductive than did their female counterparts.

The fact that men not only perceive women's friendly behavior as seductive and flirtatious, but also their own, as well as other *mens'* behavior, deserves attention. It appears that this type of biased perception is not limited to the behavior of females, but occurs for *all* behavior. As Abbey explains, "this appears to be merely one manifestation of a broader sexual orientation" (1982, p. 830).

Indeed, women and men are attaching different meanings to the very same cues in the exact same situation. Are certain cues within the interaction causing more of the difference than others? There are many factors that could potentially lead to the contrast in perceptions between males and females, especially on a date. For example, if the woman wears revealing clothes, men are more likely to see her as more sexual (Abbey, Cozzarelli, McLaughlin, & Harnish, 1987). As a consequence, a man may perceive that his date who dresses in a revealing way actually intends to have sex with him. The same types of perceptions probably occur for many types of behaviors. If a woman sits close to her date, reveals something personal about herself, or even smiles a lot, the man may get the wrong idea. These may be considered "suggestive" behaviors. In fact, high school males in one study were likely to regard *every* dating behavior asked about to be an indication that the other person wanted sex (Goodchilds, Zellman, Johnson, & Giarrusso, 1988)!

Traditional dating norms may not be fair but they are present, and women must be aware of the possibility that men may indeed misinterpret their behavior, both nonverbal and verbal. After an incident of sexual aggression has occurred between a man and a woman, both are likely to agree that the man had felt "led on" (Muehlenhard & Hollabaugh, 1988), especially when she wore revealing clothing. Though women agreed that their behavior had been interpreted in such a way, almost *all* of these women said that their actions were not intended to lead their date on in any way. Nevertheless, men reported believing that she really did want sexual contact.

Summary

The above discussion takes a somewhat optimistic view of explaining date rape because it removes some of the intention of rape away from the rapist. It is true that dating and sexual scripts, miscommunication, and misperceptions can—and often do—lead to rape. There is also research, however, to support the contention that the same motivations behind stranger rape underlie the motivations of an acquaintance rapist: power, anger, and sadism. Furthermore, Shotland argues that different causes of date rape may be a function of different types of dating relationships.

5 Spousal Rape

Prior to 1978, most people had not thought about the possibility of a man raping his wife. Even professional people ignored the matter; Finkelhor and Yllö (1985) found that of 31 textbooks on marriage and the family published in the 1970s, only one mentioned anything related to marital rape. But suddenly the mass media informed the public of the relationship between John and Greta Rideout.

The Rideout Case

In 1978 the Rideouts were in their early twenties. They had met 4 years before, in Portland, OR, and had been married for 2½ years. Their relationship had been an acrimonious one, punctuated by John's violence, Greta's escapes (she left him three times), and the couple's reconciliations because of their young daughter.

But on October 10, 1978, the conflict culminated in a series of acts that led to a nationally publicized rape trial. According to

---

AUTHORS' NOTE: This chapter relies heavily on two excellent recent books dealing with spousal rape: Finkelhor and Yllö's (1985) *License to Rape: Sexual Abuse of Wives,* and Diana E. H. Russell's (1990) *Rape in Marriage,* (rev. ed.). A chapter by Russell (1991) in *Acquaintance Rape: The Hidden Crime* (Parrot & Bechhofer, eds.), is adapted from her book.

Greta's testimony at the trial, John awoke from a nap that afternoon and demanded that she have sex with him. She stated: "He was highly obsessed with sex; he wanted it two or three times a day. No matter what I gave him, he was never totally satisfied" (Russell, 1991, p. 131). Violent sex, including slapping and slugging, seemed to give John the most pleasure.

So Greta said no. When he began to attack her, she ran from the house; trying to hide, she was caught. John dragged her back, locked her in a room and began to beat her again. He tore her pants off, forced her to the floor, and began to rape her. Finally she submitted, she later testified in court, out of fear that he would break her jaw.

After the coerced sex, Greta did manage to escape and fled to a neighbor's home. When she told the police she was informed that under Oregon law, she would have to wait 2 days to file a rape charge. But a counselor at the local women's crisis center helped Greta get to a hospital so that her charges could be documented by doctors' reports of bruises and signs of a sexual assault on her vagina. Two days later Greta did file charges against her husband; a week later, John Rideout was arrested and charged with rape. (A year before, the spousal immunity clause had been deleted from Oregon's rape law; in 1978 it was one of only three states in which a cohabiting husband could be prosecuted for rape.)

The trial of John Rideout began in December of 1978. It was *not* the first instance in the United States of a man being prosecuted for the rape of his wife; 6 months earlier a New Jersey man, Daniel Morrison, had been found guilty of raping his wife and was sentenced to 4 to 12 years in prison (Finkelhor & Yllö, 1985). But Rideout was the first husband still living with his wife to be prosecuted, and hence the trial drew national media attention—in fact, in the words of Finkelhor and Yllö (1985, p. 172), it became "a true national spectacle."

The defense attorney portrayed Greta as a disturbed and vindictive woman and tried to discredit her testimony. The jury of eight women and four men chose to discount medical evidence about a violent assault, and on December 27, 1978, found John Rideout not guilty of the first-degree rape of his wife (Finkelhor & Yllö, 1985; Russell, 1991).

Less than 2 weeks later, the Rideouts announced a reconciliation. A conciliatory John Rideout was quoted as saying: "The law is right; its a hard thing for a person like me to come back and say he believes the law is right when the law was used against me" (Russell, 1991, p. 132). Advocates seeking reform of the antiquated rape laws of most states were disappointed and angered, for the reconciliation corroborated "the arguments of skeptics who claimed it proved that vindictive wives would only use rape laws to harass husbands and waste prosecutors' time with cases that were better handled in divorce court or marriage counseling" (Finkelhor & Yllö, 1985, p. 173).

But 2 months later, matters took another turn; in March, 1979, the couple separated again. Greta was quoted as saying: "I was going to go mad if I stayed there any longer; he has some pretty wild ideas about marriage" (Russell, 1991, p. 132). Greta obtained a divorce and resumed using her maiden name.

John was not satisfied. Five months later, he broke into his ex-wife's home. He was given a 9-month suspended jail sentence, placed on 2 year's probation, required to pay $15 for the door he damaged, and submit to a psychiatric evaluation. Despite all of this, he continued to harass his ex-wife. Finally, in February 1980, he was sentenced to 9 months in jail, and spent 3 months there.

The national public, however, was not aware of the continued attacks by John Rideout on his ex-wife; instead, they remembered only the reconciliation of the apparently happy, handsome couple.

History of Spousal Rape and the Law

Yes, the outcome of the Rideout trial was disturbing to those who wish to reform rape legislation, but it was still a step forward, because at its time—a decade and a half ago—a man could not even be prosecuted for raping his wife in most states. This section describes the origins of the legislation that prevailed until a decade ago.

Most countries of the world and most of the states, until recently, included what is called "the marital exemption" in their rape laws. These laws defined rape as "the forcible penetration of the body of a woman who is not the wife of the perpetrator" (Russell, 1991, p. 129).

The origin of this exemption is usually traced to the often cited argument of Matthew Hale, Chief Justice in England in the 17th century, who wrote:

> But the husband cannot be guilty of rape committed by himself upon his lawful wife, for by their mutual matrimonial consent and contract the wife hath given up herself in this kind unto the husband which she cannot retract. (Russell, 1991, pp. 129-130)

According to Finkelhor and Yllö, "It is now generally acknowledged that Hale, for all his legal erudition, was a rabid woman-hater who made his mark among contemporaries by burning women at the stake as witches" (1985, p. 163). It is also argued that the conception of matrimony and the rights of women have changed dramatically in the 350 years since Hale's pronouncement.

But until recently, legislators were reluctant to intervene for two reasons, according to Finkelhor and Yllö (1985). One is the belief that marriage implies a special agreement for sexual intimacy. When the state of Florida considered renouncing the marital rape exemption, one of its legislators, Tom Bush, claimed: "The state of Florida has absolutely no business intervening into the sexual relationship between a husband and a wife. . . . We don't need Florida invading the sanctity and intimacy of a relationship" (Russell, 1991, p. 130).

The second belief is that for rape to occur there must be an absence of consent; "if a form of consent exists between a husband and a wife when intercourse occurs, a rape cannot be said to have taken place" (Finkelhor & Yllö, 1985, p. 164). Apparently acceptance of marriage vows "to love, honor, and obey" is interpreted to mean a blanket acceptance of intercourse on demand, or "permanent consent," as it has been labeled.

But, as modern critics of Hale's conception note, even if a woman—by marrying—is consenting to sex, she is not consenting to rape (Griffin, 1980). In other words, she is not giving her husband permission to harm her or humiliate her.

Emphasis should be on *modern* in the above paragraph. In one English case barely more than 100 years ago (*Regina v. Clarence*, 1888), the extent to which Hale's doctrine was applied was astounding. A woman brought her husband to trial because he had knowingly infected her with gonorrhea. She stated that if she had realized that he was diseased, she would have never consented to have sexual intercourse with him. Eleven judges disagreed, ruling that the husband was not guilty of harming her because "it was not illegal for him to force his wife to have intercourse even if he was knowingly hurting her" (Finkelhor & Yllö, 1985, pp. 164-165).

In contrast, modern law in general does not allow people to consent to harm (Stecich, 1977). For example, when a fraternity pledge is injured during a "Hell Week" hazing, the courts have rejected the counterargument that he "consented" to harm when he pledged the fraternity.

Furthermore, no one is allowed to take the law into his or her own hands and enforce rights through violence. Joanne Schulman, of the National Center on Women and Family Law, offers the following analogy:

> Suppose you have a contract for the delivery of some tools by a certain date, but your supplier fails to make his delivery on time. Of course he is in violation of his contract. But that does not give you the privilege of breaking into his warehouse and taking the tools by force. You have to go to court to enforce your contracts (Finkelhor & Yllö, 1985, p. 166).

The Changing Scene Regarding Laws About Marital Rape

The shift by the states and the federal government to make spousal rape a crime is truly an extraordinary achievement and testimony to the hard work of feminists and others who have dealt effectively with the resistance of mostly male state legislators (Russell, 1991). These actions have also had to deal with incorrect stereotypes about spousal rape; see Box 5.1.

Laws Against Spousal Rape

In 1980 only 3 states had laws against marital rape, although 5 more had some restrictions. A little more than a decade later, husbands could be prosecuted for raping their wives in 43 states, the District of Columbia, and on all federal land. States differ in whether conditions restrict this rule. About one third of the states have abolished the marital rape exemption entirely. About 25 other states have partially abolished the exemption or have created a special category of marital sexual assault (Stead, 1990). As of 1992, marital rape is not a crime, if a couple is living together, in only 2 states: North Carolina and Oklahoma. The marital rape exemption

BOX 5.1

The Stereotypes of Spousal Rape

Finkelhor and Yllö (1985) observe that for most people, forced sex in marriage is not "real" rape. When asked to describe marital rapes, respondents often provide descriptions that reflect two false stereotypes: the "sanitary" rape and the "healthy" rape.

In the "sanitary stereotype" the rape of a spouse is pictured as a petty conflict, a disagreement over sex that the husband wins. One respondent described it as follows:

> Husband and wife are newly separated. He comes for a short visit and forces her to make love because he really does love her and misses her. (Finkelhor & Yllö, 1985, p. 13)

In the second myth-stereotype, the husband is a "healthily sexual" man. For example, in *Gone With the Wind*, Rhett Butler (Clark Gable) overcomes the resistance of the proper and frightened Scarlett O'Hara (Vivian Leigh). The next scene shows Scarlett the morning after, glowing with barely suppressed satisfaction and love. Such depictions present "a most dangerous image of marital rape, for (they powerfully advertise) the idea that women secretly wish to be overpowered and raped, and that, in fact, rape may be a good way to reconcile a marriage" (Finkelhor & Yllö, 1985, p. 14).

has been abolished in Canada, Israel, Scotland, New Zealand, parts of Australia, and, most recently, in Great Britain. Furthermore, the highest courts in several states have struck down the marital rape exemption as an unconstitutional denial of equal protection for wives (Russell, 1991). If rape of an unmarried woman is considered a crime, then the principle of equity should require that it be so for married women, too. Feminist attorneys have urged that in the 33 states that do not have a rule against spousal rape or have an unsatisfactory law, class action suits should be organized to have the courts abolish the exemptions as unconstitutional.

Does Abolishing the Marital Rape
Exemption Increase Litigation?

One of the arguments used by traditionalists opposed to abolishing the marital rape exemption was that doing so would encourage frivolous suits by vindictive wives. Records indicate that this has not happened. Sweden has had a law making marital rape a crime for more than 20 years. Gilbert Geis, in 1979, searched the police records and found only four examples of such prosecutions for the year 1970 and two for the year 1976. No one in Sweden thought the new laws were being abused.

In the United States, the record is similar: Nebraska eliminated the exemption in 1976 but had not had a single prosecution under it 6 years later (Finkelhor & Yllö, 1985). Oregon only had four, including the Rideout case. California, the most populous state, had 42 cases for the years 1980 and 1981. The National Clearinghouse on Marital and Date Rape gained as much information as possible about each of these cases. They are "almost entirely made up of well-documented and brutal crimes, not quarrels between spouses that happen to spill into the courts" (Finkelhor & Yllö, 1985). They include one in which the husband raped his wife with a crowbar and a tire iron and then attacked her breasts with the same instruments. In another, a man forced his wife to have sex with other men and with dogs. The use of knives and guns was also a common feature; several included very extreme beatings.

The analysis of the 42 cases produced another important finding. The majority of rapes (82%) occurred for spouses who were separated, sometimes very recently so (Finkelhor & Yllö, 1985).

The fact that the abolishing of the marital rape exemption does not cause a flood of charges may be reassuring to some. But the "noneffect" can be seen in another light. Reporting a rape by a spouse—even by a spouse who is living separately—is probably very hard for most victims to do. These victims are aware of community beliefs about a "wife's obligations." Threats of reprisals for reporting are not to be ignored. And some wives may have second thoughts. (In the 1980-1981 survey of 42 California reports, charges were dropped in 28% of the cases.) Our best indication is that the limited number of charges does not mean that the incidence of spousal rape is infrequent. In fact, it is substantial. Finkelhor and Yllö (1985) found that 10% of their sample of 323 Boston-area women said that their husbands had "used physical force or threat to try to have sex with them." Russell's (1984) survey found 14%.

Conviction Rates for Marital Rapists

When a man is charged with the rape of a woman who is his wife, and the charge proceeds past arraignment and to trial, it is quite likely that the man will be convicted. Russell (1991) reports on the National Clearinghouse on Marital and Date Rape's survey of the outcomes of 210 spousal rape cases reported to the police between 1978 and 1985. Charges were dropped in 48 of the 210 cases, or 23% (a percentage close to the California figures described earlier). But 88% of the resolved cases (104 of 118) ended in a conviction. This is considerably higher than the conviction rate for *non*marital rapes, and is encouraging to those who seek reassurance that the new laws have teeth in them.

Furthermore, men who are convicted of spousal rape are now getting sentences that include extended prison terms. The first two men convicted of spousal rape in Kansas after the institution of the new law received prison sentences of 10 years to life and 7 to 21 years, respectively. The first convicted spousal rapist in Georgia was sentenced to 5 years in prison.

The Motives for Spousal Rape

Why would a man rape his wife? What kind of needs does such an act reflect? Chapter 3 described the three-part typology developed by Groth (1979) based on his interviews with convicted rapists. Most of Groth's subjects raped strangers; none were convicted of raping their wives. Does his typology apply to husbands who rape their wives?

For many of the husbands who rape their wives, coercive sex is a standard procedure. The wives of about half of them report having been sexually assaulted 20 times or more. Some women could not remember how many times it had happened; "it happened half of the time we had sex during those three years," said one (Finkelhor & Yllö, 1985, p. 23). Finkelhor and Yllö (1985) interviewed 50 women who were victims of sexual assault by their husbands. Like

Groth, they classified the perpetrators into three types: Battering rape, force-only rape, and obsessive rape.

Battering Rape

Chronically battered wives are also at high risk for being raped by their husbands. As the researchers observe, "The kind of man who beats his wife is also more likely to rape her. If he is not deterred by the social conventions against punching and hitting, he will probably not be inhibited by social conventions against forcing sex, either" (Finkelhor & Yllö, 1985, p. 37).

But we should not assume perfect overlap between the two. In her exemplary book *Rape in Marriage,* Diana Russell (1982) cautions: "Wife rape cannot and must not be subsumed under the battered woman rubric" (p. 101).

The spouses of about half of Finkelhor and Yllö's interviewees were battering rapists. These men repeatedly attacked their wives physically; it was a way of life. "These men hit their wives, belittled them, called them names, took their money, and, as another way of humiliating and degrading them, resorted to sexual violence" (1985, pp. 22-23). Wives were raped with objects. They were subjected to a variety of abuses in lieu of intercourse. Often the rape was an extension of the beatings, which might last for an hour, or a day. "At some point, usually toward the end of the beating, the husband would either strip his wife or force her to disrobe and then have intercourse" (p. 23). Of the victims interviewed by Finkelhor and Yllö, 40% described at least one such combination.

Many times the violent incidents occurred with suddenness; the wives could not identify what led up to them. On other occasions the instigating aspect was something minor like a difference of opinion over which television show to watch. Finkelhor and Yllö say the attacks seemed like capricious expressions of anger and resentment; although they were sexual acts, they were not sparked by sexual disagreements. This type thus resembles Groth's classification of anger rape.

Anger as a motivation is exemplified by the fact that the wife's leaving or threatening to leave her marriage frequently provoked a marital rape. "These husbands, furious that their wives had gathered the courage to leave, used the assault as a way to express their anger and punish their wives" (Finkelhor & Yllö, 1985, p. 25).

Force-Only Rape

About 40% of spousal rapes were of a type labeled by Finkelhor and Yllö as force-only rapes, because husbands used only as much force as necessary to coerce their wives into sex. Often no physical or verbal abuse occurred; in other couples violence was unusual.

Other factors distinguished between battering-rape couples and force-only couples. The latter were a more educated, middle-class group; their relationships were less likely to have been based on traditional roles of husband as decision maker and wife as caretaker. The victims of force-only rapists did not characteristically face long-lasting and continual abuse. The rapist's goal was to accomplish the sexual act, not to hurt the woman. In fact, "the force-only rapes were more often prompted by a sexual conflict, whereas the battering rapes were not usually preceded by any conflict over sex" (p. 46). The men in these marriages appeared to be acting on some specific sexual complaint, perhaps a long-running disagreement of frequency or appropriateness of certain sexual acts. "At some point the long-standing disagreement spilled over into coercion" (Finkelhor & Yllö, 1985, p. 46).

Thus the force-only rapes by husbands seem consistent with Groth's classification of power rapes; sexuality is a means of compensating for the husband's "underlying feelings of inadequacy and serves to express issues of mastery, strength, control, authority, identity, and capability" (Groth, 1979, p. 25). Later expressions of regret and tenderness by the husband may reflect a desire to regain control, rather than love (O'Reilly, 1983).

Obsessive Rape

About 12% of Finkelhor and Yllö's marital rapists did not fit either of the above categories. What was common to them was that their sexual interests ran toward the bizarre and perverse, and they were willing to employ force to fulfill them.

These men were preoccupied with sex. They not only collected pornography but often created it, usually by taking pictures of their wives. Their predilection was for unusual sexual activities: emphasizing anal intercourse, tying their wife up, or inserting objects into her vagina.

Groth's third category, based on convicted rapists, was the sadistic type; Finkelhor and Yllö prefer *obsessive* as the label for their marital rapists, but they acknowledge some overlap. They note that some of the married men did not seem to be aroused by the pain and suffering they caused "but actually by the perverse acts in which they forced their wives to engage" (p. 55). It was "the element of obsession, not sadism, that stood out as the most common feature of this final category of marital rape" (p. 59).

Despite the difference in terminology, the analysis of types of spousal rape offers consistency across settings and relationships, with regard to the motivations of men who sexually abuse women. Anger is the most frequent instigator; needs for dominance and control are frequent; sadistic urges are less often the primary motivation, although they are the major influence in a tenth of the cases.

Conclusions

More than one thousand residents of San Antonio, TX, were shown a card with a description of a rape incident on it, and then they were asked some questions (Williams & Holmes, 1981). Incidents included a rape by an acquaintance, a rape by a stranger, a prostitute being raped, and the rape of a wife by her husband. By a large margin, these respondents rated the spousal rape as the least serious of the incidents; only half were even willing to define it as rape. Slightly more than a fourth of the men and around 40% of the women thought that the husband should be prosecuted.

A survey of the residents of Baltimore (Rossi, Waite, Bose, & Berk, 1974) asked them to rate the seriousness of 140 crimes. "Forcible rape of a former spouse" ranked 62nd, near "driving while drunk" (66th) and blackmail (59th). Unfortunately, this survey did not ask for rating of the seriousness of "forcible rape of a current spouse" because it was not a crime in Maryland at that time.

These surveys were done between one and two decades ago; perhaps public attitudes have shifted. For example, younger adults are more in favor of criminalizing forced sex in marriage than are older ones. Yet, all of the surveys consistently find a gender difference, with men less willing to prosecute a married rapist than are women.

Prosecutors are aware of the direction of public sentiment and are reluctant to prosecute cases in which the strength of the evidence is in conflict with community standards. The assistant district attorney of a metropolitan county, in charge of prosecuting rape cases, told one of us that she would not take a marital rape case to trial—unless other charges such as assault, death threats, or kidnapping were also present—because she doubted that any jury would convict a husband of raping his wife. Susan Estrich (1987), a law professor who has written a book on rape laws, concludes that "it seems that a wife rape must be aggravated in every respect other than the identity of the rapist to qualify as a real rape" (p. 78).

The future of spousal rape is hard to predict. On the one hand, the advance in legislation on this topic in the past decade is truly remarkable, given the prediction made a little more than 10 years ago that removing the spousal rape exemption was "one of the most difficult issues to lobby through the state legislatures" (Bienen, 1980, p. 187). Some state courts have recently made ground-breaking decisions in support of the cause of marital rape victims; see the description of the *Liberta* case in Box 5.2. But this may be an issue in which governmental action has advanced beyond public support for it.

Summary

Although ardent strives have been made in the past two decades in the legal system's treatment of spousal rape, the problem itself remains. Somewhere between 10% and 14% of wives are raped by their husbands, and the rape of a spouse can be among the most brutal of rapes. Despite its prevalence and the recent public awareness, victims of spousal rape often remain silent.

BOX 5.2

The *Liberta* Decision

One of the first state courts to reject the logic that a prior relationship means less harm to the victim of coercive sexual intercourse was the Court of Appeals of the State of New York, in the *People v. Liberta* decision (1984).

Mario Liberta was the first husband in New York to be convicted of raping a woman to whom he was legally married, even though they were living apart under a court order (Estrich, 1987). He forcibly raped and sodomized his wife in the presence of their 2½-year-old son. Even though New York law at the time defined *female* in its rape statute as "any female person who is not married to the actor," Liberta was found guilty of rape.

He appealed, claiming among other things that the court order to stay away from his wife did not mean that he was "not married" for purposes of the rape law. He also claimed that constitutional issues of equal protection under the Fourteenth Amendment of the Constitution were pertinent.

The court decided, first of all, that under amendments to the marital exemption rule passed by the New York legislature in 1978, if a couple was living separately under a court order, they were no longer "married" with regard to this statute (Estrich, 1987). Furthermore, the court ruled that the claim of "equal protection" (i.e., an equal right of unmarried men to commit rape), although arguable, should not stand in the way of a recognition that a marital rape may have consequences equally or more severe than other rapes. Rather than abolishing "the law's prohibitions as applied to unmarried men, which is what Liberta had sought, the court chose to extend the law's prohibitions to *all* married men who committed rape in the future" (Estrich, 1987, p. 78, italics in original). The conviction was upheld.

6 Attitudes Toward Rape and Rape Victims

Among all the imaginable crimes, rape holds a unique status. Brownmiller (1975), among others, has noted the profusion of myths and incorrect stereotypes about rape, rapists, and rape victims in our society. These take three general forms: (1) women cannot be raped against their will, (2) women secretly wish to be raped, and (3) most accusations of rape are faked.

Myths About Rape

Some of the prevalent myths are, of course, inconsistent with each other. We are told that: "Only bad girls get raped." But we are also told that "All women want to be raped" and "Women ask for it." The mythology of rape also promises that "Any healthy woman can resist a rapist if she really wants to" and that "Women 'cry rape' only when they've been jilted."

These falsehoods create a climate hostile to rape victims, portraying them as often-willing participants in furtive sexual encounters, or even instigators of them. In fact, these attitudes often function as self-serving rationalizations and excuses for blaming the victim. A portion of this chapter will therefore be devoted to society's tendency to put the onus of cause on the survivor of rape rather than on the perpetrator.

Examples of Rape Attitude Surveys

In providing a much-needed scientific perspective on the truth about forcible rape, social scientists can provide a number of methodological skills and theoretical constructs. Rape means many different things to many different people, and these differing attitudes and perceptions affect behaviors toward both offenders and their victims (Feild, 1978). Some observers feel more empathy toward rape victims than others do; some feel empathy toward defendants charged with the crime of rape (Deitz, Blackwell, Daley, & Bentley, 1982; Deitz, Littman, & Bentley, 1984; Deitz, Russell, & Hammes, 1989). (See Box 6.1 for amplification.) Thus the conceptualization and measurement of attitudes about rape can make a contribution by clarifying what different people are talking about.

In his ground-breaking efforts here, Herbert S. Feild (1978, 1979; Barnett & Feild, 1977; Feild & Barnett, 1978; Feild & Bienen, 1980) hypothesized that attitudes about rape are multidimensional rather than unidimensional; that is, a person's view on rape cannot be simply summarized by one score on a single scale. Rather, Feild proposed that a number of separate components or factors comprise attitudes about the general topic of rape. After constructing a 75-item Attitudes Toward Rape questionnaire and analyzing responses to it, he concluded that a number of specific attitude clusters contribute to our overall perspective. These factors, as identified and named by Feild, are the following:

1. Women's Responsibility in Rape Prevention. Sample attitude items concerning women's responsibility in rape prevention are "A woman should be responsible for preventing her own rape" and "A raped woman is a responsible victim, not an innocent one." Individuals scoring high on this factor subscale seemingly attribute the completion of rape as partly the result of the woman's acquiescence. This attitude permits rapists to indulge in their

BOX 6.1

The Measurement of Rape Empathy

The program of research by Sheila Deitz and her associates has enabled us to understand the concept of *rape empathy*. The measurement of this concept is achieved through the use of the Rape Empathy Scale (Deitz, Blackwell, Daley, & Bentley, 1982), which is composed of 19 paired statements. Each statement represents extreme empathy with either the rape victim or the rapist. Subjects are asked to read two statements, choose which they prefer, and indicate their degree of preference on a 7-point scale. A typical item is:

a. In deciding whether a rape has occurred or not, the burden of proof should rest with the woman, who must prove that a rape has actually occurred.
b. In deciding whether a rape has occurred or not, the burden of proof must rest with the man, who must prove that a rape has not actually occurred.

Research findings indicate that, compared to women, men had more empathy for the rapist and rated victims more negatively (Layman & Labott, 1992).

desires while not even having to think of themselves as rapists. People with this attitude, if serving as jurors, would not be likely to convict an alleged rapist.

2. Sex as Motivation for Rape. Sample attitude items concerning sex as the motivation for rape are "The reason most rapists commit rape is for sex" and "Rape is the expression of an uncontrollable desire for sex." A high score reflects a rather traditional view that the motive for rape is sexual release. The fact that this cluster of statements emerges as a separate factor means that it is largely independent of the first factor; that is, a person who believes that rapists are sexually motivated may or may not feel that a woman should be held responsible for preventing her own rape.

3. Severe Punishment for Rape. Sample items concerning severe punishment are "A convicted rapist should be castrated" and "A man who has committed rape should be given at least 30 years in prison." Here again, high scores, reflecting beliefs in strong retribution for such crimes, are not necessarily correlated with either low scores or high scores on the first two factors.

4. Victim Precipitation of Rape. A sample item concerning victim precipitation of rape: "Women provoke rape by their appearance and behavior." Though appearing somewhat different in content from Factor 1, this attitude cluster concentrates on beliefs about the instigation of the rape and the supposition by some that women's "flirtatious" behavior or "scanty" dress are the real causes of rape.

5. Normality for Rapist. A sample item regarding normality of rapists is: "Rapists are 'normal' men." Characterizations of the degree of mental illness are separate attitudes from the preceding factors.

6. Favorable Perception of a Woman After Rape. This factor is concerned with the perceived attractiveness of a woman after the rape. A sample item is "A woman should not feel guilty following a rape."

7. Resistance as Woman's Role During Rape. A high score on resistance as a woman's role indicates a belief that a woman should try to resist during a rape attack, a matter to which we will return later.

Note that for some of these factors it is possible to characterize a high score as reflecting either a pro-rape or an anti-rape attitude. But on Factors 2, 5, and 6, this is not possible—further evidence for the multidimensionality of our attitudes toward rape.

What Accounts for Holding Myths and Stereotypes About Rape?

Despite the multitude of components, several of these factors reflect an attitude that may be characterized—in its virulent form—as unsympathetic to victims and tolerant of the existence of rape because it excuses rapists from being responsible for their actions. (Feild labeled high scores on these factors as "pro-rape.") For people possessing such attitudes, belief in the myths described earlier in this chapter would serve as justification for their attitudes. Burt (1980) has proposed that such persons who believe in rape myths have developed a broad ideology of values and beliefs that encourages the acceptance of myths about rape. Among the aspects of this ideology are the following:

1. Sexual Conservatism. Emphasis here is on restrictions in the appropriateness of sexual partners, sexual acts, and circumstances under which sexual activity should occur. Burt observes: "Since many instances of rape violate one or more aspects of this conservative position, a sexually conservative individual might feel so strongly threatened by and rejecting of the specific circumstances of rape that he or she would overlook the coercion and force involved, and condemn the victim for participating" (1980, p. 218).

2. Adversarial Sexual Beliefs. Adversarial sexual beliefs refers to the expectation that sexual relationships are fundamentally exploitative, that each participant in them is manipulative, sly, cheating, opaque to the other's understanding, and not to be trusted (Burt, 1980). Again, rape is "understood" within the implications of this ideology; to a person holding this ideology, "rape might seem the extreme in a continuum of exploitation, but not an unexpected or horrifying occurrence, or one justifying sympathy or support" (p. 218).

3. Acceptance of Interpersonal Violence. Another important part of the underlying ideology is the belief that force and coercion are legitimate ways to gain compliance and specifically that they are legitimate in intimate and sexual relationships. This ideology approves of men's dominating women and simply overpowering passive partners with violence and control. (This perspective reminds us of the controversy over whether rape is a sexual or an aggressive act.)

4. Sex-Role Stereotyping. The last component of Burt's ideology places limits on the expectations for the two genders, especially females (who are placed in an inferior and passive role). It casts each gender into the mold of behaviors that is traditional for that gender and denies the possibility of androgyny.

Burt constructed a set of attitude statements and administered them to a sample of 598 Minnesota adults in order to determine whether each of these components contributed to acceptance of myths about rape. Examples of the attitude statements can be found in Box 6.2, and items from the Rape Myth Acceptance Scale appear in Box 6.3.

When the subject's responses on the attitude-ideology clusters were compared with their answers to items from the Rape Myth Acceptance Scale, Burt found that three of the four clusters had an impact; sexual conservatism did not. The strongest predictor of believing in the myths was the acceptance of interpersonal violence. Those subjects—whether men or women—who felt that force and coercion were acceptable in persuading others were the ones who agreed with items such as those in Box 6.3.

Burt also collected other information from her sample of adults, but little of it predicted which individuals would subscribe to the myths about rape. Generally, the less educated people more often agreed with the myths. Sex-role satisfaction played only a minimal role, self-esteem none. Relevant experiences (e.g., knowing rape victims or assailants, or being a victim oneself) had little impact.

More recently, many of these qualities have been collapsed into what has been labeled the macho personality constellation, or hypermasculinity, described in Chapters 1 and 2. For example, in a recent study (Leak, Masciotra, Panza, & Unruh, 1992) those individuals who accepted myths about rape were also likely to possess other undesirable social attitudes such as prejudice against various out-groups, and undesirable personality traits such as rigidity and a lack of empathy.

Blaming the Victim

Many persons reflect negative attitudes toward crime victims, to such an extent that the term *blaming the victim* has emerged to summarize the phenomenon (Lerner & Miller, 1978).

The phenomenon of blaming the victim may take several forms, but most projects that have investigated this reaction to victims include in their study some type of negative response to an individual who has experienced a negative life event—hence the term *victim*. The response of "blaming the victim" can be applied to all

BOX 6.2

Sample Items From Burt's Ideology Components

Sexual conservatism:

1. People should not have oral sex.
2. A nice woman will be offended or embarrassed by dirty jokes.
3. A woman shouldn't give in sexually to a man too early or he'll think she's loose.
4. A woman who initiates a sexual encounter will probably have sex with anybody.

Adversarial sexual beliefs:

1. In a dating relationship a woman is largely out to take advantage of a man.
2. A man's got to show the woman who's boss right from the start or he'll end up henpecked.
3. Most women are sly and manipulating when they are out to attract a man.
4. Women are usually sweet until they've caught a man, but then they let their true self show.

Acceptance of interpersonal violence:

1. Sometimes the only way a man can get a cold woman turned on is to use force.
2. Being roughed up is sexually stimulating to many women.
3. Many times a woman will pretend she doesn't want to have intercourse because she doesn't want to seem loose, but she's really hoping he will force her.

Sex-role stereotyping:

1. A woman should be a virgin when she marries.
2. A wife should never contradict her husband in public.
3. It looks worse for a woman to be drunk than for a man to be drunk.
4. A man should fight when the woman he's with is insulted by another man.

Source: Burt, 1980, p. 222.

BOX 6.3

Sample Items From Burt's Rape Myth
Acceptance Scale

1. A woman who is stuck up and thinks she is too good to talk to guys on the street deserves to be taught a lesson.

2. If a woman gets drunk at a party and has intercourse with a man she's just met there, she should be considered "fair game" to other males at the party who want to have sex with her too, whether she wants it or not.

3. If a girl engages in necking or petting and she lets things get out of hand, it is her own fault if her partner forces sex on her.

4. Any healthy woman can successfully resist a rapist if she really wants to.

5. Women who get raped while hitchhiking get what they deserve.

6. In a majority of rapes, the victim is promiscuous or has a bad reputation.

Source: Burt, 1980.

types of victims—of car accidents, of serious illnesses, of petty crimes. But it seems especially applicable to rape victims. No other crime offers a similarly personal and intimate violation of the self. As Bard and Sangrey (1979, p. 19) note, "short of being killed, there is no greater insult to the self." And the rape victim is unique, in another sense, in that no other crime looks upon the victim with the degree of suspicion and doubt that the rape victim must face (Williams, 1984). Such suspicion and doubt may ultimately result in attributions of responsibility, or even blame (Deming & Eppy, 1981).

This section explores the psychology of blaming the rape victim. Specifically, two critical questions will be examined in detail. First, can "blaming the victim" be identified as an objective and distinct reaction? Is there a real psychological reaction to rape victims that does, in fact, constitute blame? The answer to this question is not as simple as past research may suggest, because important distinctions between blame and other related concepts within the literature are profoundly lacking (Shaver & Drown, 1986). For example, someone may react negatively to a rape victim but may not believe that she is blameworthy. Or the respondent may believe that she is somewhat responsible for her victimization but that the blame resides in the rapist. A second more involved question that arises, then, is if negative reactions—of any kind—to victims of rape do indeed occur, how can they be explained? Why do victims of rape face public scrutiny? Several different theoretical explanations have been proposed to answer this question. The explanations include both motivationally oriented and cognitive hypotheses, both of which will be examined for their applicability to this phenomenon.

Blame, Causality, and Responsibility: Conceptual Distinctions

The research that addresses reactions to rape victims generally deals with three distinct but related concepts. First, is the victim, by virtue of either her character or her behavior believed to have *caused* her fate? In contrast to causation, a second question deals with responsibility; do observers find that the victim should bear some *responsibility* for being victimized? Finally, do observers actually believe that the victim should be *blamed* for her misfortune? To be sure, these are not the only reactions investigated. Finding the victim to be less attractive or likable, for example, have both been found to comprise part of the gamut of negative reactions to rape victims (e.g., Deitz et al., 1984). But it is these three concepts—causality, responsibility, and blame—that demand special attention here because it is these terms that have been so thoroughly confused in the literature (Shaver & Drown, 1986). The terms are often used interchangeably as if they were one and the same. They are not. And the conceptual distinctions among these three terms are extremely important. Without such distinctions in empirical investigations, evaluations of the empirical work as a whole will remain problematic (Baumgardner, Kenniston, Becker, & Beaulieu, 1989).

1. Defining Blame. According to Shaver and Drown (1986, p. 701), the concept of blame occurs when an offensive act has occurred, and the actor's justifications or excuses for the act are found to be invalid and unacceptable. This definition provides both a thorough definition of blame, and seeks to clarify the concept of blame from both causality and responsibility. By this definition, in order for blame to be assigned, two important dimensions must be present. First and most obvious, one must perceive that a negative event has occurred. As Shaver (1985, p. 3) points out, "people are never blamed for doing good," and without an outcome found to be offensive, the need for blame does not exist. Such an offensive act also demands justification. It is expected that such a justification or an excuse will follow and be evaluated for its acceptability. A second important criterion for establishing blame is intentionality. Theoretically, blame will not be assigned if it is perceived that the offending person did not intend for an unfavorable outcome to occur.

To apply this definition of blame to the case of a rape victim, then, we find that two things should be present before it should be decided that the victim is blameworthy. First, a negative event has occurred that demands explanation, and this clearly is present. The second criterion for blame to exist is intentionality. Did the victim somehow intend, or as some may say, "ask" to be raped? This, to be sure, is less clear. As McCaul, Veltum, Boyechko, and Crawford (1990, p. 6) note, "It would be rare for people to say that the victim 'intended' or 'consented' to be raped." For this reason, if one accepts this definition of *blame*, then the use of the term *blaming the victim* may not accurately represent most observers' reactions to rape victims.

2. Defining Causality. Blame should be distinguished from both causality and responsibility. *Causality* quite simply refers to those antecedent(s) sufficient for a particular event to occur (Shaver & Drown, 1986). If you turn your computer on during a lightning storm and your computer gets zapped, then that action, at least in part, caused the demise of your computer. In this situation, you may be perceived as having caused the downfall of your computer, but you cannot be blamed because you did not intend for this outcome to occur. Because antecedents are present for any outcome, attributions of causality may be the most common for any particular event, negative or positive. And in the case of a rape, a rape victim will invariably have engaged in some kind of behavior before being victimized, some of which may be perceived of as causing the rape. If antecedent behaviors of the rape victim are assumed by others to have led to the rape, then attributions of causality are present.

3. Defining Responsibility. The definition of *responsibility* is a little more involved. Early critiques of the attribution of responsibility research (e.g., Burger, 1981; Fishbein & Ajzen, 1973; Vidmar & Crinklaw, 1974) have acknowledged that the general term *responsibility* has been used to refer to many, often different, things. Heider (1958), in fact, has outlined five distinct ways that the term *responsibility* may be interpreted. These include:

1. *association:* a person may be held responsible for any action that is connected with him or her, however remote the association may be;
2. *commission:* a person is responsible for anything he or she causes, even though he or she could not possibly have foreseen or intended the consequences;
3. *foreseeability:* a person is held responsible for an event that may have been foreseen, even though it was not intended;
4. *intentionality:* a person is held responsible *only* for consequences of actions that were intended;
5. *justification:* a person is held responsible for an action even if the behavior constitutes a justifiable response to a situation (e.g., anyone would have responded similarly). In this case, the situation is taken into account, but the person is still found responsible for the behavior itself. Using this analysis, then, a victim of any mishap may, at the most primitive level, be found responsible for his or her misfortune merely by association.

Just as the research fails to distinguish clearly between the concepts of causality, responsibility, and blame, it also fails to distinguish between the more specific levels of responsibility. When investigators include the issue of responsibility in their dependent measures, only the general term is used. Therefore, we cannot discern with any confidence the different levels of responsibility that may be being assigned by subjects in the research when they assign general responsibility to the victim.

Shaver (1985) has also developed a definition of responsibility. In his theory of the attribution of blame, he defines *responsibility* as "a judgment made about the moral accountability of a person of normal capacities, which judgment usually but not always involves a causal connection between the person being judged and some morally disapproved action or event" (1985, p. 66). Unlike causality, which is dichotomous (e.g., the antecedent behaviors are either present or not present), responsibility is variable; a "more or less" label that is applied to an outcome after various aspects are taken into account. Basing his analysis on work of the philosopher H. L. A. Hart (1968), Shaver concludes that the attribution of responsibility is dependent upon: (a) perceptions of the stimulus person's causal contribution to the outcome, (b) awareness of the consequences, (c) intentions for the event to occur, (d) degree of volition, and (e) appreciation of the moral wrongfulness of the action taken. As each of these components increase, so will attributions of responsibility. Responsibility is also different from blame; it is not required that one *intended* for an outcome to occur for one to be found responsible for that outcome, although intentionality is taken into consideration. Nor is it required that the action being considered must be offensive.

The work on the concept of responsibility by Heider (1958) and by Shaver (1985) do not completely overlap. Heider, for example, recognizes more fully the "primitive" nature of potential attributions. Hence, merely by being associated with a negative outcome, one may be held responsible by a perceiver for that outcome, at least to some degree. On the other hand, both theories acknowledge that it is possible to be causally responsible for an outcome—although the two concepts are distinct, they may be related. Both Heider and Shaver, as well as others (Fincham & Jaspars, 1980; Fishbein & Ajzen, 1973; Shultz & Schleifer, 1983) recognize the multidimensionality of responsibility and call for researchers to distinguish among the different possible levels of responsibility.

Researchers are beginning, in fact, to identify the conceptual distinctions between blame, causality, and responsibility, and to direct their research with these distinctions in mind. Such research does find, in fact, that attributions of causality, responsibility, and blame are moderately correlated, but clearly are not identical (Baumgardner, Becker, Beaulieu, & Kenniston, 1988; Critchlow, 1985; Shaver, 1989). Baumgardner and his colleagues (1988), for example, gave subjects definitions of each respective term as defined by Shaver, and found that attributions of responsibility and blame for a rape victim were significantly correlated. Judgments of causality, however, were not correlated with attributions of blame or with attributions of responsibility. This suggests that in this study, subjects were recognizing the prior behavior of the victim as somehow related to the outcome (causality), but were not necessarily using that behavior as a criterion for her responsibility and blame. For *rapist* attributions in this study, significant attributions were found between causality and responsibility and between causality and blame. And this makes sense. Issues of causality deal with the behavior of an individual; blame deals with the cognitions of that individual. Responsibility may involve both behaviors and cognitions of an individual.

Though it is important for psychological research to distinguish among these distinct concepts, the question remains whether lay individuals do the same. Does it even matter to the naive perceiver whether these are distinguishable terms? Consider the rape victim who is being judged as he or she testifies in court. Members of the jury—naive perceivers—must decide whether the defendant is guilty or not guilty. They are not afforded the opportunity to assign levels of causality or levels of responsibility and blame in their ultimate decision. For a victim who has undergone the trauma of testifying only to see the defendant walk away, it cannot matter whether jurors were making attributions of causality or attributions of responsibility or attributions of blame—the point is moot.

It is common, however, for public figures, when explaining an event (e.g., a police officer shooting an innocent bystander) to accept responsibility, but not to accept blame. And it is common for the majority of the public to accept this rationale (e.g., from President Reagan, when the Marines were killed in Lebanon). This suggests that the lay public can distinguish between these concepts. Research as well suggests that lay individuals can learn the conceptual distinctions, and that such distinctions can make a difference in ultimate attributions.

Borek and Shaver (1988), for example, found that by merely reading *one sentence* definitions of each term, correlations between attributions of either causality or responsibility and blame for another individual were significantly reduced. This finding suggests promising implications, for if individuals may be taught the conceptual distinctions between these concepts—particularly the fact that in order to assign blame, one must be found to have intended the outcome—then it is possible that such attributions could be diminished. This research, as well as research that indicates that the approach used in measuring causality, responsibility, and blame can affect overall results of a study (Baumgardner et al., 1989) supports the argument that it is critically important for not only researchers to "share the same conceptual language," but that researchers and study participants, and even jurors, should have the same understanding.

Is the Victim Blamed?

With these important conceptual clarifications in mind, the question that must be addressed is whether "blaming the victim" occurs. Recall that more than 25 years of research has led both investigators studying rape and the media repeatedly to apply the term *blaming the victim* to the general phenomenon of reacting negatively to a victim, including a victim of rape. This suggests that this phenomenon is extremely robust. And the research demonstrates that some subjects do, in fact, blame the victim. The research also shows, however, that this phenomenon is not as common as is currently thought. Furthermore, although victims are sometimes blamed, the more prevalent phenomenon that seems to be occurring is the assignment of attributions of both causality and responsibility to the victim for this misfortune.

1. Blame. The idea that a victim somehow wanted, or asked, to be raped is not a new one. Freud, in 1924, argued that the essence of femininity included masochism. This juxtaposition of femininity with masochism created the notion that females are *innately* masochistic. Despite arguments to the contrary (Caplan, 1987), the idea that women not only invite, but may enjoy sexual aggression remains (Bond & Mosher, 1986). Even today, the primary defining element of rape remains that of *nonconsent* (Estrich, 1987; Loh, 1981). In effect, the victim of rape must prove that she did not solicit the rapist in order to prove that she is innocent and he is guilty (this is also discussed in Chapter 10).

In order directly to assess the existence of blaming the victim, researchers must have directly asked respondents in their study whether or not the victim should be blamed. Of the numerous studies that have investigated reactions to victims of rape, only a handful have actually used as a dependent measure the existence of blaming the victim independent of causality and responsibility.

Some studies have labeled their dependent measure as constituting victim blame, but an examination of the actual measures indicates that what was being measured was not blame at all. Janoff-Bulman, Timko, and Carli (1985), for example, created 10 questions, half of which were intended to measure "behavioral blame" and half intended to measure "characterological blame." The questions they asked, however, did not actually assess blame; the word *blame* was never even used. Instead, the "behavioral blame" questions are clearly assessing perceived causality, and included items such as "She should not have let him kiss her," "She should not have gone up to his apartment," and "She should have insisted that he take her home" (p. 166). Such attributions of causality would make the victim liable for not having known better, for not having foreseen the outcome (the knowledge dimension of responsibility; Shaver, 1985), but they cannot constitute attributions that the victim intended her misfortune—which is necessary theoretically for blame to occur.

Conversely, questions in this study that constituted "characterological blame" included items that measured internal qualities of the victim: "She's not assertive enough; she doesn't seem to be able to say no or fight back when she has the chance," "She's naive and doesn't seem able to take care of herself; she trusts people much too easily," and "She's not self confident enough," are examples. Unlike Janoff-Bulman et al.'s behavioral blame, which infers causality, this characterological blame may actually deny it (Shaver, 1985); by virtue of her character, she somehow *could not* have known better. Although agreement with these items would clearly reflect a derogation of the victim, they should not be labeled "blame." Even though this study is a good illustration of the conceptual confusion that appears in the literature, it should not be assumed that this is the only study that is subject to this type criticism (see Bulman & Wortman, 1977; Pagel, Becker, & Coppel, 1985; Pugh, 1983; Shotland & Goodstein, 1983; Taylor, Lichtman, & Wood, 1984; Thornton, Ryckman, & Robbins, 1982; Wohlers, 1982).

The studies that have investigated victim blaming (and actually operationalize blame consistently with the proposed definition) have found it to exist, but to a lesser degree than might be currently thought; these include Baumgardner et al. (1988), Howells et al. (1984), Karuza and Carey (1984), Krulewitz and Payne (1978), Luginbuhl and Mullin (1981), and McCaul et al. (1990). Krulewitz and Payne (1978), for example, distinguished in their study victim blame from victim responsibility. Victim blame was observed to some extent, with scores ranging from 3.69 to 4.49 on a 19-point scale (1 = low, 19 = high), depending upon which condition subjects were exposed to. Clearly, most of the blame was assigned to the rapist, who received blame scores ranging from 13.88 to 15.56 (again, by condition) on the same scale. This finding seems to generalize to other research. In another study respondents were asked to assign a finite amount of blame to the victim, the rapist, and/or to the situation (McCaul et al., 1990). Results indicated that although respondents willingly assigned the victim about 10% of the blame, they recognized that the rapist deserved the vast amount of blame, at more than 75% (the situation received about 13% of the blame).

Other research has distinguished between types of blame. Basing their work, and their dependent measures, on Janoff-Bulman's (1979) distinction between behavioral and characterological self-blame (and explicitly asking subjects whether the victims should be blamed for various reasons), Karuza and Carey (1984) found that behavioral blame—blame assigned to the victim for actions she engaged in prior to or during the rape—was strongly preferred over characterological blame, blame assigned to the victim for her character or personality. This is important because subjects in this study could have assigned *both* behavioral and characterological blame to the victim, but they chose not to. And this finding has been replicated (Luginbuhl & Mullin, 1981).

Perhaps the cleanest measures of blame come from Baumgardner et al. (1988). In this study, a total of 24 statements defining causality, responsibility, and blame were written based on Shaver and Drown's (1986) definition of the terms. This study clearly indicated that the attribution of choice for observers of rape victims was not blame. Though they argue that their results provide no evidence of blaming the victim, their data indicate that some blame was, in fact, present, as there was enough variance in the measure of blame to produce significant differences between males and females. Blame attribution scores in this study generally ranged from 4.5 to 8.0 on a 24-point scale, with higher numbers indicating stronger attributions. Nevertheless, attributions of blame were much lower than attributions of responsibility or causality, which averaged about 9 and 16, respectively, on the same scale, for the victim or the assignment of blame to the rapist, which averaged about 18 on the 24-point scale.

The research generally shows, then, that although blaming the victim does indeed exist, the phenomenon is not robust. And this makes sense. Individuals who are forced to distinguish blame from other attributions, as were subjects in the Baumgardner et al. study, should have difficulty finding that the victim "intended" to be raped (see also McCaul et al., 1990). And though victim blaming is clearly strongly associated with mitigation of the rapist's guilt (Acock & Ireland, 1983), what may be more important, because of their increased prevalence and similarly negative implications, is to investigate other possible attributions about the victim. Do individuals believe that rape victims may in some way be the cause, or more importantly, share a significant part of the responsibility for their own misfortune?

2. Causality and Responsibility. The research shows that attributions of both causality and responsibility are consistently and heartily assigned to the victim of rape. In fact, this is such a robust phenomenon that the focus of concern in the research has shifted to what factors influence the extent to which such attributions are made. Numerous variables have been investigated and found to affect these attributions. They include aspects of the observer, the relationship between the victim and the rapist, and characteristics of the victim.

The characteristics of the observers (i.e., study participants) that have been studied include the gender and attitudes of the observers. As will be discussed, many different theoretically relevant attitude constructs have been investigated for their predictive utility in attributions of responsibility, including both general attitudes and more specific attitudes concerning women and rape. Numerous characteristics of the victim have been studied as well, including her "respectability," the amount and type of resistance she puts forth, as well as her attractiveness. All of these characteristics, as well as the relationship between the victim and the rapist, have been found to play a role in attributions.

Characteristics of the Observer

Observer's Gender

The general question as to whether males or females react more harshly to the rape victim is a long-standing one. An examination of the findings generally suggests, however, that males react less favorably to the victim, usually reflected in males' greater attributions of responsibility to the victim (Bridges & McGrail, 1989; Calhoun, Selby, Cann, & Keller, 1978; Cann, Calhoun, & Selby, 1979; Deitz, 1980; Deitz & Byrnes, 1981; Deitz et al., 1984; Feldman-Summers & Lindner, 1976; Feild, 1978; Fulero & DeLara, 1976; Howells et al., 1984; Jenkins & Dambrot, 1987; Johnson & Jackson,

1988; Kanekar & Vaz, 1983; Kanekar & Kolsawalla, 1977; Luginbuhl & Mullin, 1981; McCaul et al., 1990; Smith, Keating, Hester, & Mitchell, 1976; Thornton, Robbins, & Johnson, 1981; Thornton & Ryckman, 1983; Thornton et al., 1982; Wyer, Bodenhausen, & Gorman, 1985), although some studies have failed to find any sex differences (Acock & Ireland, 1983; Janoff-Bulman et al., 1985; Jones & Aronson, 1973; Krahe, 1988; L'Armand & Pepitone, 1982; Shotland & Goodstein, 1983; Villemur & Hyde, 1983). In only one known study have females been found to attribute more responsibility to the victim than did males (Krulewitz & Payne, 1978). Although research reviews tend to claim that the results are clearly mixed on the issue of whether males or females react more harshly to rape victims (e.g., Shotland & Goodstein, 1983), these studies measuring attributions of responsibility clearly show that females are generally more favorable to the victim. This is consistent with data that indicate that males have a greater tendency to believe in rape myths (Jenkins & Dambrot, 1987; Malamuth & Check, 1981) and generally report less empathy for a rape victim (Deitz et al., 1982). Females also report stronger identification with victimization in general than do men (Krulewitz, 1981).

Attitudes of Observers

The attitudes of respondents in their judgments toward rape victims have also been studied quite extensively by researchers interested in this area. Shaver (1975) has argued that the attitude of the observer may be the critical factor in predicting dispositional judgments, and social psychologists are certainly aware of the importance of attitudes on an individuals' thoughts and feelings toward other people, and toward objects and issues in their environment (Deaux & Wrightsman, 1988). Gordon Allport has described attitudes as "the keystone in the edifice of American social psychology" (1935, p. 798).

The literature on reactions to rape victims indicates that many different theoretically relevant attitudes have been investigated for their ability to predict judgments toward such victims. And consistent with the research on attitudes and behavior that shows that the more specific the attitude, the more powerful its ability to predict behavior (Fishbein, 1980; Fishbein & Ajzen, 1975; Weigel, Vernon, & Tognacci, 1974), the research investigating attitudes and reactions toward rape victims indicates that the more specific the attitude toward rape, the more predictive it is in assessing judgments toward rape victims. The more general attitude constructs that have been studied include locus of control orientation, personal-environmental attributional tendency, juror-bias, authoritarianism, dogmatism, and belief in a just world. The more specific attitudes that have been addressed in the research include sex-role attitudes and attitudes toward rape. Each of these is evaluated in the following sections.

General Attitudes Relevant to Rape Judgments

The general attitudes that have been examined show mixed results. Locus of control orientation, or the extent to which a person believes that he or she has control over what happens in his or her life, has not been found to predict attributions of responsibility in a rape case (Thornton et al., 1982; Villemur & Hyde, 1983), even though it has been found to predict attributions of responsibility in events such as crimes and accidents (e.g., Kauffman & Ryckman, 1979; Phares & Wilson, 1972; Sosis, 1974). Because the Internal-External Locus of Control Scale (Rotter, 1966) measures perceptions of control in one's own life, Lowe, Medway, and Beers (1978) developed the Personal-Environment Causal Attribution Scale to tap individual differences in causal attributions concerning other people. Two studies have been done to determine the predictive utility of this construct, with mixed results. Thornton et al. (1981) found that it was indeed predictive of attributions of responsibility for a rape victim. This finding, however, has failed to replicate (Thornton et al., 1982). Finally, neither authoritarianism (Adorno, Frenkel-Brunswik, Levinson, & Sanford, 1950), nor juror bias (Kassin & Wrightsman, 1983), which refers to pro-prosecution or pro-defense biases in potential jurors, have proven relevant to attributions of guilt in a rape case, despite the fact that a pro-prosecution orientation has been found to be negatively related to empathy for a rape victim (Kassin & Wrightsman, 1983).

Dogmatism refers to a quality possessed by a generally closed-minded person who prefers simple solutions to problems, shows intolerance for ambiguity, and seeks less supplemental information (Robbins, 1975; Rokeach, 1960). Dogmatic individuals should be less likely to take extenuating circumstances into account (Shaver, 1975). Support has been found for the hypothesis that highly dogmatic observers focus more attention on the rape victim and consequently attribute more responsibility to the victim in a rape case (Thornton et al., 1982).

A final general construct that is theoretically relevant to attributions of responsibility is "belief in a just world" (Lerner, 1970). This construct reflects a general belief that people get what they deserve and deserve what they get. Therefore, one who believes in a just world should be more likely to assign attributions of responsibility to a rape victim, as a means of making his or her own world safe. Several studies have investigated the relationship between belief in a just world (using the Just World Scale; Rubin & Peplau, 1975) and attributions of responsibility in a rape case. Miller, Smith, Ferree, and Taylor (1976), as well as Zuckerman, Gerbasi, Kravitz, and Wheeler (1975), have found that those with a strong belief in a just world perceive the rape victim as more responsible for her fate. Another study, however, assessing this same relationship, did not replicate this finding (Thornton et al., 1982). Finally, Weir and Wrightsman (1990) have found that belief in a just world does not predict attributions of guilt in a rape case. It appears, then, that although one's belief in a just world may affect perceptions of the victim's responsibility in a rape case, it may not affect one's attributions for the rapist, as reflected in verdicts of guilt. It is, after all, the victim who has experienced such a traumatic event and therefore threatens one's sense of justice in the world.

Specific Attitudes Toward Rape

More specific attitudes toward rape or the treatment of women have also been investigated for their predictive utility in judgments toward rape. It has been consistently argued by some that we live in a "rape culture," in which traditional beliefs and attitudes toward women and their appropriate roles actually support and condone rape (Brownmiller, 1975; Clark & Lewis, 1977; Griffin, 1971; Weis & Borges, 1973). Such attitudes may take the form of attitudes toward appropriate roles for men and women in society, or explicit attitudes toward rape. Attitudes about appropriate sex-roles for men and women are, in fact, strongly positively correlated with attitudes toward rape (Costin, 1985; Fischer, 1987).

The research on the relationship between sex-role attitudes and causal attributions in a rape case consistently shows that traditional individuals react more harshly toward rape victims than do feminists. Traditional males, for example, generally consider rape more justifiable if they believe the woman wanted sex (Muehlenhard, Friedman, & Thomas, 1985). Feminist respondents have been found to cite more societal reinforcement of male aggression as an explanation for rape, to agree that society's encouragement of women to act passively is an important factor in rape, and to be more likely to agree that a rape did occur (Burt & Albin, 1981; Krulewitz & Payne, 1978; Malamuth, 1981; Shotland & Goodstein, 1983). Feminist subjects also attribute less causality and responsibility to the victim (Burt & Albin, 1981; Howells et al., 1984; Jenkins & Dambrot, 1987; Krahe, 1988; Shotland & Goodstein, 1983) and recognize the victim as suffering more (Howells et al., 1984). No differences between traditional and feminist individuals in the assignment of blame to the victim, however, have been found (Krulewitz & Payne, 1978). This finding only strengthens the argument that dependent measures should distinguish between causality, responsibility, and blame.

One's attitudes toward sex-roles and rape have also been found to affect how information about the rape, and more specifically the rape victim, are interpreted. Traditional individuals are more likely to take a victim's behavior prior to the rape into account, possibly creating causal attributions to mitigate the rapist's responsibility (Deitz et al., 1984; Krahe, 1988; Krulewitz & Payne, 1978; Weir & Wrightsman, 1990). These traditional individuals are also likely to interpret the behavior of the victim in a way that is consistent with their own beliefs. In one study, for example, subjects who reported low empathy with a rape victim were more likely to view the victim's avoidance of eye-contact as indicative of the rapist's lack of guilt whereas subjects who reported high empathy with a rape victim interpreted this same information in a more favorable light (Weir & Wrightsman, 1990).

It is clear that the effect of attitude orientation upon attributions and reactions to a rape victim is extremely robust. The effect of the attitudes of respondents has, in fact, been found to attenuate, if not eliminate, the effects of gender on attributions toward the rape victim (Shotland & Goodstein, 1983; Weir & Wrightsman, 1990). It appears that although males in general do have a bias against the rape victim, a feminist attitudinal perspective in a male may at least partially remove this bias. Conversely, more traditional women have been found to be quite negative toward rape victims (cf. Weir & Wrightsman, 1990).

In summary, it is clear that the characteristics of those observing a scenario depicting rape bring with them their own set of predispositions that guide their perceptions and interpretations of the event. Specifically, males more often react harshly to victims of rape than do females. However, the existing attitudes of men and women play a strong role in their perceptions. Finally, the interaction between gender and attitudes may ultimately produce the differential responses to rape victims that the numerous studies reported here have found.

Characteristics of the Victim

Numerous characteristics of the victim have been studied for their effects on attributions about the rape. Those most often studied deal with the "respectability" of the victim, the relationship of the victim with the rapist, the amount and type of resistance put forth by the victim, the physical attractiveness of the victim, as well as the pre-rape behavior of the victim. Results of these studies suggest interesting main effects as well as interactions among the variables. Each of these will be discussed below.

Respectability of the Victim

Perhaps no variable has been investigated for its effect on attributions as much as perceived "respectability" or "character" of the rape victim. If observers of a rape situation are using information about the rape victim rather than the rapist to explain the deplorable event, then the internal qualities of the victim may be important. Interestingly, the first study to address this question found that the *more* respectable the victim was (operationalized by varying the marital status of the victim: She was either a virgin, married, or divorced), the more responsible she was found to be for the rape (Jones & Aronson, 1973). The just world hypothesis was used to explain this outcome (see also Chapter 7). Attempts to replicate, however, have proven futile (Feldman-Summers & Lindner, 1976; Kahn et al., 1977; Kanekar & Kolsawalla, 1977; Karuza & Carey, 1984; Kerr & Kurtz, 1977; Luginbuhl & Mullin, 1981; McCaul et al., 1990; Paulsen, 1979; Pugh, 1983; Smith et al., 1976). The more consistent finding, rather, shows just the opposite;

the more perceived respectability for the victim, the less she is held responsible.

There is a problem with research that addresses the issue of the "respectability" of the victim. Specifically, the term *respectability* (sometimes referred to as *moral character;* Pugh, 1983) of the victim has been used as a generic term to refer to many different dimensions of the victim. Furthermore, such dimensions of the victim are often confounded as variables in the research. Aronson and Jones (1973) clearly confounded marital status with the sexual history of the victim. Kanekar and Kolsawalla (1977) also varied status of the victim using five levels: unmarried virgin, married woman, widow, divorcee, and prostitute, thereby confounding who knows how many variables (a few are marital status, sexual history, and age of the victim). Other research is not immune to this problem. Karuza and Carey (1984) operationalized respectability by varying three entirely different aspects of the victim's life in the same condition: arrest record, current relationship status, and history of venereal disease. Smith et al. (1976) used three levels of respectability: the victim was either a topless-bottomless dancer, a social worker, or a Catholic nun. Yet other research does not report their operationalization of the term (Luginbuhl & Mullin, 1981).

To use such elements as marital status, sexual history, and so forth, as components of general respectability is not entirely meaningless. However, to use such diverse and disparate operationalizations and use them to refer to the same thing—respectability—is misleading. Manipulation checks indicating that subjects did, in fact, perceive less "respectability" in expected conditions would be reassuring, but they are missing in many of these studies (e.g., Jones & Aronson, 1973; Kanekar & Kolsawalla, 1977; McCaul et al., 1990; Smith et al., 1976). Instead of "extending the parameters of respectability," as Smith et al. (1976, p. 347) proposed to do, such manipulations actually cloud the issue. It seems more appropriate to be more specific when discussing the effects of that which is studied, and say, for example, "the effects of marital status of the victim on attributions are . . ." or, "the effects of past sexual history of the victim are . . . ," as others have done (e.g., L'Armand & Pepitone, 1982).

Relationship of Victim With the Rapist

As discussed in Chapter 4, recent surveys of victims find that the majority of rape victims actually knew their attacker (Koss, 1988;

Russell, 1984). The extent of the acquaintanceship may vary, from casual acquaintances to married partners; there is no relationship barrier to rape. Nevertheless, it is quite difficult for the public to define forced intercourse between acquaintances for what it is—rape (Bridges & McGrail, 1989; Koss et al., 1988). Respondents may thus agree that a scenario represents a form of "forced sex," but are less likely to agree that the forced sex was rape, despite the fact that rape *is* forced sex.

Studies addressing differential reactions to rape victims as a function of victim-rapist relationship produce mixed results. Some studies have found that the victim is attributed more responsibility when she is acquainted with her attacker than when she is not (Bridges & McGrail, 1989; Calhoun, Selby, & Warring, 1976; L'Armand & Pepitone, 1982; Smith et al., 1976). Other studies find no differences in attributions (Howells et al., 1984; McCaul et al., 1990). One study has found an interaction between subject gender and victim-rapist relationship, with females reacting more favorably to the victim of stranger rape, and males react more harshly to this victim (Tetreault & Barnett, 1987; see also Chapter 4).

What may be the critical determining factor in increased attributions of responsibility is the perceived level of intimacy between the victim and rapist. Willis and Wrightsman (1990), for example, varied four levels of acquaintanceship—strangers, co-workers, friends, or a dating relationship. Results indicated that when the victim and rapist were either friends or involved in a dating relationship, attributions of responsibility increased for the victim. What is especially interesting here is that despite the fact that the co-workers in this study were acquainted with each other, this was not enough to increase the responsibility of the victim. An examination of other research seems to support this, which may explain the mixed results. In L'Armand and Pepitone's (1982) research, for example, attributions of responsibility for the victim were increased if the dating couple had had sex previously, as opposed to the couple just dating. It is possible that subjects perceived a high level of intimacy between the former couple. Howells et al. (1984), who found no differences as a function of victim-rapist relationship, described the victim who knew the rapist as the baby-sitter of his children. This effect may be stronger for females, who are all too aware of their role as "gatekeeper" in society. In addition to Tetreault and Barnett's (1987) interaction effect reported earlier, Jenkins and Dambrot (1987) have found that the type of dating situation affects females' attributions of responsibility of a victim, but does not alter the opinions of males.

Victim's Resistance

How the victim responds to an attack is looked upon with special scrutiny by those judging her. In fact, as noted earlier, the primary definitional element of rape remains that of nonconsent (Loh, 1981). In essence, the victim must prove that she resisted her attacker; that she did not want it. Even today, 38 states still require that the victim put forth "reasonable" resistance in order for the event to be considered rape (Largen, 1988). Because of this, her behavior during the attack is considered especially important by others.

Not only is some resistance required by law in most states, but lay individuals give it careful consideration in judging whether rape occurred. The research in this area indicated that there is a fine line between what is appropriate resistance to a rape attack and what is appropriate behavior in general. Specifically, it appears that women are expected to resist, but to resist in a stereotypically appropriate manner. For example, Branscombe and Weir (1990) found that either too little or too *much* resistance increased attributions of responsibility to the victim. Apparently, when the victim crosses the line to the point of behaving stereotypically inconsistent—by strongly resisting in both a verbal and physical manner—she is derogated. Although no other research has directly investigated this hypothesis, other research indicates support for this phenomenon. Deitz et al. (1984) found that subjects reported more positive feelings for the rapist when the victim was either too passive or too resistive. And an interaction effect was found in this latter study, indicating that an unattractive victim (versus an attractive victim) who strongly resisted was rated the most unfavorably. Krulewitz (1981) found that, though subjects are more likely to agree that an event was actually a rape when the victim strongly resisted, female subjects rated the resisting victim as *less* intelligent and *more* at fault than the less resisting victim. Finally, Acock and Ireland (1983) have also shown that a victim's norm violation (though operationalized as a female all-night gas attendant who offers a man a ride) somewhat decreases her respectability and increases her blame.

Some research does show positive reactions to victims who resist. An analysis of the operationalization of such resistance, however, indicates that the resistance put forth by the victim is neither too much nor too little. Krulewitz and Nash (1979), for example, found that strong physical resistance without any verbal resistance generally lowers attributions of responsibility to the victim, and increases the assignment of punishment for the rapist (see also Scroggs, 1976). Strong verbal resistance, without physical resistance by the victim, similarly influences judgments (Krulewitz, 1981). Finally, McCaul et al. (1990) have found the victim to be more credible when she resists by "screaming and fighting to break free"–an action that is quite stereotypical of females.

Finally, it appears that passivity on the part of the victim may be differentially interpreted, depending upon the source of passivity. Baumgardner et al. (1989) included two passive conditions, one in which the victim attempted to "talk" her way out of it, and one in which the victim was so consumed by fear that she could not react. Only in the latter condition were attributions of responsibility to the victim decreased. This may indicate that judgments about the victim may also be a function of whether it was perceived that the victim was in control of the outcome or not, as the former passive condition may have been interpreted as an intentional strategy used by the victim, whereas the fear-induced passivity may have been perceived as an involuntary response (Baumgardner et al., 1989).

Victim Attractiveness

Although the physical attractiveness of the victim should ostensibly have absolutely no impact on whether she is held accountable for her actions, it does affect attributions. Generally, society associates physical attractiveness with other "good" qualities, and treats attractive individuals accordingly (Dion, Berscheid, & Walster, 1972). The effect that attractiveness has on attributions assigned to a rape victim, however, is not a simple one, and the research shows no consistent pattern of effects. Two studies have found no effect of victim attractiveness on attribution of responsibility (McCaul et al., 1990; Thornton, 1977). Seligman, Brickman, and Koulack (1977) found, on the other hand, that although attractive women were perceived as more likely to become rape victims, the unattractive victims were found more responsible for provoking their victimization. In line with this study, Deitz et al. (1984) found that subjects tended to identify with, and have more positive feelings toward, the attractive victim and reported the most negative feelings toward the unattractive victim who resisted. Villemur and Hyde (1983) did not find a main effect for attraction, but did find an interesting three-way interaction with sex of subject, age of victim, and attractiveness of victim. Females found the attractive woman to be more responsible, despite the age of the victim. Males in this study, however, assigned less attributional fault to victims who were either young and attractive, or old and unattractive. Only one study has reported that physically attractive women are found to play a greater role in their rape (Calhoun et al., 1978).

The fact that physical attractiveness of a victim does not, by itself, play a strong role in attribution of responsibility is consistent with other research not investigating rape per se. Sigall and Ostrove (1975), for example, have shown that whether the attractiveness of a defendant was advantageous or not depends on the crime committed. When the crime is perceived as the type in which the perpetrator's attractiveness contributes to the success of the outcome (e.g., swindling), the defendant may be found to have tried to use his attractiveness and is treated more harshly. Whether an attractive rape victim is treated favorably or not seems to depend on other demographic characteristics (e.g., her age) as well as her own behavior (e.g., resistance).

Pre-Rape Behavior of the Victim

Finally, another factor that has been found to play a very strong role in attributions includes behaviors that the victim engaged in before she was attacked. Many different aspects of her behavior are scrutinized, too, whether the behavior immediately preceded the rape or not. For example, research documents that accused rapists receive less severe penalties when the victim was described as promiscuous (Barber, 1974; Clark & Lewis, 1977; Holmstrom & Burgess, 1978; Kalven & Zeisel, 1966; LaFree, 1980). In fact, prior sexual history of the victim of any kind leads to a reluctance to convict an alleged rapist and the perception that the rape is less serious (Borgida & White, 1978; L'Armand & Pepitone, 1982). Similarly, less severe penalties are also given when the victim had been involved in unconventional living arrangements (e.g., living with a man; Clark & Lewis, 1977), or when the victim is described as a chronic alcohol user (Kalven & Zeisel, 1966). Especially when the issue in a rape trial is that of consent–when the fact that intercourse took place is not in question–do these factors play a strong role. LaFree, Reskin, and Visher (1985) documented that in actual rape trials where consent is the issue, any evidence of victim's drinking, drug use, or sexual activity outside of marriage led jurors to doubt whether rape had occurred.

Other research indicates that observers find date rape to be more justifiable if the victim went to the apartment of the man who raped her (as opposed to going to a religious function with him), if she initiated the date (compared to the rapist initiating the date), and if the man paid all of the dating expenses rather than both sharing them (Muehlenhard et al., 1985). In another study, 54% of high school boys agreed that if a girl "leads a boy on," then raping her should be at least somewhat justifiable. Victims who are seen as engaging in behaviors that are generally provocative or nonconforming to the female role are also attributed more responsibility to the rape (Acock & Ireland, 1983; Best & Demmin, 1982; Krahe, 1988). Weir and Wrightsman (1990) presented a rape trial to subjects and asked them to indicate how important various factors of the rape were in their decision whether or not to convict the defendant. It was found that those subjects reporting low empathy with the victim identified the fact that the couple had previously dated, that she had danced with the defendant on the night in question, and that she had accompanied the defendant to a friend's home as significantly more important to their decision than those who reported having empathy for the victim. Finally, research indicates that when the victim does not protest early enough (Shotland & Goodstein, 1983) or appears ambiguous in her desire for sexual intercourse (Johnson & Jackson, 1988) attributions of responsibility increase and perceptions of the victim become more negative. Even when the rape is violent, if it is suggested that the victim was attracted to the man, the rape is seen as less serious (Shotland & Strau, 1976).

Summary

A review of the literature on attributions of blame, responsibility, and causality to rape victims points to three conclusions. First, although attributions of blame are not as common as may be thought, they do exist. Second, attributions of responsibility and causality assigned to the rape victim are common and widespread. It seems that individuals exposed to a rape situation willingly assign the victim some role in her own victimization. Finally, many factors affect the extent to which such causality and/or responsibility will be assigned to the victim, including both aspects of the observer and aspects of the victim.

7 Explaining Negative Reactions Toward Rape Victims

When Mike Tyson was charged with rape, whispers echoed through the conversations: What did the victim think she was doing going out with this bully at 2:00 in the morning? Where was her common sense? For the alleged victim of William Kennedy Smith, people were not so subtle. Many of the characteristics that lead to attributing responsibility to the victim that were discussed in Chapter 6 were present in this case: Her character was called into question, what she was wearing on the evening of the incident was displayed at the trial, her past relationships were scrutinized, as was her behavior that occurred just prior to the incident. In the Tyson trial, scrutiny of the victim failed to uncover any flaws that might serve as viable alternative explanations for the incident, but this was not the case in the Smith case. The point here is not whether each of the verdicts was just. The point is that the victims of each of these cases were both thoroughly scrutinized, not just at the trials but in daily conversations and throughout the media. Take a moment to ask friends what they remember about these cases. Chances are that they will be able to tell you more about the victims in each of these cases than about the behavior of either Tyson or Smith during the respective incidents.

Chapter 6 has reviewed the pervasive tendency for others to blame the rape victim for her rape, or to conclude that her behavior somehow caused the attack. Why do these reactions occur? This chapter reviews three theoretical explanations for why the victim is assigned a role in her own victimization. These theories are: the belief in a just world, defensive attribution, and the more cognitive attributional explanations.

Belief in a Just World

According to Lerner (Lerner & Miller, 1978; Lerner & Simmons, 1966), individuals are committed to the belief that people get what they deserve, and conversely, deserve what they get. A belief in a just world centers around the notion that if one either behaves appropriately or is a good person (and one who behaves appropriately is usually considered to be good), then good outcomes will occur. In effect, one's outcomes can be controlled. This belief may be extended to say that if one behaves "inappropriately" or is a bad person, then bad things will result. Such propositions create a fit between the character and actions of an individual and his or her outcomes, and are considered just. When the character or actions of an individual do not match his or her outcome, then a threat to such a belief occurs. And when one observes another suffering unjustly—either directly or indirectly—his or her *own* belief in a just world is threatened.

The consequence of this threat is an attempt to restore justice (Lerner & Simmons, 1966). Individuals may behaviorally restore justice to the victim by helping the other person. But if this is not possible, then, according to Lerner, the observer will *cognitively* restore justice by inferring that because of either the victim's behavior or character, the victim must have deserved the outcome. If the victim's behavior can be construed as the cause of suffering, then no derogation of the victim's character is needed (Lerner & Miller, 1978). But if behavioral responsibility cannot be inferred, then at this point rejection or derogation of the victim's character will occur. *What is critical for a threat to occur is that either the actions or the character of the victim do not clearly correspond to the outcome.* A rape victim has experienced an ultimate injustice—the violation of her intimate self. For someone else to observe such an injustice should, theoretically, create a threat to the observer's just world and a need to restore justice. To reject the rape victim by deciding that she deserved her fate by virtue of either her character or her actions would restore the other's sense of justice as well as the belief that we can control our own outcomes.

Several specific predictions can be made from the just world hypothesis. All predictions relevant to reactions to a rape victim that are derived from this perspective hypothesize that the greater the threat to one's just world, the stronger one's reaction to the victim will be. Lerner and Miller (1978) have noted that as an event becomes more relevant to a person, his or her concerns with justice will become more salient, as will the need to explain apparent injustices. Therefore, because females are at a much greater risk of rape and because the research examining reactions to rape uses primarily females as the victim in their scenarios, the threat to one's just world should be more severe for females. Their predicted reactions, therefore, should be that females should reject the victim more than males. As reviewed in Chapter 6, this effect is clearly not evident. Males react more negatively to rape victims than do females.

A second very clear prediction involves the character of the victim. If a woman of seemingly good character is raped, the fit between what that person seemingly deserved and what that person got is much more mismatched than when one observes a woman of seemingly bad character who has been raped. The former situation, then, should elicit a stronger threat than the latter. The explicit prediction has been tested, via the victim's "respectability" many times. And again (see Chapter 6), although the initial test of the hypothesis generated support, attempts to replicate have been futile.

Here are, then, two very clear instances where the just world theory cannot explain negative reactions to rape victims. To be fair to the theory, however, we should note the gap between what the theory actually predicts and what the research measures. The theory predicts that upon being exposed to an injustice in which a victim does not get what is deserved, in order to restore justice the victim will be "rejected" (Lerner & Simmons, 1966) or "derogated" (Lerner & Miller, 1978). In essence, it is the character of the victim that will ultimately be devalued in order to restore justice. The initial experiment on rejecting the innocent victim (not of rape) used measures of attractiveness and a "social stimulus value" measure assessing the general "likability" of the stimulus person. Measures of blame, responsibility, or causality were not included in this experiment. Nor does the just world hypothesis necessarily predict that such measures would be affected by one's belief in a just world, despite assumptions to the contrary (e.g., Jones & Aronson, 1973). That is, if subjects assign a causal role to the person or assign behavioral responsibility to a victim for her fate, then they may, in fact, be agreeing that her actions corresponded to her fate. In effect, no threat has occurred and individuals can go about their business (Lerner & Miller, 1978). If one assigns blame to an individual, then, according to the definition of *blame,* one is assuming that the victim somehow *intended* for the outcome to occur. And it is precisely when an observer witnesses a situation that was clearly unintended that a threat most strongly occurs.

This creates quite a paradox. The very research that is cited so often as having premised the existence of "blaming the victim" cannot, or does not, attempt to explain "blaming the victim" as it has been defined by Shaver. One may say that this is only a conceptual issue and past research did not carefully define the concept of blame as Shaver (1989) argues it should be. But future research should take careful note of what is being studied before trying to explain the findings. And though the theory does not explain "blaming" it is still quite relevant to the research on reactions to rape victims. Specifically, the theory proposes that a threat to one's just world will result in devaluation or rejection of the victim when no other explanation seems plausible.

It should be pointed out, however, that assigning behavioral responsibility is not always done logically (Lerner & Miller, 1978). Observers are willing to assign such responsibility in instances where it is not reasonable (e.g., Lerner & Matthews, 1967). According to Lerner and Miller (1978), these irrational attributional reactions to victims indicate that respondents are, in fact, reducing their perceived threat to a just world. And Lerner and Miller actually cite studies using only attributional dependent measures as support for their theory. This creates a somewhat circular argument for sustaining the viability of the theory. If subjects do assign responsibility to a victim, then this is support for the theory, but if subjects do *not* see a victim as deserving her fate, then proponents of the theory can, and do, argue that this is not relevant to the theory, because no threat has occurred. Future research should attempt to discern whether behavioral responsibility is assigned as a precondition to threat or to alleviate threat and restore justice. Though the latter instance would be support for the just world hypothesis, the former would not demand rejection of the theory, as again it could be argued that no threat occurred, so the theory is not relevant. Because the hypothesis predicts that experiencing threat to one's just world creates arousal (Lerner & Miller, 1978) that one is motivated to reduce, measures of arousal should be incorporated into future research.

Unfortunately, then, not much research has addressed the validity of a just world hypothesis in this domain, as most of the research has used basic attributional measures to the exclusion of characterological responsibility measures. Only a few studies that addressed the issue of the "respectability" of the victim included in their dependent measures an item concerning the likability of the victim. Contrary to the predictions of this hypothesis, Luginbuhl and Mullin (1981) found the respectable victim was liked *more* than the victim who was not respectable, despite the fact that she was seen as suffering more, which presumably would have created a greater threat to the respondents' just world. Similarly, Karuza and Carey (1984) also found this pattern for derogation measures, which included general likability of the victim. Another study (Stokols & Schopler, 1973) varied the perceived carelessness of the victim, as well as the seriousness of the consequences. In this study, the "careless" victim was found to be more responsible. The severity of the consequences also had an effect; the more severe the consequences, the more likely subjects were to find the victim to be less attractive, despite her carelessness. Though Lerner and Miller cite this very study as support for the just world theory, what actually should have been found in order to validate the concept would be an interaction between carelessness and severity of consequences for the victim's attractiveness. If assigning behavioral responsibility to a victim alleviates the threat, as they say it does, then no characterological derogation of this victim should have been necessary.

Perhaps the just world hypothesis is too specific in its focus, as it relates to derogating the victim. One cannot rule out the possibility that attributions of causality, or behavioral responsibility, or even blame, are assigned as result of a desire to restore justice. Proponents of this hypothesis need to explicate more clearly under what conditions characterological derogation occurs, and when (and if) behavioral responsibility attributions are a product of the motivation to restore justice. It is quite possible that this occurs, because subjects show a clear preference for assigning behavioral fault over characterological fault. In fact, when one's belief in a just world is taken into account, it is only behavioral fault that has been found to be related to preserving adaptive beliefs as "my world is just" (Karuza & Carey, 1984).

Clearly what is also needed are cleaner measures of derogation. Although the just world hypothesis, as it is stated, cannot explain why men generally derogate the victim more than women do, or deal with the findings on the "respectability" of the victim, it could very well explain why victims are reacted to so negatively at all (McCaul et al., 1990).

Defensive Attribution

The defensive attribution hypothesis, outlined by Shaver (1970), argues that issues of *harm avoidance* should be distinguished from issues of *blame avoidance*. When one is confronted with a threatening situation, one is not likely to assign attributions of responsibility to a victim who has experienced an event that very well could happen to *oneself*. The inference that such an event could happen to oneself will be based on the similarity of the observer to the victim. If the observer is *personally* similar, then the observer perceives that the situation that has befallen the victim may some day happen to him or her. If both personal and situational similarities exist between the observer and the victim, instead of increased responsibility, the observer will actually *minimize* the responsibility of the victim, presumably in order to assure that when the observer finds him- or herself in a similar situation, he or she will not be blamed either.

Some evidence from rape attribution research supports the defensive attribution hypothesis. Gender differences that have been observed are consistent with this view. Females, who may perceive the possibility of being raped themselves, may decrease the responsibility of the victim in order to avoid blame if it should happen to them. A study that varied the similarity of a rape victim to college-student subjects found that subjects were less likely to assign responsibility when the victim was a similar college student than when the victim was a dissimilar housewife (Fulero & DeLara, 1976). Wohlers (1982) has shown that feelings of threat are highest when the victim is of the same sex. Other research finds that identification with the victim decreases attributional responsibility (Deitz et al., 1984).

This hypothesis, like the just world hypothesis, proposes that the minimization of responsibility in the case of both personal and situational similarity is a motivated distortion of reality. Unlike for the just world hypothesis, however, research has been done to provide support for the existence of this motivation. Thornton (1984) varied both personal and situational similarity, as well as the presence or absence of cues that could serve as a possible alternative explanation for any arousal that subjects may have experienced upon being exposed to a rape scenario. In this study, when alternative explanations for arousal were present, subjects assigned less responsibility to victims of rape than when no alternative explanation was made available. Presumably, the arousal was labeled in accordance with the provided explanation, and not assigned to the rape victim. When this attributional cue was not present, the arousal was attributed to the rape victim, as reflected by higher responsibility attributions. In a second study, Thornton (1984) increased the arousal of subjects and found that such an increase in arousal also increased the responsibility assigned to the victim. These two studies also supported the similarity effect—the more similar the respondent was to the victim, the less responsibility was attributed to her.

The defensive attribution hypothesis, then, is able to predict some findings in the research literature that the just world hypothesis cannot. There is also evidence that responsibility is assigned as a result of motivation. But several findings cannot be explained—for example, differences in responsibility as a function of resistance, or level of acquaintanceship with the victim. This hypothesis would predict that females would be especially lenient to victims who have been raped by someone the victim knew or were dating because they are very likely to find themselves in such a social situation. But this is not the case (Tetreault & Barnett, 1986). Shaver (1985) points out, however, that perceivers are rational information processors most of the time. And this is an important point. But it is equally important to point out, according to Shaver, that the perceiver's motives in making attributions can never be dismissed. Heider

(1958) also noted the importance of motivation in the attribution process when he stated that "the reason has to fit the wishes of the person" (p. 172).

Choosing Between Explanations
That Use Motives

Two motivational explanations for reacting negatively to a rape victim have been presented. Although neither one can be ruled out entirely, neither the just world hypothesis nor the defensive attribution hypothesis can accurately explain all of the findings in the research literature. The lack of research documenting that observers actually experience a just world threat precludes support for the just world hypothesis in the domain of rape. Furthermore, specific predictions made by the just world hypothesis have not been supported. The defensive attribution hypothesis, on the other hand, is more consistent with some of the findings of the research and therefore does a better job of explaining why rape victims are found accountable for their own rape. In addition, data exist that document a direct relationship between arousal and activated defensive attributions—the more arousal one has, the stronger are the attributions (Thornton, 1984). For this reason, one should not be inclined to disregard the motivational bases for such reactions. As Gordon and Riger (1989) point out, the only crime women fear more than rape is murder. Conversely, rape laws reflect the fear in men of being falsely accused of rape (Estrich, 1987). There is little doubt that being exposed to the very nature of rape demands an explanation that an individual will be motivated to make.

The question that remains, then, is what purpose is served by the explanation that is created by an observer? When an individual finds fault in the rape victim, is he or she doing so out of self-protective needs? Or is the observer merely trying to make sense out of something that does not make sense—trying to explain that which demands explanation? The motivational explanations would propose the former view—that individuals make such attributions in an attempt to preserve their own safety; to keep their self-protective beliefs secure. However, the very assumptions and predictions of the defensive attribution hypothesis run counter to what is known about potential rape victims (including all women and not excluding all men). Specifically, there is a predominant belief among these individuals that "it won't happen to *me!*" (Janoff-Bulman, 1985a; Janoff-Bulman & Frieze, 1983). They, in effect, do not recognize themselves as potential rape victims. Furthermore, individuals may go to great lengths to ensure that it will not happen to them (Gordon & Riger, 1989). In order to activate a defensive attribution, according to the hypothesis, one *must* acknowledge the probability that it may happen to them. We would argue that this is not likely. This is particularly not likely when the victim is both personally and situationally similar, which requires one to discard this belief altogether—to say "yes, this not only may happen to me, but is likely to happen to me"—in order to avoid blame when it does occur. The self-protective belief does exist, but is too strong to be rejected that easily and quickly.

The status, therefore, of these specific motivational explanations, as they relate to explaining reactions to rape victims, is currently vulnerable to criticism. Specifically, little evidence exists that individuals find a rape victim accountable for the rape because they are trying to save themselves. Instead, perhaps what they are doing is simply trying to make sense out of what may be perceived as both an extreme and negative outcome that demands an explanation. Both attributional principles and cognitive explanations may elucidate the judgment process of observers who are exposed to a rape situation.

Attribution and Social Perception

Another type of explanation for the pervasive negative reactions emphasizes cognitive rather than motivational processes. It relies on attributional theory. The very essence of attribution involves linking an event to its causes (Ross & Fletcher, 1985). When one encounters an event, attributions allow understanding of that event, as well as the ability to react to the event, either directly or indirectly. Several basic perceptual and attributional principles may yield much insight into why individuals so often find a victim responsible for her fate.

Heider (1958) was the first to observe systematically that all individuals act as "naive perceivers." That is, given an outcome, they attempt to find the causes of that outcome; they seek explanation, prediction, and control in their surroundings. Although most individuals are not psychologists, most do psychologically analyze events. Perhaps Heider's greatest contribution was actually stating that which was obvious. And though he made many contributions, perhaps the contributions most useful here were his hypotheses on perceptions of responsibilities.

Recall that it was proposed that there are five levels of responsibility that determine how accountable one is for an outcome. First, merely by being *associated* with an outcome, one may be found responsible. Responsibility via *commission* occurs when the person caused the outcome, despite the preclusion of foreseeability. If it is perceived that an event should have been *foreseen,* one may also be held responsible. Finally, an individual is held responsible for actions that were *intentional.* The intentional behavior may well be *justifiable,* but the individual is still held responsible for the behavior, although the behavior would be considered justified by the situation.

At the most primitive level, then, a rape victim may be found responsible for her behavior merely because she was physically present during the rape. She may also be found responsible for her behavior before the assault (e.g., going up to the apartment of the rapist) whether she thought of the possibility of rape or not. If it is perceived that the rape victim *should* have anticipated the actions of the rapist, then she may also be found responsible. These forms of responsibility are perhaps those most commonly made by perceivers of rape victims, and may help to explain their existence, as Heider notes that even mature individuals often make primitive attributions. The latter two, assigned when the behavior is considered intentional, or intentional but justified, would deal with attributions of blame, which have been shown to be less common as responsibility attributions.

Unfortunately, though it is easy to imagine that individuals do use these levels of responsibility when determining responsibility, little research has been done to identify directly which levels are used under which circumstances, or if they are even used in making responsibility attributions to rape victims. The studies investigating the pre-rape behavior of the victim, as well as those studying the effects of the victim-rapist relationship, suggest that respondents are taking both the victim's association with the rapist as well as her pre-rape behavior into account. This may be reflected by the more negative evaluations of her, higher attributions of her responsibility, and less severe penalties for the rapist when she engages in certain pre-rape behaviors (e.g., drinking, initiating interaction), or when she had been involved with the rapist, in comparison to reactions when such factors are not present.

One study (McCaul et al., 1990) has directly assessed the extent to which subjects believe that the victim should have been able to foresee the rape and the subsequent attributions of responsibility. As predicted, judgments that the rape should have been foreseeable were significantly related to stronger attributions of blame for the victim. In addition, this study investigated the perceived intentions of the victim, although not directly. Hypothesizing that because "sexual relationships are by their very nature participatory—one *intends* to engage in sex with another" (McCaul et al., 1990, p. 5)— the authors investigated the extent to which subjects perceived that the victim found some pleasure in the event and how such perceptions would affect attributions of blame. In two studies, they found that perceived pleasure felt by the victim and blame of the victim were strongly positively correlated.

Hence, in addition to the indirect evidence obtained from research on the victim-rapist relationship and pre-rape behavior of the victim that support Heider's ideas, McCaul et al. (1990) provide a direct test for two of the five levels of responsibility, and find both foreseeability and intentionality to be positively correlated with attributions of responsibility and blame to the victim. This suggests that observers of a rape may indeed use the different levels of responsibility, as hypothesized by Heider. The research also suggests correspondence with Shaver's (1985) analysis of responsibility, described in Chapter 6. In general, the more actions in which the victim willingly engages preceding the rape (presumably producing perceptions of causality in observers), the more the victim is held responsible. Furthermore, the more the victim is expected to have been able to foresee the outcome, the more she is held responsible and even blamed. Finally, perceptions of victim intentions, measured through perceptions of victim-pleasure, are strongly related to victim blame.

Given this general support for both Heider's and Shaver's ideas, it is quite likely that individuals do use these criteria for determining the responsibility of a rape victim. Support especially exists for a strong positive relationship between foreseeability and responsibility—the more it is believed that the victim should have or may have known what would happen, the more she is found responsible. This may be an important part of any attributional/cognitive explanation for why victims are held accountable. Specifically, these findings suggest that not only is the behavior of the victim scrutinized, but her psychological state is also analyzed. The rape victim, in effect, receives a good deal of an observer's attention when it comes to explaining why the rape occurred. However, these findings cannot explain *why* the rape victim receives so much attention from observers when it is the rapist who rapes. Nor can it explain what is going on in the minds of observers as they produce their judgments. In order to explain these questions, further work is needed.

The Focus of Attention on the Victim

The remainder of this chapter explores these very questions. First, work that describes why the focus of attention may turn to the rape victim is discussed. The final portion of the chapter is devoted to using cognitive explanations in order to understand just what types of cognitive processing may be going on.

According to Nisbett and Ross (1980), people expect "great" events to have great causes, and such events guide the attributional processes accordingly. This "resemblance criterion," as Nisbett and Ross call it, may explain why perceivers do not appear satisfied with a simple, "the rapist is to blame." The very word *rape* carries extremely negative connotations. It is bad. It is dirty. To blame the rapist may just not be enough "reason" for such an extreme outcome.

Similarly, Kelley (1972) has identified *causal schemata* to help explain perceptions of single events in which information about the event is incomplete and inferences are required. Specifically, he describes two types of causal schemata: the multiple necessary causal schema and the multiple sufficient causal schema. The multiple sufficient causal schema is used to explain outcomes that are not particularly unusual or extreme and assumes that any one of several potential causes could be sufficient to produce an outcome. The multiple necessary causal schema, on the other hand, is required to explain outcomes that are more extreme, and would therefore be most applicable to this discussion. This schema, which all individuals may use, assumes that for such extreme outcomes to occur, more than one cause is *necessary* to explain its occurrence. Therefore, individuals may assume that although a rapist was capable of rape, and intended to rape, he could not have raped without the participation of the female—that both causes were necessary in order for the outcome to occur.

The very focus of the research on attributions of responsibility in a rape case usually involves aspects of the rape victim; her "respectability," her attractiveness, her behavior. In essence, the research is making the rape victim perceptually *salient*. The effects of a salient figure on subsequent judgments are extremely robust (McArthur, 1981; Taylor & Fiske, 1978). Salient stimuli lead to increased attention. Such increased attention, in turn, has been found to lead directly to perceptions of causality (Taylor & Fiske, 1975). That is, when particular attention is paid to a particularly salient individual, then that individual will be found to have played a more causal role in an outcome than one who is not salient.

Taken together, it becomes clear that the situation of a rape victim demands considerable explanation (possibly due to the "resemblance criterion" or through one's causal schema). This, as well as the saliency of the victim—in research as well as through the media and in the courtroom—may increase the focus of attention on the victim. It is possible that if the focus of attention were placed on the rapist, attributions of responsibility would be altered, at least somewhat. This is a hypothesis that needs to be tested.

It could be argued that the increased cognitive thought that is triggered when one is presented with a rape event would lead to the insight that it was, in fact, the rapist's fault—that he raped her. But we know that this does not happen, and there are theoretical explanations that can help to understand why.

Norm Theory

Specifically, it is possible that individuals who are presented with such a negative event as rape may engage in a cognitive search for a way that it could have been different. Kahneman and Miller (1986) have documented considerable research that supports what they call *norm theory*. This theory predicts that when an event is considered "abnormal," then individuals will engage in a search for possible alternative behaviors or outcomes that could have occurred. Abnormality, in this theory, is not defined through statistics or probabilities. Instead, if the perceiver is surprised or finds the event unusual, then the event is considered abnormal and a search for alternatives begins. If it is possible for the perceiver to create in his or her mind possible alternatives to the event (either causes or effects), then the particular causes or effects that were cognitively noted as those that could have been different will play a particularly important role in judgments. Let us apply this theory to the case of rape—which most perceive as both abnormal and unusual. If one is presented with a situation of rape, and the preceding behaviors did not lead to an expectation of rape (e.g., a woman goes on a date with a man, has a nice time, and gets raped), then that event will evoke a search for possible alternatives to the event. Could the outcome have been different? How could the outcome have been different? *"Could the victim have behaved differently?"* (And, ultimately, *should* the victim have behaved differently?)

If it is possible to create in one's mind alternatives to particular behaviors (a process called *counterfactual thinking*), then *those particular behaviors* will strongly affect judgments about the event. Ultimately, this process could lead to increased attributions of responsibility assigned to the victim. Respondents may be cognitively producing alternative scenarios for how she could have behaved differently, and consequently find fault in the victim.

Norm theory further elaborates on which aspects of a situation are most likely to create counterfactual thinking. Specifically, it is those aspects of the situation that are most *mutable* (i.e., changeable) that are most likely to produce alternative scenarios. Some aspects are simply easier to change than others, and are consequently more likely to be changed. For example, it is more likely that action will create counterfactual thinking, rather than inaction—when a victim has gone to the apartment of a man who rapes her, it is much easier to think about how she should not have done that, as opposed to thinking about something she should have done in addition. It is also more likely that changes will be made for those aspects of the situation that have been attended to most, rather than other aspects. Given the apparently predominating tendency of observers for focusing their attention on the rape victim, norm theory would predict that it would be precisely her behavior that would most likely be considered mutable.

It could be argued that because the rapist has been found actually to receive *most* of the responsibility or blame, that it is, in fact, his behavior that is being viewed most clearly as mutable and therefore the basis for counterfactual thinking. This is not likely, however.

Especially in this society, misconceptions about the rapist prevail. Rapists are considered to be sex-starved, insane, or both. Males are not expected to be able to control their sexual urges as well as women are. These assigned characteristics are stable and not very amenable to change.

Norm theory may, then, explain the cognitive processes that may be going on in the minds of observers. Support for this view has been obtained by Coleman and Branscombe (1991). In this study, all subjects received the same scenario depicting an acquaintance rape. Subjects were then asked to change only certain aspects of the event. They could either change only the behavior of the victim, or they could change both the behavior of the victim and the outcome. (Subjects were never instructed to change the behavior of the rapist.) When subjects were able to change the behavior of the victim, and at the same time produce a different outcome, measures of responsibility increased. They were, in effect, constructing a story for how she could have avoided being raped. Conversely, measures of responsibility decreased when subjects were instructed to change the victim's behavior without altering the outcome. These subjects apparently realized that no matter what the victim did, she would be raped—her behavior did not matter!

This research, though promising, is the only work that has investigated the validity of norm theory as it relates to rape victims and responsibility. Other findings that have tested norm theory are also relevant to this discussion. For example, Miller and McFarland (1986) found that subjects reacted more strongly to a victim of a shooting when an alternative to that outcome was more easily imagined. In this situation, subjects offered more compensation to the victim; Miller and McFarland point out, however, that the theory does not predict the direction of the response, only the strength of the response. Therefore, the more easily observers can think of how a rape victim could have avoided rape, the more likely they should be to find her accountable. Gleicher et al. (1990) have also shown that counterfactual thinking is more likely to occur when the event is negative, as rape is, than when the event is neutral or positive, unless possible alternatives are provided and made salient. This could be because people are more likely to anticipate more positive or neutral outcomes than negative outcomes (Wells, 1980).

Norm theory may best explain why the behavior of a victim prior to the rape is considered so important to observers. It may also explain why the relationship between the victim and rapist is important. A victim who is raped by someone she knows well may be considered more abnormal to respondents (despite its increased prevalence statistically), which is likely to evoke more counter-factual thinking. In addition, traditional individuals may consider this event to be more abnormal than feminists and be more likely to create alternative scenarios. Research on the effects of victim resistance on judgments may also be explained by this theory. For example, Branscombe and Weir's (1992) finding that those who resisted in a stereotypically inconsistent fashion were judged more harshly may be the product of its abnormality that would be more likely to produce counterfactual thinking. Although the rape of a respectable woman may also be considered more abnormal to the lay observer, her behavior may be less mutable because of the behavioral constraints placed on a "respectable" woman. This could potentially be an explanation for why the respectable woman is held less responsible, as it may be assumed that a respectable woman would do all of the right things in order to avoid being raped. In this case, her relatively immutable behavior would not elicit counter-factual thinking, despite the abnormal nature of the event. Unlike the just world hypothesis and defensive attribution hypothesis, this theory is potentially consistent with most of the findings in the research. More research is nevertheless needed to establish direct relationships among perceived abnormality, counterfactual think-ing, and attributions in various situations of rape.

The creation of counterfactual thinking is dependent upon the evocation of a norm that is not considered normal. Theoretically, it might be evoked from either a cause, an effect, or the cause-effect relationship. Any of these can produce a story in the minds of observers for how things could have been different. However, another phenomenon that relates specifically to the cause-effect relationship may add further insight to the judgment process. *Hindsight bias* has been demonstrated by Fischhoff and his col-leagues (Fischhoff, 1975, 1980, 1982; Fischhoff & Beyth, 1975; Fischhoff, Slovic, & Lichtenstein, 1977) and involves strengthening the relationship between events and their outcomes. Because of the strengthened relationship, once an outcome is known, it actually appears to have been inevitable, given the preceding events. And, in hindsight, people assume that what they perceive as inevitable should have been foreseeable by the individual in question. Thus the victim is held responsible—once the outcome is known—for not having foreseen the possibility of rape.

The hindsight bias has been shown to exist when the situation is rape (Janoff-Bulman et al., 1985). In one study, subjects all read the same scenario, but half were told that the outcome was rape and half were presented with a more neutral outcome (that the man took the woman home). Subjects were then asked to judge the likelihood of several different scenario outcomes. Results showed that the outcome that was considered most likely was the one they had been exposed to, demonstrating the hindsight effect—subjects had strengthened the relationship between the outcome and the preceding events. A second study indicated that when the outcome is rape (as opposed to a neutral outcome), subjects were more likely to "blame" (recall that this study's questions actually measured issues of causality) the female for her behavior than when a neutral outcome occurred, despite the fact that the females in both scenarios engaged in exactly the same behaviors.

It is likely, then, that observers judging a rape victim are engaging in some "Monday morning quarterbacking." They know the outcome, they see how the victim behaved, and they find the relationship causally clear.

The hindsight bias complements norm theory and creates a possible explanation for what types of cognitive processes occur when observers make judgments about rape events. Once the outcome of rape is apparent, individuals may both produce in their minds what they perceive to be the inevitability of the rape, given the preceding behaviors, and view the behaviors of the victim as those that could most likely have been different. Hence, the link between actual behaviors and actual outcome is strengthened, as is the link between other potentially different behaviors and a different outcome. This may ultimately produce the belief that because it is obvious to the observer how the rape occurred and how it could have been prevented, then it should have been obvious—foreseeable—to the victim, who after all, was there at the time.

Summary

Rape victims are not only victimized by the rapist, but by those who judge the rape as well. Chapter 6 and this chapter have shown that although attributions of blame are not nearly as common as previously thought, attributions of both causality and responsibility prevail. Several different factors may affect such attributions, including both characteristics of the observer as well as characteristics of the victim and her behavior. Although being exposed to a situation involving rape may, indeed, motivate one to explain the occurrence, the motivation is most likely not one of self-protection, because the research does not support most of the predictions of either the just world theory or defensive attribution hypothesis. Instead, the more cognitive perspectives (e.g., the issue of foreseeability, norm theory, and the hindsight bias) produce predictions that are more consistent with recent research findings.

8 The Reactions of Rape Victims

Two years ago and 11 years after being raped, a 29-year-old university student and mother of two small children sat down and put her experience in writing. She titles her work:

In Defense of Hating Pink Floyd

Everyone was drinking, getting stoned, and tripping on acid. This was something I had never tried and at the time I was what everyone considered to be a "prude." I didn't want to trip, said so, and thought that would be that. I was given a rum and Coke and joined the party. I talked, laughed, and had fun when suddenly I felt odd. I sat down and finished my drink. I became more and more quiet. They were playing Pink Floyd over and over. It began to irritate me, I wanted to say something and found I couldn't. I found myself laid back on the couch staring at the textured ceiling. Suddenly the nodules changed into Christmas tree ornaments and descended down from the ceiling on beautiful satin ribbons. They began to serenade me. I don't remember what they sang, except it sounded wondrous to me. In the back of my mind this concern was lurking, how did I get so high when I haven't had anything but a rum and Coke? I looked at the table where the glass was sitting and saw what looked like a postage stamp glued to the bottom of the glass. At the time I didn't think anything of it. I was intensely cold. I found I couldn't move, strangely enough, this didn't frighten me. I figured I could ride my high out and come down. I tried to talk, I couldn't. So I spaced out. When I came back I noticed there were only a few people left at the party. I noticed my purse had been dumped on the floor, contents scattered, this bothered me, but not much. I noticed the girl who was throwing this party was talking to some guy, who I vaguely remembered being the one who was the acid dealer. They were off to one side talking. They were both looking at me. She gestures at me and shrugs, he walks over to me, and picks me up. I was like a sack of potatoes. He carries me into the bedroom. I remember thinking, great, I can go to sleep . . .

It was painful, humiliating, degrading, and frightening. "Guess that six hits of acid knocked your ass in the dirt, huh?" he says. "Well that's okay, it doesn't bother me. I hear you're a virgin, let's find out."

He undresses.

What a way to visually experience your first sight of an erect penis. . . . He tied my hands together—"case you start to come down too soon." He kept referring to me as a snotty, stuck-up squaw. To this day the term *squaw* makes me want to puke. He liked to play rough. He tore my shirt off. Having one's clothing torn off I found out, is *painful*. Unfortunately I was very capable of experiencing pain. He didn't tear off my pants, he merely pulled them off. Rip went the underwear. I was terrified. I knew it was going to happen and I couldn't even *fight*. I wasn't asked. I didn't have the opportunity to say *NO!*

Clinically speaking, my vaginal tract was so dry he tore my urethra, an impossible thing to do when he pierced my hymen. At the time I was in accelerated English (Sophomore year) and we had just finished *Beowulf*. In *Beowulf* is a monster Grendel, who killed Englishmen by tearing them apart. At the time I was certain this was Grendel, I wondered if I would live. He was rutting like a pig. Disgusting. Putrid. Vile.

I viewed my rape for the most part dispassionately and somewhat objectively. He finished. "Guess you *were* a virgin. Slut." He left. I passed out. About 3 a.m. I came around. The rope had loosened from my wrist and I got loose. I did have rope burns though, probably from his not-so-gentle approach. I picked up what was left of my purse and contents, missing were my wallet, my bag of weed, and my pipe.

I was still tripping. On my way home I found I couldn't tell the difference between green, red, or yellow. However, I remembered which light was what on the stoplight sequence, so my drive home went okay. I didn't realize I was in shock.

I arrived at home about 4 a.m. My mom was up and furious. She sat at her antique oak table playing solitaire in the living room. She lectured me about partying and staying out late. I was atypically quiet. Her lecture lasted until 6 a.m. Her final word was "since you stayed out all night, you can go to school today!" I remember watching her face change shape during the lecture. I shrugged. I went into the bathroom not bothering to lock it, undressed, got in the tub. I thought it was odd how much blood was running down my legs, I'd just menstruated the week before. She walked in on me. "You must have started," she said stiffly, and left. I often wonder how she could not have seen all the pieces. . . . A slight bruise on one side of my face, scratches, torn shirt, bruises up and down my leg, me silent, withdrawn, usually locking the door—how could she not see? I theorize it's because she did not want to. After all, she knew I never performed any function in the bathroom without locking the door . . .

I was stupid. I went to school the next day. I could have easily ditched, it didn't occur to me. A couple of days later I did go to [the medical center]. I had severe infection. My urethra was stitched up. I got an enormous amount of antibiotics. They fixed me physically, but emotionally I was a wreck. I had a small, quiet breakdown.

Propriety! How I hate this word! This mere social convention kills far more than it ever cures. Propriety bound me up and gagged me. I was not allowed to talk about this event in my life. Why are people so "conventionally" stupid? When things are not allowed to flow outward, they go inward into deeper levels. I changed, practically overnight. I became obnoxious, hateful, vulgar, crude, and I felt desolate. Oh, I did come out of it a bit. I went to a shrink, which helped a little. Yet every time I feel cornered or insecure this "defense mechanism" comes trotting out. It gives me a false sense of security. I feel if I can push people away they can't hurt me, but in *reality* they still can.

My aversion to such trivialities of things like the term "squaw" or the music of Pink Floyd are really secondary. What I hope is in the foremost of anyone's mind is what is really going on in cases such like this. If no one is willing to listen, how then can the story be told? Do not be dogmatic, blaming circumstance or drugs or innocence. . . . Instead, focus on the loss of an individual that no one was truly there to help or cared to. Perhaps if we were not so condemnatory we would be better prepared to listen. Perhaps.

Like this woman's experience, and as in the case of several other crimes, such as theft or a mugging, the time it takes to commit an act of rape may be quite brief. But from the perspective of the victim, the effects of this short interaction may last for months, for years, even forever. As this woman describes, the event is painful; in every sense of the word the event is painful. Because the act can never be forgotten, in one sense the victim is forced to be a different person for the rest of a lifetime. At another level, recovery does occur but estimates of the time necessary for its completion vary, depending upon the circumstances of the rape, the particular symptoms, and the characteristics of the individual victim. Researchers and therapists believe that for some victims the deleterious effects may last for months (Calhoun, Atkeson, & Resick, 1982), or even years (Burgess & Holmstrom, 1985; Kilpatrick, Veronen, & Best, 1984, 1985). Kilpatrick (1988) observes that some victims may never return to normality.

As Greenberg and Ruback note, "The hurt that victims experience is more than physical and material. They suffer psychologically and emotionally, and the recovery process is slow and difficult" (1984, p. 6). As we repeatedly note throughout this book, victims of rape are in a special category, because no other crime offers a similarly personal and intimate violation of the self. The rape experience has been described as "involving a total loss of control over one's life, one's body, and the course of events" (B. Katz, 1991, p. 253). Bard and Sangrey put it eloquently: "Short of being killed, there is no greater insult to the self" (1979, p. 19).

The theme of this book is, as noted in Chapter 1, that rape had been, and continues to be, a misunderstood phenomenon. A news article in *The New York Times* in early 1990 described the rape of a 17-year-old Columbia University student and stated that the victim was "cut on her arms and hands but not seriously injured" (Bamberger, 1990). Despite such callous reactions, we detect signs of improvement in society's level of understanding. Prior to the 1970s, much of research and writing speculated about false accusations by purported rape victims (Chappell, Geis, & Fogarty, 1974). In the last decade and one half, the shift has mobilized in support of a greater recognition of the legitimacy of a victim's need for help. This emphasis was first detected in the early 1970s, when several groups of researchers in the social sciences began to document the severity of the consequences of rape (e.g., Burgess & Holmstrom, 1974a; Sutherland & Scherl, 1970). More recently, victims, led by

Nancy Ziegenmeyer of Grinnell, IA, are beginning to speak out about their reactions, in the hope that others might learn from their experiences (Canon & Brandon, 1990).

A major purpose of this chapter is to synthesize these observations about the responses (both psychological and physical) expressed by victims of rape.

Shattered Assumptions

All of us make assumptions about the nature of the world and the people who occupy it. The world is so complex and we confront so many people every day that we can not cope unless we "simplify" our environment through the use of generalized assumptions. These expectations are often not explicit; that is, we are generally unaware of their role in helping guide us in our responses to our environment. For most of us, the basic content of these expectations is benign; even though we are vigilant when it comes to the occasional suspicious person in our neighborhood or the occasional erratic driver on the freeway, we assume that most people and events in our world are positive and beneficial, or at least not negative. Furthermore, we tend to believe that we are less likely than our peers to experience negative events (Taylor & Brown, 1988). But there are events and people that may shatter these accommodating assumptions; being a rape victim is one such event.

Psychologist Ronnie Janoff-Bulman (1985a, 1985b; Janoff-Bulman & Frieze, 1983) has argued that stress reactions, such as rape trauma syndrome and post-traumatic stress syndrome, are the result of these basic assumptions having been shattered.

The Assumption of Invulnerability

We are all aware that disasters occur, often unexpectedly, in all parts of the world. We often read or hear about people being diagnosed as having terminal illnesses, about others being harmed in assaults or robberies. Despite the deluge of exposure we receive about such traumatic experiences, we as individuals may still feel that "it won't happen to me" (Taylor & Brown, 1988). Several studies have shown that people do, in fact, experience this sense of invulnerability. In a clever study C. R. Snyder (1978) discovered that most of us believe we possess more "good" and less "bad" than others do. He reported the results of an in-class demonstration in which college students were given data on life expectancies supposedly obtained from life-insurance company records. After considering the projected death rates for people of differing ages, including their own, these students concluded that they would live, on the average, for 10 years longer than the age predicted from actuarial tables.

Other research shows that people tend to believe that they have a less-than-average likelihood to become the victims of disease (Harris & Guten, 1979; Kirscht, Haefner, Kegeles, & Rosenstock, 1966; Weinstein, 1980) or to become victims of a crime. They also believe that crime in their own neighborhood is less serious than in other neighborhoods (Hindelang, Gottfredson, & Garofalo, 1978; Skogan & Maxfield, 1981). This "illusion of invulnerability" may stem from a strong need for personal control over our environment; most of us want to have some say over what happens to us.

The experience of having been raped (as well as other examples of victimization) shatters this sense of invulnerability. Rape victims can no longer say "it won't happen to me" because it *has* happened to them. Having been forcibly placed in the role of a victim, furthermore, makes it easier to envision oneself as a victim again. Janoff-Bulman (1985a, 1985b) believes that this reaction may contribute to the massive levels of fear reported by victims even months after their victimization had occurred. They no longer feel safe; the world is no longer benignly predictable. In the case of a rape victim, the consequences of this shattered assumption may be the most severe because it was another human being who did the shattering. People in general can no longer be trusted.

The World as Meaningful

Recall the just world theory from Chapter 7. It relies heavily on the belief that many of us hold dear to our hearts—that the world is not an unpredictable place. Most of us do prefer to believe that everything happens for a reason. Furthermore, many of us adamantly assume that if we are patient enough or if we work hard enough, good things will come to us. A fundamental credo in our society is that people get what they deserve. A logical converse of this belief is that people deserve what they get; this extension of the fundamental credo is especially adhered to in Western culture (Bard & Sangrey, 1979).

With respect to relatively routine events, this type of rationalization serves as an explanation and gives meaning to the world. For example, if Susan gets an "A" on her psychology exam, she may generate several attributions. Probably she will assume that she deserved the "A" because she is a hardworking, relatively intelligent person. Although other attributions are possible, research indicates that this internal attribution (i.e., "I possess qualities within myself that cause this outcome") is most common (Miller & Ross, 1975; Zuckerman, 1979).

After a rape, victims may spend a massive portion of their waking hours trying to come up with explanations for why *they* were raped. According to Janoff-Bulman, the mental focus is *not* on the question "Why did this event happen?," but on the question "Why did this event happen to *me?*"

Thus we confront the second major assumption that is shattered in the process of victimization; no longer secure is a belief that things occur for just reasons. Explanations for why they were victimized will initially be absent, especially among victims who consider themselves to be good people, who are appropriately cautious in response to danger. As we will describe in the next section of this chapter, the resulting pressure to create new explanations may lead to self-blame and other erosions of self-esteem.

Positive Self-Perceptions

The third assumption affected by having been raped is that "I am a good and decent person." Most of us are motivated to establish and maintain a high level of self-esteem by possessing a positive self-image. Being raped may act as a catalyst for the emergence of latent negative self-images (Horowitz, Wilner, Marmar, & Krupnick, 1980). One rape victim has written: "I still feel insignificant. When people turn to listen to me, I freeze. Don't listen to me! Why should anyone care what I have to say?" (Barr, 1979, p. 107). Victims may come to see themselves as helpless and defenseless in an aberrant society. Not only do rape victims find themselves questioning their own personal worth, but they now see themselves as radically different from everyone else. No longer does anyone—even those close to them—understand.

When these fundamental assumptions collapse, the person can no longer function as before. To summarize, for rape victims: they are no longer invulnerable, the world is not just, and they are not worthy or decent. These changes inevitably have consequences; Janoff-Bulman argues that the symptoms that inexorably appear may be described by the term *rape trauma syndrome*. It is to that phenomenon to which we now turn.

Rape Trauma Syndrome and Post-Traumatic Stress Disorder

In 1974, Ann Wolbert Burgess, a psychiatric nurse, and Lynda Lytle Holmstrom, a sociologist, coined the term *rape trauma syndrome* to describe a collection of the consequences of rape. According to Burgess and Holmstrom, all rape victims suffer from rape trauma syndrome to some degree. Some show severe symptoms, others not so severe, but all suffer. The rape trauma syndrome may be divided into two phases, but each can adversely affect all facets of the victim's life: physical, psychological, social, and sexual.

The first phase of the rape trauma syndrome deals with the immediate reactions of the rape victim. To refer to these as "short-term" responses possibly diminishes their importance, for they may last for days or weeks, and are usually quite severe. The second phase of the rape trauma syndrome reflects the long-term process of reorganization; that is, coming to terms with the reactions and trying to deal with the pain and hurt in an effective manner. Although exactly which symptoms will predominate in an individual victim will depend on both the nature of the rape and the characteristics of the victim, some responses are so frequent that the term *syndrome* seems justified.

Phase I: Acute Crisis Phase

The first phase, initiating immediately after the act, is also known as the phase of *impact* (Bard & Sangrey, 1979). Victims are in a state of shock; it is not an exaggeration when they report that everything has fallen apart inside (see Box 8.1 for one example).

One of the most frequent responses is that of anxiety or fearfulness (Gidycz & Koss, 1991). As one victim put it, "Only the terror repeats itself constantly, again and again" (Barr, 1979, p. 46). That

BOX 8.1

An Acquaintance Rape Victim's Reaction

Georgette was a student in her first year at a university in North Carolina when she was raped by the resident advisor in her dormitory. While standing outside her room, she was approached by him; she repeatedly rejected his advances but he dragged her into her room and raped her. She described her experience to Warshaw (1988), as follows:

> I didn't tell anyone. In fact, I wouldn't even admit it to myself until about four months later when the guilt and fear that had been eating at me became too much to hide and I came very close to a complete nervous breakdown. I tried to kill myself, but fortunately I chickened out at the last minute.
>
> There's no way to describe what was going on inside me. I was losing control and I'd never been so terrified and helpless in my life. I felt as if my whole world had been kicked out from under me and I had been left to drift all alone in the darkness. I had horrible nightmares in which I relived the rape and others which were even worse. I was terrified of being with people and terrified of being alone. I couldn't concentrate on anything and began failing several classes. Deciding what to wear in the morning was enough to make me panic and cry uncontrollably. I was convinced I was going crazy, and I'm still convinced I almost did. (p. 54)

is, the fear can become so salient and demanding that it overpowers the lives of its victims. Many sufferers relive the event over and over again in their minds. They have great difficulty in getting to sleep, and when they finally do, the sleep—instead of being a relief—is accompanied by nightmares in which the rape is reinstated.

The immediate consequences of being raped have been documented by one investigation in which victims were asked to complete a checklist of symptoms only 2 or 3 hours after the rape (Veronen, Kilpatrick, & Resick, 1979). Profound cognitive and physiological symptoms of anxiety were manifest. Of the victims, 96% reported feeling scared, a similar percentage reported being worried, and 92% said they were terrified and confused. Four

fifths of the respondents reported that thoughts were racing
through their minds. Accompanying these all-but-unanimous cognitions were physiological manifestations of anxiety that were equally
negative; these included shaking or trembling (reported by 96% of
the victims), a racing heart (80%), pain (72%), tight muscles (68%),
rapid breathing (64%), and numbness (60%).

Although fear and anxiety are most common, they are not the only
immediate consequences. Others include the following:

*1. Denial, Shock, and Disbelief: "This Couldn't Be Happening to
Me."* One woman later recounted her thoughts during the ordeal:
"Thoughts pounded through my head as I tried to understand what
was happening. Was this a joke? Was this someone I knew being
cruel? It couldn't be real" (Barr, 1979, p. 18).

2. Disruption. Victims may respond with varying degrees of personality disorganization (Bassuk, 1980). Some may appear confused
and disoriented; they often are fearful and trembling. Other victims
do not exhibit observable emotional symptoms. In contrast to the
above so-called expressive victims, these "controlled" respondents
are often dazed and numb, and hence appear to be unresponsive to
their environment.

3. Guilt, Hostility, and Blame. Janoff-Bulman (1979) suggests that
responding by blaming oneself may be the second most common
reaction after fear. For example, many victims will reason that
things would have been different "if only I hadn't been on that
street" or "if only I wouldn't have left the window open." Others
may direct their hostility and blame at men in general, or at society
for permitting sexual assaults to occur. One study reported that 11%
of rape victims reacted in this manner, by agreeing to statements
like "Men have too little respect for women" or "There is never a
policeman around when you need him" (Meyer & Taylor, 1986).
Among this same sample of respondents, only slightly more than
half (56%) assigned blame to the rapist.

Self-blame, as a reaction in some victims, can be so strong that
they believe the rape was their fault or that the man cares for them.
Ruth, an acquaintance rape victim interviewed by Warshaw (1988),
even married the man who raped her.

4. Regression to a State of Helplessness or Dependency. The feeling that one is no longer an independent person is a common one. Former senses of autonomy and competence are replaced with self-doubt. Victims report being confronted with feelings that they no longer have control over their lives and what happens to them, that they may have to rely on those close to them to make even the most insignificant decisions.

5. Distorted Perceptions. The impact of being a victim of a sexual assault cannot be overestimated; it often re-creates the world into a scary place to live. Feelings resembling paranoia result. One victim told Warshaw (1988): "One thing I'll never get over is my distrust of men" (p. 75). Koss (1988) discovered that 41% of acquaintance rape victims who were college students believed that they would be raped again.

Phase II: Long-Term Reactions

Following the immediate terror of a rape, victims are faced with the challenging job of putting the broken pieces of their lives together. During this second phase, also known as the *recoil* stage of the rape trauma syndrome, victims have the task of restoring order to their lives and reinstituting a feeling of mastery over their world (Burgess & Holmstrom, 1985). This task can take anywhere from a few months to years for completion, if, indeed, completion and closure ever do occur.

During this period of reorganization, victims must strive to understand what has happened to them, and how they are feeling as the process of restoration tries to proceed (Bard & Sangrey, 1979). Their collection of feelings may contain some that are contradictory with others; experiencing fear, sadness, guilt, and anger all at the same time is not uncommon. Some develop an overriding belief that because they have become victims, they will always be victims. As one woman wrote 4 months after her rape, "I am so sick of being a 'rape victim.' I want to be me again" (Barr, 1979, p. 105). Major symptoms of this phase include phobias, disturbances in physical functioning including sexual behavior, and changes in life-style.

Phobias. A phobia is an irrational fear, the possession of which interferes with effective adaptation to one's environment. Most persons with phobias will go to great lengths to avoid the object of their fear. A study that included a one-year follow-up (Kilpatrick, Resick, & Veronen, 1981) found that victims continued to report manifestations of fear and anxiety. Measures of paranoia and phobic anxiety given at that time led to continued high scores.

How might we explain the continuation of phobic responses long after the event? Psychologists usually consider phobic reactions as learned associations with a painful or unpleasant stimulus. For example, Kilpatrick et al. (1981) view a rape itself as a classical conditioning stimulus. Thus anything associated with the rape will come to be feared, as a result of the association. Furthermore, associations may be generalized; if a knife was used in the assault, then the victim may fear knives. Recipients of sexual assaults may become afraid of being alone, or of going out at night.

These fears may force the victim into what seems to be a no-win situation. If she stays home alone, she is afraid. If she goes out, she is also afraid. Many victims leave the lights on in their homes 24 hours a day. Clearly, the nature of the conditioned associations to the rape leads victims to alter their lives in may ways.

The cumulation of these fears may be one cause of the fact that relatively few victims report a rape to the police. As we noted previously, Russell (1984) has estimated that only about 10% of all rapes are reported by the victim. Fear of being embarrassed in court (Flynn, 1974) or simply not believed (Griffin, 1971) contributed to these estimates. As one victim put it, "I felt more vulnerable in court than I had on the street" (Bard & Sangrey, 1979, p. 103). Evidence also exists that these fears may be valid ones, as employees of the criminal justice system have tended to disbelieve many rape victims (Feldman-Summers & Palmer, 1980).

Disturbances in General Functioning. It is quite common for victims of sexual assault to experience resulting problems in dealing with routine aspects of living. Many are not able to eat on a regular basis, whereas some may eat ravenously and continuously. Changes in sleeping patterns, including insomnia, occur frequently. Once the person goes to sleep, nightmares about the rape may intrude.

One victim reports:

> At first, I had no appetite. I didn't eat anything for three whole days. It hurt to swallow for some reason. Then I began to eat a lot, you know, and gained weight. I don't think I slept for the same three days

that I didn't eat. I remember not going to bed the first two nights. After that I couldn't sleep more than a couple of hours at a time for a week or so, and that still happens two or three times a week. I've had nightmares, but I can't remember what they are. Only that I wake up feeling like I'm about to be hurt. (Rowland, 1985, p. 146)

For many rape victims, intimate relationships suffer and deteriorate as they withdraw from the outside world. Others may wholeheartedly rely on one individual to guide them from hour to hour. One victim has described her dilemma as follows:

Jon and I had known for months that he would have to make a business trip to California in December. Originally, before things had changed, we had all planned to go. I loved California, I wanted to go away with Jon, I didn't want to be left alone, but as the trip approached we had to face the reality . . . I didn't think I could leave the little security I found in my house, for strange motels. Camping was out of the question. We gave up the idea and I tried not to think about how I would survive a week without Jon. (Barr, 1979, p. 83)

Sexual Problems. Frequent among the long-term reactions to rape are changes in the enjoyment of sexual behavior. Feldman-Summers, Gordon, and Meagher (1979) evaluated the impact of being raped on a victim's sexual satisfaction, and supported an expectation that rape has a strong negative impact on the victim's sexual life. Differences between rape victims and other women who were not victims were not in regard to *frequency* of sexual activities but rather in the subjective quality of such experiences. Rape victims reported that they did not enjoy sex with their partner as much as they had before they were raped, and their level of satisfaction was not as high as that of the control group for almost every type of intimate relationship. The only exceptions were, first, those activities considered primarily as affectional (such as holding hands and hugging) and, second, masturbation. Frequency and satisfaction for both these activities were unaffected by the rape. Of importance is the fact that victims report less desire to engage in sexual activity (Becker, Skinner, Abel, Axelrod, & Treacy, 1984). Judith Rowland (1985), a prosecuting attorney questioning a victim, reports the following exchange:

"Jill, . . . how is your relationship with Alan now, and since the assault?"

"We broke up about four months later."

I learned that she had slept with no one but Alan for over a year before the rape, but had not been able to have satisfactory intercourse with him, or anyone else, since. She never attempted it again in her own apartment, and at his place she had cried the two or three times they had gotten close to making love; so they stopped trying, and their relationship had deteriorated through the summer.

"Alan was kind to me, but I couldn't let him back in, emotionally or physically." (p. 259)

Another rape victim explains her reaction to subsequent sex with her husband: "Evenings with Jon were spent watching TV or going to bed early, but our frenzied sex life had abated. With all its intensity, it did not reassure me that I was still desirable. It reassured me that Jon cared and loved me in spite of it" (Barr, 1979, p. 75).

Changes in Life-Style. Although some victims may make only small changes in their everyday activities, others may make drastic ones. Some rape victims, for example, may restructure their activities, change their jobs, or even change their appearance (Warshaw, 1988). Some may move to another home or even to a completely different city. Other victims may find themselves frequently engaged in compulsive behaviors, such as taking long showers two or three times a day, or intermittently checking doors and windows to make sure they are locked.

Victims often complain that their problems are exacerbated by a lack of understanding or compassion for them by their family and friends. Such reactions create a self-perpetuating escalation of deteriorating relationships. McCahill, Meyer, and Fischman (1979) describe one example:

After the rape, the victim's previously excellent sex life deteriorated, as did the rest of her marriage. Her husband accused her of being too emotional about the rape and insisted that she not think or talk about it. He was also annoyed that she had told so many friends and neighbors about the incident, feeling embarrassed that others knew about it. . . . Their marital relations, which had been strong and healthy before the rape, continued to decline. (p. 33)

Even though it is usually unintentional, friends and family may adhere to the rape myths described earlier in this book; many conclude that the victim was in some way responsible for the assault and that the rape could somehow have been avoided. (Chapter 11 discusses how friends and family members can help the victim cope more effectively.)

The pattern of recovery during the long-term phase is not necessarily a continuously improving one. Yes, at times during this phase some victims will appear as if things are back to normal and they are able to deal with the experience. At other times, denial or shock may reappear as if these same victims had regressed back to the earlier, impact phase. Such shifts are quite characteristic of the recovery process, and collectively they have been called the "waxing and waning of tension" (Caplan, 1964).

Exactly how long, then, does it take for a rape victim to recover? Interviews and assessments by Kilpatrick et al. (1981) suggest that most improvement by rape victims occurs somewhere between 1 and 3 months after the rape, as no significant differences in functioning were reported by victims between 6 months and a year after.

But the above figures do not indicate that recovery is complete so soon. Only 20% to 25% of the victims reported no symptoms one year after the event. Some victims even reported being slightly worse on some measures one year after the assault than they had been at 6 months, suggesting that some regression had taken place. Furthermore, one year after the rape the victims as a group were more anxious, fearful, suspicious, and confused than were nonvictims.

To be sure, individual differences in recovery rate always exist. No two victims will respond in the same manner just as no two people are alike and no two rapes are exactly the same. Scheppele and Bart (1983), for example, found that those women who had been assaulted in places that they originally perceived to be safe suffered from "total fear reaction." Their basic assumptions—those identified by Janoff-Bulman at the beginning of this chapter—were totally shattered.

It appears, however, that if significant recovery is going to occur, it will mostly occur in the first few months. Because Burgess and Holmstrom found that 25% of the rape victims they studied had *not* significantly recovered several *years* after the rape, we can question whether they ever will. Further follow-ups are needed in order to know for sure, but some researchers (cf., Kilpatrick, Veronen, & Best, 1985; Sperling, 1985) would offer a tentative "no" to the question of eventual complete recovery.

Post-Traumatic Stress Disorder

Revised in 1987, the American Psychiatric Association's diagnostic system known as DSM-III-R (for *Diagnostic and Statistical Manual of Mental Disorders-Revised*) (American Psychiatric Association [APA], 1987) recognized the presence of a psychological disorder that is the direct result of a stressful event. This disorder, termed post-traumatic stress disorder (PTSD), is defined as "the development of characteristic symptoms following a psychologically distressing event that is outside the range of usual human experience" (APA, 1987, p. 247). Although PTSD can, by definition, result from any of a number of stressful events including disasters of nature and combat in war, rape also fulfills the first criterion—a stressor of significant magnitude. In fact, DSM-III-R advises that PTSD is "apparently more severe and longer lasting when the stressor is of human design" (APA, 1987, p. 248). Being recognized as a mental disorder by the national organization of psychiatrists increases the likelihood that the lay public and other professional organizations will understand that the traumatic effects reported by victims are real. For example, prosecuting attorneys have brought experts to the courtroom to testify that an alleged rape victim's post-traumatic stress syndrome serves as evidence that she actually was raped (Frazier & Borgida, 1985).

Besides having experienced the recognized "psychological traumatic event," the victim must display several symptoms before being diagnosed as suffering from post-traumatic stress disorder. The first of these is a repeated experiencing of the traumatic event; this may be in the form of intrusive thoughts or emotions, or in recurrent nightmares. Associated with this symptom is an active avoidance of those situations, ideas, and feelings that are related to the rape. The second primary symptom intrinsic to the diagnosis is a "psychic numbing" or a reduced responsiveness to the environment.

Along with these two primary symptoms, the DSM-III-R diagnosis specified that one must be experiencing at least two of the following:

1. difficulty falling or staying asleep
2. irritability or outbursts of anger
3. difficulty concentrating
4. hypervigilance

5. exaggerated startle response

6. physiological reactivity upon exposure to events that symbolize or resemble an aspect of the traumatic event

Note that similarities exist between the post-traumatic stress disorder and rape trauma syndrome. Researchers have documented that PTSD is present in rape victims. Horowitz, Wilner, and Alvarez (1979) developed the Impact of Event Scale (IES) to measure the first primary symptom (either event-related intrusions of thoughts and emotions, plus avoidance of event-related situations) identified with PTSD. Later, Kilpatrick and Veronen (1984) administered this scale to victims whose rapes had occurred earlier (either 6-21 days before, 3 months, 6 months, 1 year, 2 years, or 3 years before). Regardless of the length of time since the rape, most victims reported experiencing significant levels of both symptoms. With regard to the symptoms of a numbed responsiveness and a reduced involvement with the environment, Kilpatrick et al. (1981) discovered in a longitudinal study that fear stemming from having been raped causes victims to restrict their daily activities and life-styles dramatically, as described earlier in this chapter.

With regard to the six other criteria, several researchers have observed that some or all of these symptoms are suffered by victims of rape (Burgess & Holmstrom, 1985; Kilpatrick, Veronen, & Best, 1985). The most frequent symptoms shown by such persons are, in fact, avoidance behaviors, hypersensitivity, difficulties in maintaining concentration, and intensification of symptoms whenever exposed to rape-related cues (Kilpatrick, Veronen, & Best, 1985).

Factors Predicting Psychological Distress Among Rape Victims

It is important to emphasize that not all rape victims suffer to the same degree with regard to rape trauma syndrome. Some show such tremendous distress that their ability to get out of bed in the morning is severely taxed. Other rape victims may seem to hold up fairly well, showing relatively few symptoms. Exactly how a person will respond after being raped may depend on several factors, including demographic characteristics, her own unique personal history, the circumstances of the rape, and the availability of later social support. The impact of each of these is reviewed below.

Demographic Characteristics

The role of demographic characteristics in recovery has been explored by several studies. With respect to marital status, McCahill et al. (1979) found that married victims currently living with their husbands did not seem to adjust as well as other victims. Although black victims do not seem to differ from whites in the recovery process (Morelli, 1981), it may be the nonwhite women who are married who experience the *most* trauma after being raped (Ruch & Chandler, 1983). Unfortunately, it is members of minority groups (blacks, Chicanos, Chinese Americans) who report less likelihood that they would report a rape (Feldman-Summers & Ashworth, 1981). One reason for this is that minorities are alienated from the public agencies of this country and are distrustful of them; moreover, Asian women are reluctant to reveal information about such personal matters.

Age of a rape victim also seems to be a factor that can affect the recovery process. McCahill et al. (1979) found that adult victims were the most likely to suffer from adjustment problems. Adolescents (those victims ages 12-17) fared somewhat better, and children had the least adjustment problems. These authors suggest several possible explanations for these age differences. First, adult victims are more likely to be married, already identified as a potential source of tension and anxiety. Another possible factor is the outside responsibilities (e.g., family and/or a career) that drain time and energy from the necessary task of actively dealing with the situation. Finally, adults are also responsible for *themselves,* who they are and what they do. When this salient part of one's life goes wrong, how do you explain having been raped?

These findings and potential explanations are provocative, but attempts to replicate and verify them have not proven fruitful. Kilpatrick, Veronen, and Best (1985) compared two groups of rape victims 3 months after the rape: those who were relatively less distressed versus those who were quite distressed; no differences emerged on *any* biographical or demographic characteristics, including race, marital status, age, amount of education, religious preference, or living arrangements prior to the rape. One message here is that rape is the ultimately personal act, and each victim is going to respond as a person who possesses a unique combination of qualities. Can such qualities be identified?

Personal History

The rape victim's personal history prior to the rape may play a role in the post-rape adjustment. Those victims who have had previous psychiatric treatment were found to have poorer adjustment to the rape than those who have not had such treatment (Frank, Turner, Stewart, Jacob, & West, 1981). McCahill et al. (1979) reported that those victims who had received such psychiatric treatment prior to being raped possessed—right after the rape—more negative feelings toward men whom they knew. But one year after the rape, no significant differences in these attitudes existed between those who had previously been in treatment and those who had not. Again, however, Kilpatrick and his colleagues failed to replicate these findings in their studies.

Other aspects of a victim's history prior to the rape have also been examined. Prior life events, or those experiences that may disrupt or threaten to disrupt a person's usual life-style or routines and require readjustment, have also been identified as affecting a victim's adjustment. Such life events are not necessarily negative events; they include any stressor that evokes a change in an individual's life. For example, events such as getting married, enrolling at a new school, or breaking up with a significant other all qualify as life events. Previous research has discovered a relationship between such life events and one's ability to cope with future life events. The relationship is an inverse one, in that the more life events the person reports, the more vulnerable that person is to both mental and physical illness (c.f. Brown, 1974; Dohrenwend, 1973; Markush & Favero, 1974; Paykel, 1974).

Ruch, Chandler, and Harter (1980) investigated the impact of other life changes on rape trauma, 2 weeks after the rape, and found a curvilinear relationship between the two. That is, those women who had experienced moderate levels of life changes prior to the rape were the least traumatized. Those who had experienced many other major life changes suffered the greatest amount of rape trauma, and those who reported *no* other life changes were between these two groups on the amount of trauma suffered. Wirtz and Harrell (1986) found that those victims who had experienced such life events reported higher levels of fear than victims who had not; their measures were taken as much as 6 months after the rape. It should be noted that these measures were objective; that is, victims responded by indicating which experiences had or had not happened to them in a one-year period. Subjective measures—how stressful the victims perceived these events to be—might be even better predictors of subsequent trauma.

Characteristics of the Rape

Just as Chapter 2 indicated that there are several types of rapists, so too are there many types of rapes. Some may be similar, but no two will ever be exactly alike. Some may be particularly violent and brutal; others may involve little or no violence. Some may last a few minutes, others hours or even days with repeated assaults. The number of assailants may vary from one to several. Some victims may know their assailants; others will be complete strangers. Some victims will be forced to comply by the threat of a knife or gun in their face, while others are overcome by the physical force of the rapist. Still others will be coerced by sheer words alone. Some rapes may occur in the victim's home, in the presence of children, while others may occur in isolated rural areas. Although vaginal inter-course usually comes to mind when one is talking about rape, other forms of sexual assault can be just as traumatic or even more so; for example, oral-genital sex, anal sex, or even forced fondling. The different possibilities are seemingly infinite. How do such differ-ences affect the adjustment process of the victim?

McCahill et al. (1979) sought to answer this specific question. In their study, they expected a positive relationship between the amount of violence and the difficulty in readjusting, with those who received the most physical and sexual aggression hypothesized to have the most problems dealing with the trauma. Instead, they found a curvilinear relationship between these variables—one, in retrospect, that was easy to explain.

The prediction was supported that those who suffered highly violent rapes would have the greatest difficulty adjusting. Each of these victims faced tremendous danger, with the threat of death. As a consequence, they reported more modifications of their life-style than did other rape victims. For example, victims of the most brutal rapes severely reduced their risk-taking behaviors; they often re-frained from walking alone or even going out. These behaviors may cause the perceptions of vulnerability to become even more salient. Victims of these exceedingly aggressive rapes also reported more nightmares. As McCahill et al. explain, "The more brutal that a rape incident is, the less likely that a victim will be able to consciously deal with it" (1979, p. 64).

What went counter to the investigator's original prediction was the reaction of victims of the least violent rapes; these victims reported just as much difficulty as those in the violent incidents. McCahill et al. suggest that these victims may be more prone to blaming themselves, and hence experiencing higher levels of guilt. They also may be blamed more by their partners than are victims of brutal rapes; they may be accused by their partner of not adequately resisting or of crying rape to cover up an affair. Consequently, they may begin to question themselves and wonder if there was not more that they could have done to avoid the situation. McCahill et al. see it as a no-win situation; "Either she suffers the trauma of a brutal rape or she is accused of complicity if she does not" (1979, p. 65).

The relationship between the type of rape (including such aspects as its duration and the kinds of sexual acts demanded) and the difficulty in readjustment was also a curvilinear one. McCahill et al. (1979) investigated eight different types of sexually aggressive behavior. The researchers view these different acts as falling on a continuum, with fondling and caressing (usually forced by an acquaintance) considered to be at one end of this dimension, and a completed act of vaginal-penile intercourse at the opposite end. Of course, any combination of activities is possible in any one sexual assault. Furthermore, one's own perception of where each sexual act should lie on this continuum may be different from the opinion of the researchers. Nevertheless, it was discovered that those at the two extremes (i.e., victims of a completed act of vaginal-penile intercourse plus those involved in fondling and caressing only) were the victims who experienced the greatest adjustment difficulties.

McCahill et al. suggest that the victim of the former type may view herself as being contaminated or no longer clean. In contrast, the case of sexual assault that involved only fondling and caressing may cause severe consequences because of its own ambiguity. Such ambiguity may make it difficult for the victim to "mentally segregate the rape from her everyday life" (1979, p. 67).

Recall that those who were victims of only unwanted fondling and caressing were usually acquainted with the assailant. Jenkins and Dambrot (1987) also suggest that date or acquaintance rape may be the catalyst for more feelings of guilt and self-blame and thus decrease the victim's overall trust in others. B. Katz (1991) concludes that women raped by nonstrangers experience longer periods of recovery, and uses the concepts of trust and closeness to explain the difference. After all, if you can't trust those whom you know and socialize with, whom can you trust?

But other studies' results are not consistent with the above. Frank, Turner, and Stewart (1980) report no differences in the responses of individuals one month after the rape as a function of different types of rapes, as did Ruch and Chandler (1983) and Kilpatrick, Veronen, and Best (1985). While the inconsistency of these findings reaffirms the point that each rape is a complex and perhaps idiosyncratic event, a recent systematic study, described in Box 8.2, adds perspective.

Availability of Social Support

Characteristically, women receive little social support after being raped, even in the most severe types including use of weapons, beatings, and life threats (Cohen & Roth, 1987; Wyatt, Notgrass, & Newcomb, 1990).

Wyatt et al. describe one brutal rape after which the victim confides in her best friend. The woman friend's reaction was: "See what men are like? That is all they want—you should get something out of it—money" (1990, p. 169). Cynical responses by potential caregivers are especially disturbing, given that victims view social support and talking about the rape as most helpful (Frazier, 1989).

Self-Blame

Until recently, it was a popular belief that any type of self-blame by a victim was maladaptive and related to psychological problems (Becker, Skinner, Abel, Howell, & Bruce, 1982; Notman & Nadelson, 1976; Rose, 1986). Janoff-Bulman (1979) suggests, however, that this is not always the case. She differentiates between two types of self-blame, behavioral and characerological, and believes that each unique type generates different psychological consequences. The primary difference between these two deals directly with one's level of perceived control.

Characterological self-blame reflects attributions about stable aspects of oneself, such as "I am too trusting" or "I am a bad person." It implies no real sense of control; in fact, an inevitability and a feeling that the attack was deserved (Meyer & Taylor, 1986). In contrast, behavioral self-blame occurs when a victim assigns the responsibility for her rape to her own modifiable behaviors, that, for example, she was hitchhiking or that she had failed to lock the front door. The use of behavioral self-blame would, according to the theory, make the future more controllable and less menacing. Based on reactions of crisis center counselors, Janoff-Bulman estimated that 74% of all rape victims who seek counseling blame themselves, with 69% saying their behavior was the cause of the rape, whereas only 19% fault aspects of their character. She hypothesized that behavioral self-blame should be related to more effective adjustment after the rape than would characterological self-blame, as long as the blame was directed at specific, controllable behaviors. She went on to suggest that internal, unstable, and specific attributions may be the most adaptive for rape victims (Janoff-Bulman & Lang-Gunn, 1988).

As Frazier (in press) notes, this is a provocative hypothesis, because generally, internal attributions for negative events are associated with heightened depression. Furthermore, the idea that some type of self-blame can be an adaptive response is inconsistent with current approaches to counseling victims of rape that focus on providing a nonjudgmental atmosphere that discourages victims blaming themselves. The conceptual distinction between blame, causality, and responsibility should also be noted here. Given Janoff-Bulman's operationalizations, we believe that *blame* may not be what subjects in Janoff-Bulman's study were reporting. Rather, most seemed to be believing that they played some causal role in the outcome, or were assuming some of the responsibility for it. Although the term *blame* is used in this discussion for purposes of consistency with the authors' terminology, it seems more appropriate for future literature to adopt less "loaded" labels for this phenomenon.

The hypothesis that some types of self-blame may be beneficial to the coping process of rape victims needs empirical study beyond Janoff-Bulman's survey of rape crisis center counselors. Meyer and Taylor (1986) were apparently the first to do so, other than Janoff-Bulman's own work. The correlations they obtained between rape victims' attributions and the symptoms they manifested indicated that both the behavioral self-blame *and* the characterological self-blame were associated with poorer adjustment after the rape. They also noted that victims don't always seem to view

BOX 8.2

**Victim's Reactions to Rape by a Stranger
Versus Rape by an Acquaintance**

Is a victim' recovery affected by the relationship with the rapist? Based on Stewart's (1982) model of adaptation to life
changes, we may expect that recovery from a traumatic event
involves several phases. First, as the chapter indicates, the victim experiences helplessness and dependence. Then emerge
attempts to control the situation. "Mastering or understanding
the event forms the basis for integrating the event and its
effects into the fabric of one's personality and life experience"
(B. Katz, 1991, p. 253). The required self-evaluation at this
phase is the domain in which, according to B. Katz (1991),
recovery from the two types of rape probably differs the most.
Rape by someone you know is an even more personal attack
than rape by a stranger. It usually is done in a situation previously associated with safety and privacy. Having been raped
by someone she knows causes a woman to question her own
judgment; her internal security checks had failed (Gidycz &
Koss, 1991).

    A woman raped by an unknown assailant may suffer more
brutal physical violence, but in B. Katz's (1991) view, "it is

character traits as unchangeable, so perhaps victims don't make
the distinctions between behavior and character that the theory
emphasizes.

The key distinction involved in this issue may be the difference
between one's perceived ability to control *future* occurrences as
opposed to past occurrences. Janoff-Bulman (1979) proposed that
behavioral self-blame is adaptive only in the absence of characterological self-blame; it is essential that a belief that future rapes
can be avoided is dominant. Using a sample of 67 female victims
who reported to the emergency room of a county medical center,
Frazier (in press) administered a questionnaire about attributions

BOX 8.2 (Continued)

probably easier for her to see her own victimization as a more random and less personal event" (p. 254).

But these are speculations. Katz (1987) collected information from 87 rape victims, women who were over age 17 at the time of the rape and who had been raped at least 6 months prior to the interview. A little more than half of the rapists (55%) were total strangers. Katz found that women raped by strangers blamed themselves less for the rape, saw themselves in a more positive light, and felt closer to recovery than did the victims of an attack by an acquaintance. Components of trust and close-ness played a role in self-evaluation of the impact of the rape and in the woman's recovery. However, women raped by an ac-quaintance showed greater recovery *over a long period of time* than did those raped by a stranger. B. Katz (1991) notes:

> The devastating personal nature of rape by a non-stranger may lead to more initial distress (here, as reflected in relatively less positive self-concept), but the process of self-evaluation that follows also could allow for a conscious reorganization that includes elements of psychological growth. Although this potential for rebuilding seems likely for both types of rape, the results of this study show evidence of it only in the group of women raped by nonstrangers. (p. 265)

3 days after the assault. Adjustment was measured by the Beck Depression Inventory (Beck, Ward, Mendelsohn, Mock, & Erbaugh, 1961). First, Frazier found that most of these victims did not blame their behavior, their character, or themselves in general—that they rated the causes of their rape as generally external. Second, her subjects did not make the distinctions between blaming their behavior and blaming their character that Janoff-Bulman's theory implied. Only 7% of the victims engaged in behavioral self-blame without blaming characterological factors as well.

Finally, Frazier (in press) found confirmation of Meyer and Taylor's (1986) results in that victims who expressed charac-terological *and* behavioral self-blame had greater degrees of depression. What was related to a relative absence of depression was a belief that one could control one's *future*, not one's past.

Summary

It is apparent that rape victims face a tough and often long road to recovery. Their basic guiding assumptions that they are generally invulnerable to negative events, that the world is meaningful, and that their personhood is positive have been shattered and must somehow be rebuilt to accommodate their rape experience. All victims will to some extent experience rape trauma syndrome, which includes a variety of symptoms ranging from depression and anger to anxiety and phobias. Although most improvement for rape victims occurs within 3 months of the rape, complete recovery over the event can take longer—up to several years. Factors that may affect recovery include the age of the victim, her personal history, characteristics of the rape, social support networks, and intrapersonal attributions concerning the cause of the rape.

9 The Rape Victim at Trial

Of the thousands of rapes that occur annually, few lead to jury trials. Some rapes are not even labeled as such by their survivors; when they are, they are often not reported to the police. If the sexual assault is by a stranger, the police may never locate a viable suspect. Even when perpetrators are captured and charged, many plea-bargain an admission of guilt to a lesser crime.

The *Victim* on Trial?

But even when the case goes to trial, specific aspects of the litigation procedure reinforce our label of rape as a misunderstood crime. It is not an exaggeration to say that the alleged victim may become suspect in the eyes of many, including possibly the jurors and even the judge. The purpose of this chapter is to identify the idiosyncratic problems in achieving valid outcomes when the purpose of the trial is to determine if a rape occurred or if the defendant is the rapist.

Part of the problem is produced by the treatment of victims—regardless of the type of crime—by the criminal justice system. A victim is often cast adrift as the forgotten "third party" in a criminal investigation or trial. Crimes become interpreted as hostile acts against the state, representing *all* people (Karmen, 1984). Ellison and Buckhout (1981) have even characterized the victim as having the status of a bit player, or being treated like a piece of evidence. For example, a victim, by law, must report a crime, but so doing will likely cost the victim time, money, and other, unexpected resources. The victim's name and address may become a matter of public record; belongings may be confiscated and kept interminably. Even worse, victims have no veto power over their own counsel, as some defendants do. The turnover is often so great in the prosecuting attorney's office that victims may justifiably lose confidence in the quality of the advocacy on their behalf. Survivors and victims' families are often not unreasonably outraged when the state agrees to a plea-bargain for a conviction to a lesser crime, such as attempted assault rather than aggravated rape. These reasons, generated by Ellison and Buckhout (1981), legitimize the label of the victim as the "forgotten third party."

But the challenges to victims of rape go beyond this unenviable litany. The truthfulness of a person who reports being sexually assaulted is more likely to be questioned, doubted, and challenged than are the statements of victims of other crimes. Recounting in public one's victimization is exceedingly stressful, but the reactions by police, attorneys, judges—including skepticism, cynicism, and in some cases, harassment—only compounds the agony. Astute observers suggest that this second victimization—by representatives of the criminal justice system and officers of the court—is just as bad as, if not worse than, the original rape (Brownmiller, 1975; Gager & Schurr, 1976; Medea & Thompson, 1974). In fact, one study found that the primary reason given by rape victims for not pressing charges against their assailant was the desire to avoid the ordeal of courtroom testimony (Holmstrom & Burgess, 1978).

Consider the chronological sequence of events after the report of a rape. The victim must tell every detail of the assault to the police time and time again. The prosecuting attorney will then want to inquire into all the intimate details of the victim's recent life, including her relationships with men, and with the rapist, if she knew him. Her personal habits will be scrutinized. Thus, at the trial, her fear of testifying is not based on imagination alone; she must again tell her story, fully aware that the job of the defense attorney is to find flaws in her testimony or otherwise impugn her personal credibility. Further adding to her frustration, important physical evidence sometimes gets lost, fermenting (further) doubt in the minds of the jurors and placing greater emphasis on assessing her credibility.

In summary, when a person claims to have been raped, the criminal justice system has always established barriers to proving the charge; these barriers exceed those for victims of other major crimes. Consider for example a legal concept unique to sexual assault crimes: nonconsent. Chapter 10 describes the history of the legal system's definitions of *nonconsent* in the crime of rape, including the central need to demonstrate that the alleged victim resisted. In addition, traditionally, corroboration of the alleged victim's account of events has been required.

In contrast, just imagine what it would be like if a victim of a holdup were interrogated in the same way as a person who reports having been sexually assaulted:

Did you struggle with the robber? Why not?

You said you didn't struggle because he had a knife. Can you show us any signs that he had a knife? I don't see any wounds.

Did you scream? Why not?

Have you ever been robbed before? If so, why didn't you take precautions to avoid it happening again?

Can you *prove* that you had $125 in your wallet? Do you always carry this much money with you?

A victim of a knifing or a mugging may or may not have a history of victimization; the police and the courts are not that curious. But the courts have long established that the prior sexual history of the complainant of rape was relevant evidence to be admitted at trial. In one appellate decision, the court's moralistic evaluation was made clear: "Who is more likely to consent to the approaches of a man, the unsullied virgin and the revered, loved, and virtuous mother of a family, or the lewd and loose prostitute, whose arms are open to the embraces of every coarse brute who has enough money to pay for the privilege" (*Camp v. State*, 1847, p. 419). A century later, the intrusion of sexist assumptions remained. A 1942 decision stated:

If consent be a defense to the charge [of rape] then certainly any
evidence which reasonably tends to show consent is relevant and
material, and common experience teaches us that the woman who
had once departed from the paths of virtue is far more apt to consent
to another lapse than is one who had never stepped aside from that
path. (*State v. Wood,* 1942, p. 49)

But prior sexual behavior is just one of the problems. It is not an
exaggeration to say that in the minds of each of the legal system's
operatives—the prosecuting attorney, the defense attorney, the
judge, and the jury—the victim is *on* trial. Thus in this chapter we
sequentially take the perspective of each central participant. We
ask: How does each treat the victim when the victim testifies? What
psychological concepts are useful in understanding the behavior of
each?

The Prosecuting Attorney

The goal of a prosecuting attorney is to obtain convictions,
preferably prior to a trial, but at the very least as a result of a trial.
The rate of convictions may become a political issue if the chief
prosecuting attorney's (or district attorney's) position is an elected
one. Metropolitan jurisdictions will, of course, have a staff of
assistant prosecuting attorneys, and in some jurisdictions a specific
assistant will be responsible for prosecuting all rapes and sexual
abuse charges. For example, in the Manhattan (New York) District
Attorney's office one deputy district attorney heads the sex crimes
unit, overseeing the disposition of as many as 700 cases a year
involving rape and sexual abuse (Bouton, 1990). The unit includes
14 full-time assistant district attorneys.

Just as defense attorneys may become inappropriately zealous in
representing their clients, so too may some prosecutors—full of
justified moral outrage—become too aggressive and use inflamma-
tory rhetoric or otherwise test the limits of acceptable courtroom
advocacy.

Defendants who are convicted may appeal the decision on the
grounds of prosecutorial misconduct. For example, one defendant,
convicted of raping three women, successfully appealed, claiming
prosecutorial misconduct based partly on the following exchange
between a California deputy district attorney and the defendant:

Q. Would it be fair to assume that somewhere in your trousers, there is a penis?

A. You could assume that.

Q. So somehow that penis came out of those trousers; is that right?

A. That's right.

Q. Now, why don't you tell us how they got out, or how it got out. I presume there's only one. How did it get out? That little bugger just pop out?

The Court: Mr. Nudelman, Mr. Nudelman. (Slind-Flor, 1990, p. 8)

The California appeals court concluded that the deputy district attorney's "prejudicial tactics" led to a "miscarriage of justice" and therefore overturned the conviction.

The Rape Trauma Syndrome in Court

One resource that recently has become available to prosecutors is the introduction of an expert witness who testifies about rape trauma syndrome. The term covers a constellation of symptoms commonly found in rape victims; these include sleeplessness, startle reactions, self-blame, headaches, and other characteristics that resemble those found in victims of other post-traumatic stress disorders. The term *rape trauma syndrome* was originally coined by Burgess and Holmstrom (1974a), whose article provides more description of the phenomenon (see also Chapter 8). In general, the symptoms characterizing a post-traumatic stress disorder include the following:

1. the existence of a recognizable stressor,
2. recollecting the event many times, hence reexperiencing it,
3. a reduced involvement in the world, or a numbing of responsiveness, and
4. at least two symptoms mentioned . . . were not present before the trauma. (Frazier & Borgida, 1985)

Evidence that the witness-victim is experiencing rape trauma syndrome is especially important in trials in which consent is at issue. When the defendant and the alleged victim both agree that sexual intercourse took place but differ regarding the alleged victim's willingness, no corroborating evidence for the complainant's charges may be present (Frazier & Borgida, 1985). Thus the presence of a psychologist testifying as an expert witness is crucial.

The courts have had to decide several issues regarding the rape trauma syndrome. First, is it a viable phenomenon? Courts around the country have differed with respect to the admissibility of testimony to that effect, and the resulting controversy has generated legal debates (Lawrence, 1984; Ross, 1983). See Box 9.1 for one example of a state court decision.

In a very useful article, Patricia Frazier and Eugene Borgida (1985) examine the evidence for the rape trauma syndrome in light of three criteria normally used to determine the admissibility of expert testimony: its scientific status, its helpfulness to the jury, and its prejudicial impact (see Box 9.1). Psychological theory and research justifies the admissibility of such testimony, but the courts have often disagreed.

Expert Witnesses: Do They Help?

A second question the courts must decide was implied above: Are jurors already sufficiently informed about the subject of rape and the reactions of rape victims? If so, judges would be reluctant to let expert witnesses testify.

To assess the helpfulness of such testimony, Frazier and Borgida (1988), in a second study, administered a sexual assault questionnaire to experts on rape and post-traumatic stress disorder and then compared their responses with those of laypersons. Results indicated that the nonexperts were *not* well informed on many rape-related issues and were significantly less knowledgeable than the experts. Frazier and Borgida's (1988) study thus provides strong support for innovations that would provide such testimony to the jury.

The Defense Attorney

Keep in mind that a defense attorney may win a case by establishing a reasonable doubt in the minds of the jurors. Practically speaking, such reasonable doubt needs only to be present in the mind of *one* juror, as a unanimous verdict is usually required in order to convict a person of rape. Establishing doubt in the minds

BOX 9.1

The *State of Minnesota v. Saldana* Case

The *Saldana* case reflects one viewpoint on the admissibility of testimony about the rape trauma syndrome. The defendant in the *Saldana* case, charged with first-degree "criminal sexual conduct," claimed that the complainant had consented to the sexual intercourse. To rebut this claim, the prosecuting attorney called a rape victim counselor as an expert witness. Not only did the expert describe what the usual behavior of rape victims was, but she also testified that she definitely believed that the complainant had been raped and that she did not believe that the rape had been fantasized.

After the defendant was convicted, he appealed, and the Minnesota state appellate court considered each of the three previously mentioned criteria:

Scientific Status: The court held that the evidence was not established to a sufficient degree in the medical or psychiatric community for it to be admitted.

Helpfulness to the Jury: The Court ruled that even if such evidence were reliable, it would not be helpful to the jury because it is not the kind of evidence that "accurately and reliably determines whether a rape occurred" (*State v. Saldana*, 1982, p. 229). Furthermore, the Court held that "evidence concerning how some, or even most, people react to rape is not helpful to the jury; rather, the jury must decide each case on the basis of the facts at hand" (Frazier & Borgida, 1985, p. 986).

Prejudicial Effects: The statement that the expert believed the complainant had been raped was seen as prejudicial in that it involved making a legal conclusion. "Credibility judgments, such as testimony that the rape was not fantasized, are regarded as within the province of the jury and are allowed only in unusual circumstances (for example, in the case of a mentally retarded witness)" (Frazier & Borgida, 1985, p. 986).

The *Saldana* case was retried and the defendant acquitted.

of jurors is not that difficult—especially in rape cases. What defense
attorney who has agreed to defend his or her client "zealously"
would not use every legal means available to ensure a verdict of not
guilty? If courts allow—or even consider relevant—evidence about an
alleged victim's past sexual life, how many attorneys would disregard this chance to free their client?

Rape Shield Laws

When a complainant takes the witness stand and is cross-
examined about her past sexual acts, it can be justifiably said that
she is being punished for *her* sexual behavior rather than the
defendant for *his* (Bohmer, 1991). Furthermore, we are aware of no
evidence that those women who have been sexually active are more
likely to be liars.

Given the great potential for abuse of the victim as she testifies
on the witness stand about her rape, the past two decades have been
deluged with demands for changes in the limits of inquiry, by both
feminists and legal reformers (Borgida, 1981). Despite vigorous
opposition from those fearing that elimination of such evidence
from the alleged victim would violate the due process clause of the
Fourteenth Amendment, as well as the confrontation and compul-
sory process clauses of the Sixth Amendment (Largen, 1988),
changes were made (at least temporarily) by most of the states of
the United States, as well as the federal government. However, some
states (e.g., Hawaii, Iowa, North Carolina, and recently, Florida)
have rescinded their rape shield laws (Berger, Searles, & Neuman,
1988).

The innovative changes made, which disallow testimony about
the victim's prior sexual history except in certain circumstances,
are known as rape shield laws. They, in effect, shield the rape victim
from verbal abuse and harassment while she testifies. Although
these laws differ from jurisdiction to jurisdiction (Borgida, 1981),
the common exceptions to this rule involve cases in which the
victim's past sexual conduct can be shown to be relevant to specific
issues at conflict in the case. For example, New York, as of mid-
1991, prevents introduction of a victim's sexual conduct even in
non-rape cases involving, for example, slashings or attempted homi-
cides (Sack, 1991). But Michigan permits the admissibility of evidence that the defendant and the alleged victim had a previous
sexual relationship if the defendant's attorney notifies the prosecu-

tion within 10 days that he or she intends to introduce such evidence (Greenhouse, 1990).

Exceptions

The exceptions typical to these laws include cases that:

1. Raise the issues of consent by showing prior sexual conduct between the victim and the defendant.
2. Show that the defendant was not the source of semen nor the contributor to pregnancy nor the cause of venereal disease.
3. Attack the victim's credibility by contradicting her earlier testimony on her past sexual conduct.

Whether or not such information about the woman's sexual history can or cannot be admitted into evidence ultimately will be decided by the trial judge and the laws of that state (see Box 9.2 for further jurisdictional variations).

Given discrepancies in the law between jurisdictions, as well as the fact that the judge is given great discretion in his or her admission of evidence, some rape shield laws may be more effective than others, depending on how radical (or moderate) the reforms are, as well as who the judge is. Despite these constraints, rape shield laws offer a buffer between the victim and the potential abuse not present before rape-legislation reform took place.

The Judge

Most rape trials are decided by a jury. In any criminal trial, however, a defendant may request that the verdict be determined by the judge (i.e., a bench trial). The question arises, does this make any difference?

A Judge Versus a Jury

The most extensive comparison of verdicts by juries or a judge was carried out by Kalven and Zeisel (1966), who asked each district court judge and federal judge in the United States to provide information about recent jury trials he or she had administered. Although only a minority responded (about 500 out of 3,500), some

BOX 9.2

Rape Shield Laws:
How Much Do They Shield?

Advocates of the reform of rape laws have found that their legislative victories are lost by the decisions of trial judges and appellate courts. Consider New Hampshire's rape shield law; it bars the admission of evidence "of prior consensual activity between the victim and any other person other than the defendant" (Freivogel, 1990, p. C-7). But when he was on the New Hampshire Supreme Court, before he became a U.S. Supreme Court justice, David Souter overruled a trial judge's decision to exclude such testimony, ruling that this rape shield law did not bar evidence showing that a complainant had encouraged sexual advances (Freivogel, 1990).

In some states, or according to the discretion of some judges, the rape shield laws do not shield the victim from very much.

Borgida (1980, 1981) has classified these new laws into three categories, based on the extent to which such evidence is excluded. Furthermore, he has determined how adult mock jurors react to different versions of rape trial reenactment that reflect these modifications.

judges provided information about a large number of trials, so that the data base amounted to more than 3,500 actual trials.

The judges were asked, among other questions, whether their verdict would have been the same as that of the jury. In criminal trials, the judges reported that their verdict would have been the same as the jury's 75% of the time. In these trials the jury convicted the defendant 64% of the time and acquitted the defendant 30% of the time. Between 5% and 6% of the juries could not reach a unanimous verdict and hence were "hung." In those same trials, the presiding judge would have convicted the defendant 83% of the time and would have acquitted the defendant 17% of the time. Thus juries were more lenient (64% convictions) than judges (83% convictions).

But this leniency effect was more pronounced for trials dealing with certain types of offenses—mostly minor offenses such as

BOX 9.2 (Continued)

Consider the following:

The complainant testifies that she met the defendant at a
singles bar, danced and drank with him, and accepted his offer
to drive her home. She testifies that at the front door he refused
to leave, forced his way into her apartment, and raped her. The
defendant wants to prove that the complainant had previously
consented to intercourse with casual acquaintances she had
met at singles bars. Is the evidence relevant? (Borgida, 1981,
p. 234)

According to what Borgida calls moderate reform statutes,
this evidence would probably be admitted; the judge would
probably rule that the evidence of the victim's past liaisons is
material to the fact at issue. But under the more restrictive "radical reform" statutes of some states (Borgida, 1981, p. 213), such
evidence would probably be excluded. These states have concluded that such evidence would be quite prejudicial (against
the complainant), and Borgida's (1981) jurors affirmed the expectation. They were reluctant to convict the defendant when
testimony was introduced regarding the victim's past sexual
relationships with other men.

violations of hunting laws or gambling. It is instructive to examine
the degree of discrepancy specifically for rape trials. For 106 cases
of forcible rape, the judge and jury agreed 66% of the time; the jury
was more lenient than the judge, acquitting the defendant in 13%
of the cases in which the judge would have convicted (the jury
acquitted in 44 cases, convicted in 58, and were undecided in 4; the
judge would have acquitted in 31 and convicted in 75).

Kalven and Zeisel (1966) offer several explanations for the reasons that juries tend to be more lenient than judges. They conclude, in keeping with the previous section of this chapter, that
the jury places more emphasis on an "assumption of risk" than the
judge does. The jury "weigh[s] the woman's conduct in the prior
history of the affair. It closely, and often harshly, scrutinizes the
female complainant and is moved to be lenient with the defendant

whenever there are suggestions of contributory behavior on her part" (1966, p. 249).

At times the point is unmistakable simply in the judge's description of the facts of the case; consider this spousal rape charge:

> Complaining witness and defendant were formerly married and had two children. During the past year they had been going together with a view toward reconciliation and remarriage. The defendant had apparently spent much time and many evenings at the complaining witness's home. She denied any prior intercourse during the period since the divorce, but he claimed it continued after the divorce. The jury was of the opinion that if it [the sexual intercourse] was in a course of conduct which she had accepted, she was in no position to complain of her leading him on. (sic) (Kalven & Zeisel, 1966, p. 250)

In other cases, in which the complainant had been at a night club or had been dancing, the jury acquitted the defendant when the judge would not. In some of these trials, the jury found the defendant guilty of a lesser charge; "the jury's stance is not so much that involuntary intercourse under these circumstances is no crime at all, but rather it does not have the gravity of rape" (Kalven & Zeisel, 1966, p. 250).

The jury's leniency toward the defendant extends beyond cases in which force was not used. In one trial, evidence was presented that the woman's jaw had been fractured in two places, but because the parties knew each other and had been drinking together on the evening in question, the jury acquitted the defendant. In what a presiding judge called "a travesty of justice," the jury found the defendants not guilty in a case in which three men had kidnapped a young woman from the street at 1:30 a.m., had taken her to an apartment, and attacked her; the woman was unmarried and had two illegitimate children.

But especially when aggravating circumstances are not present (e.g., violence, several assailants, parties are strangers to each other), the judge was much more likely to convict the defendant than was the jury. Kalven and Zeisel, writing more than 25 years ago, noted that the jury—if not given the option of finding the defendant guilty of a lesser crime, will tend to find him not guilty, because of the assumption-of-risk principle. We return to this point in Chapter 10, in a review of new laws that provide levels of classification of sexual assault crimes.

The Judge as an Influence

The preceding section has concluded that in a rape trial, a judge is more likely to be responsive to a complainant's position than is a jury. Unfortunately, Kalven and Zeisel's comparison of judge and jury verdicts, published more than 25 years ago, has not been repeated, so we do not know if this difference in reaction still holds.

But even if the jury is the decision maker, the judge plays a significant role as an influence on the outcome of the trial. He or she has great discretion in decisions about the admissibility of testimony and the choice of instructions given to the jury. The judge may terminate testimony or unintentionally convey his or her evaluation of certain attorneys or witnesses. Peter David Blanck, a law professor at the University of Iowa, has demonstrated how juries in criminal trials accord even the most subtle behavior of judges (such as eye contact, head nods, and posture) great weight and deference (Blanck, 1991; Blanck, Rosenthal, Hart, & Bernieri, 1990).

Judges are human, like jurors. They, too, may have false assumptions about the nature of rape. For example, a judge in South Carolina gave convicted rapists the choice between castration and imprisonment, a choice that, in Susan Estrich's words, "makes sense only if their crime (in that case, a rape by two men who also burned cigarettes on the victim's body) is understood as a problem solely of excessive, abnormal, sexual desire" (1987, p. 82).

Judges have sentiments and biases leading them to make judgments about the credibility of a defendant, a witness, or an alleged victim. Regardless of whether the decision maker is a judge or a jury, the complainant who has reported a rape and is willing to testify at a trial runs risks of having her credibility and judgment questioned. Prior to further focus on jury decision making, we examine the victim's behavior as a witness in court and its effects on decision making.

The Victim as a Witness at Trial

As indicated above, it is not only the defendant who stands trial when the alleged crime is rape. Behaviors that a victim manifests while a witness in a court of law will either enhance or detract from her credibility, because in a crime of rape much of the evidence is intangible. Usually no witnesses are present other than the victim. No bruises may be found on the woman's body.

The Victim-Witness's Nonverbal
Behavior While on the Stand

The type of nonverbal behavior shown by an alleged rape victim while testifying under oath may provide substantial amounts of information to the decision makers. For example, the type of eye contact used by an alleged victim may help jurors either to confirm or disconfirm her statements. In mock trials (not rape trials), the following were found to influence the jury:

1. a witness avoiding eye contact with a questioning attorney (Hemsley & Doob, 1978)
2. level of confidence shown by an eyewitness (Wells & Murray, 1984)
3. powerful versus powerless style of speech (Erickson, Lind, Johnson, & O'Barr, 1978)

In general, when the relationship between two people reflects negative feelings, a decrease in eye contact occurs (Knapp, 1980). Depressed people, those feeling a sense of shame, or people who wish to hide something may also avoid eye contact. So lack of eye contact is usually interpreted unfavorably by observers.

On the other hand, those who express frequent amounts of eye contact with others are usually seen in a better light than those who avert their gaze. Kleck and Nuessle (1968) report that those who look at another at least 80% of the time are seen as more sincere, friendly, self-confident, natural, and mature. Mehrabian and Williams (1969) found speakers who gazed at others more frequently to be more persuasive, truthful, sincere, and credible.

So far, the implications seem clear-cut. But matters may not be so simple. Knapp (1980) suggests that other motivations may be present for extensive eye-contact that do not reflect sincerity in the looker. He suggests that those who continually gaze may be doing so as the product of anger or in an effort to manipulate the situation. The act of staring certainly is often interpreted as a sign of hostility.

Now consider an alleged rape victim testifying as a witness in a trial. While on the witness stand, giving her testimony, she steadfastly stares at the defendant, the man she claims assaulted her. How does the decision maker—the jury or the judge—interpret such behavior? Is it seen as a sign of truth telling and confidence, or an expression of hostility? Or is it an attempt to manipulate?

Let us say that a second alleged rape victim, while on the witness stand, averts her gaze from the defendant. Is this seen as a sign of lying? Or lack of confidence? Or shame and embarrassment over being a victim of rape?

Weir and Wrightsman (1990) set out to see which of these attributions operates in a case where the witness-victim gazes intensively or where she completely avoids looking at the defendant. A total of 338 college students read portions of a modified trial transcript titled *State v. McNamara*. In this case the defendant, Greg McNamara, is charged with raping Sheryl Palmer in his car after conversing with her in a bar. The fact that sexual intercourse took place was not disputed. The defense claimed that Palmer consented to the act and, in an effort to hide that fact, told her boyfriend that McNamara had raped her. Subjects read only the portion of the trial transcript in which the alleged victim testified. The 12-page transcript excerpt took approximately 15 minutes to read.

Besides a control condition in which no additional material was added to the transcript, 10 different versions of the transcript excerpt were prepared. These transcripts varied by type of eye-contact (avoiding or staring) and whether it was the attorney for the prosecution or for the defense who called attention to her eye contact in the transcript (prosecution or defense). The remaining versions included additional attributions made by the attorney and the response of the witness to his questioning. These versions of subsequent attributions were added for two reasons:

First, to make the manipulation more meaningful and believable for the subjects, and second, to be able to determine if subjects were making their own attributions or relying on those of the questioning attorney. All manipulations were added at the end of the attorney's (direct or cross) examination. Those subjects in the *avoided* condition read the following excerpt as spoken by the attorney:

> Ms. Palmer, I notice that all through your testimony, you've been looking away from the defendant. Even when you were asked to identify him, you barely could look at him. And even then, you did it very quickly, and then you looked away. Is this not true?

In contrast, those subjects in the *staring* condition read:

Ms. Palmer, I notice that all through your testimony you've been
staring intently at the defendant. Instead of looking at me, or looking
at the judge, or at the jury, you've been looking at the defendant the
whole time. Is that not true?

If no attribution was made by the attorney, the alleged victim
would reply, "I didn't realize I was," and there was no more mention
of the eye contact. In the remaining six conditions, she affirmed the
inquiry, offering the rationalization in four of the conditions that
she was behaving this way because he had "hurt her." In the final
two of these six conditions, the defense attorney offered his own
negative attribution of why she was staring or avoiding the defendant. In the *avoiding* condition, he stated:

And isn't it true, Ms. Palmer, that you can't look him in the eye
because you're lying—that no rape took place. That instead you
consented to have sexual intercourse with him and now you're trying
to keep your boyfriend's good opinion of you. Isn't that why you can't
look at the defendant?

But in the *staring* condition, he stated:

And isn't it true, Ms. Palmer, that you are doing that to try to convince
the jury that a rape really took place? That you assume that when the
jury sees you staring so intensively at the defendant, you think they'll
believe your story about a rape taking place?

In both conditions, the alleged rape victim replied:

No. (pause). Er, uh, no, he did rape me. He hurt me; that's why I'm
looking at him.

All questioning was concluded at this point by the attorney.

The eye contact that the alleged rape victim displayed toward the
defendant did, indeed, have an effect on the verdicts of mock jurors.
Specifically, when the victim avoided eye contact with the defendant, female mock jurors rendered more guilty verdicts, thus indicating that for them, the gaze avoidance was an indication that the
woman was, indeed, hurt.

But this effect was not found for male subjects. No amount of
differentiated eye contact seemed to affect the verdicts of male
subjects, a theme to be found in studies reported later in this

chapter. Rosenthal, Hall, DiMatteo, Rogers, and Archer (1979), in their studies of males' and females' sensitivity to nonverbal cues, consistently find that females have the advantage when it comes to receiving and judging nonverbal cues; they are better able both to notice nonverbal cues and to explain or interpret them.

Although, in general, avoiding eye contact is perceived as more sincere by female mock jurors, the prior attitudes of these subjects are very influential in their interpretations. Interestingly, it is the staring condition that produces the most differential effects. When the witness's behavior involves staring, those women who score high on the Rape Empathy Scale tend to find her just as, or slightly more, credible than when she avoids gaze. But women who are low scorers on the Rape Empathy Scale differ dramatically from the above in how they interpret eye contact. If the alleged victim stares at the defendant throughout her testimony, women low in rape empathy tend to find the defendant not guilty. The speculated doubt that low empathizing women have about women who claim they have been raped is clear, but when the alleged victim emits constant staring, that doubt all but disappears. In fact, women who report low empathy for rape victims are harsher in their reactions to such alleged victims than are low-empathizing men.

The Relationship of the Witness-Victim and the Defendant

Prior research and writing has indicated that attributions of responsibility for rape are influenced by the relationship of the alleged rapist and victim. L'Armand and Pepitone (1982) found that previous sexual experience of the victim had a significant effect on ratings of seriousness and blame. The more sexually experienced the female, the less seriously was the damage viewed; and as sexual experience increased, the attribution of blame increased for the victim but decreased for the rapist. Furthermore, an examination of the impact of victim/defendant relationships (strangers, dating, dating with prior consensual intercourse) on attributions of blame found that increased intimacy between the victim and the defendant resulted in decreased ratings of blame for the rapist but increased ratings of blame for the victim.

Wyer et al. (1985) also found a bias in attributions of responsibility for different relationships between victim and defendant. They manipulated whether the relationship was one of strangers (they had seen each other once), acquaintances (they had eaten lunch together several times), or a control condition (no mention made of any relationship) and also whether the woman resisted or not. Results indicated that male subjects' ratings of how responsible the victim was increased with an increased acquaintanceship. In contrast, increased acquaintanceship led females to decrease how much they saw the victim as being responsible for the act. Moreover, acquaintanceship increased the ratings of the victim's responsibility when the victim resisted but decreased ratings when she did not. The latter finding was interpreted in terms of violation of positive norms for appropriate behavior between males and females in a relationship, such that females should not resist men they know. Apparently, resistance is only viewed positively when the assailant is a stranger.

The factors underlying the tendency to assign more responsibility to rape victims who had known the assailant were investigated by Johnson and Jackson (1988). Although the ambiguity of the victim's desire for sexual relations and attraction levels (i.e., dislike, friends, dating) between the victim and rapist were both manipulated, only the presence of ambiguity appeared to be an important factor. Ambiguity led to subjects expressing less likelihood that the defendant was guilty of rape. Johnson and Jackson (1988) concluded that ambiguity about the victim's desire for sexual relations may be more important in making attributions than the relationship between the persons.

Willis and Wrightsman (1990) had 232 college students watch one of 12 videotaped versions of a victim testifying in a rape trial. Four types of relationship were portrayed in various versions of the tape (strangers, co-workers, friends, or dating partners). A statistically significant effect was found for the degree of intimacy; a defendant who had been a friend was seen as less guilty than a defendant who had been co-worker or stranger. Similarly, a victim who had been a friend was seen as less truthful than a victim who had been a co-worker or stranger.

Thus, when the victim has had a close relationship with the defendant, the latter's culpability is discounted by jurors. Kelley's (1972, 1973) attribution model, focusing on multiple causes for behavior, proposes that intimacy may make it more likely that both the defendant and the victim are seen as contributing causes to the final outcome. Hence, discounting occurs for the defendant's culpability. When no intimacy is present, it is less likely that there are additional and plausible causes for the outcome, other than the dispositional attributions that can be made concerning the defendant. The discounting of the intimate defendant can also be explained in terms of the dimensions that outline the use of covariation information (Fiske & Taylor, 1984). When intimacy has been present in the victim-defendant relationship, people may believe that the defendant does not usually rape (high distinctiveness), has not raped the victim in the past (low consistency), and no one else has raped the victim (low consensus). Thus a circumstance attribution is possible, the defendant's culpability is discounted, and the victim is seen as part of the circumstance.

In a rape case in which no intimacy is present, however, there is the possibility of low distinctiveness, high consistency, and low consensus. People may assume that the defendant has probably raped before (low distinctiveness), he probably would have raped the victim given another circumstance (high consistency), and no one else has raped the victim (low consensus). This covariation information would lead to a personal attribution—the defendant is at fault.

The Jury

We have already described some of the jury reactions to the rape victim when she is a witness at the trial. At this point we review this material by systematically examining the jury decision-making process. We divided the latter into three stages: (1) jurors' predispositions and pre-trial biases, (2) jurors' processing of trial information, and (3) jury deliberations.

Jurors' Attitudes Prior to Trial

A person's attitudes toward rape are especially important when that person is confronted, as a juror, with the charge of rape. Jurors' empathy with rape victims has been found by Deitz and her colleagues and other researchers (Deitz et al., 1982; Deitz et al., 1984; Weir & Wrightsman, 1990) to be a reliable predictor of juror verdicts. (But Wiener, Feldman-Wiener, & Grisso, 1989, in a study described in the next section, failed to find a Rape Empathy Scale-verdict relationship.) Mock jurors' ability to empathize with an alleged rape victim (or, conversely, the rapist) in a rape case has been found to be predictive of their attributions of responsibility, social perceptions, and judgments of guilt in a rape case. An ability to empathize with an alleged victim corresponds with the ability to take the psychological perspective of a rape victim. In the next section, we propose that such predispositions affect the processing of evidence.

Jurors' Processing of Information

How does a juror's sympathy with rape victims or suspicions about their truthfulness interact with the actual evidence in the trial? Numerous pieces of evidence, facts, and observations of behavior—such as the previously described eye-contact of the alleged victim—are "out there." How are they put to use?

Deitz and her colleagues (Deitz et al., 1989) found that when victim-empathic mock jurors were asked to focus on the defendant in the case, they still assumed the victim's perspective on the crime and attended to subtle manipulations of the defendant's characteristics in attributing responsibility for the incident. In contrast, defendant-empathic subjects were consistent in their attributions of responsibility for the incident, regardless of the defendant's characteristics. Similarly, when asked to focus their attention on the victim in the case, victim-empathic jurors were consistently positive in their ratings of the victim, whereas defendant-empathic subjects attributed responsibility differentially based on subtle manipulations of the victim's characteristics.

This implies that jurors' predispositions to favor the defendant or the victim lead to their acceptance of different versions or "stories" of what happened. Pennington and Hastie (1986, 1988) have proposed that the formation of such stories early in the trial determines how later evidence is processed. Olsen-Fulero, Fulero, and Wulff (1989) explored the cognitive processing of jurors using Pennington and Hastie's story model. Their procedure was to have college-student subjects view a videotape of a rape trial and then "think out loud" as they each arrived at an early verdict. These oral accounts were then transcribed and coded. Clear differences in structure were found between the stories of jurors who later ruled guilty and those who later ruled not guilty.

Further evidence for the operation of a story model in at least some subjects comes from an innovative study by Wiener et al. (1989), who summarized the testimony in an actual rape trial and then presented arguments for the prosecution and the defense to mock jurors. The latter were asked to answer a series of questions about attributions of responsibility after they received each portion of the testimony summaries, and then at the conclusion of the trial they were asked to state a verdict. Thus the 4-item attribution questionnaire was administered to each subject 25 times.

Previous findings in this program of research (Wiener & Vodanovich, 1986) discovered that when attributing responsibility to the defendant, subjects distinguished between physical causality (whether or not the alleged rapist forced the alleged victim to have sexual intercourse with him) and psychological causality (the extent to which the defendant's thoughts and actions caused him to rape the victim). Wiener and Reinhart (1986) concluded that for most subjects psychological causality included judgments of the accused's intentions to do violence and the extent to which his thoughts were attributable to the victim.

These attributions of responsibility, for some types of jurors, get established early in the trial. Surprisingly, it was not empathy with the victim or the defendant that determined this, as in previous research. Rather, prior acquaintance with a victim of rape was the differentiating factor. Wiener et al. (1989) found the decision processes of those subjects who were acquainted with a rape victim to be different in several ways from those not so acquainted. Those who knew a victim attributed greater responsibility to the defendant; they were more likely to convict him. (Of 26 victim-acquainted subjects, 20 (77%) found the defendant guilty, but only 12 (38%) of the 32 subjects not acquainted with a victim did so.) Given that scores on the Rape Empathy Scale did not predict these verdicts, the authors propose that attitudes based on direct experience (i.e., knowing a victim personally) contribute to the processing of trial evidence more than do attitudes based on cognitive reconstructions.

The second difference is relevant to the viability of a story model. The analysis of the responses to the 25 sets of attribution questions shows that prior acquaintance with a victim leads to a different processing of conflicting evidence. The two types of subjects did not differ in their rating of the attacker's level of responsibility at pretrial or following the first argument in the case for the prosecution. But after that point the ratings by the victim-unacquainted subjects began shifting away from attributing responsibility to the defendant, and continued in that direction for the rest of the trial.

In contrast, the ratings of responsibility given by subjects who knew a rape victim remained rather constant on all the repetitions after the first one.

Carroll and Wiener (1982) hypothesized that people, including jurors, use early information to form initial hypotheses. Jury decision making may rely on schematic processing; jurors use schemata, or thematic frameworks, that guide them in their processing and interpretations of actual testimony presented later in the trial. Once a schema has been activated, it directs additional processing about the topic at hand. For example, those subjects in the Wiener et al. (1989) study who had known a rape victim finished the trial with the same rape script with which they began.

But others did not. Even those who did not, however, made use of an initial script to initiate their story. Note that Pennington and Hastie (1986, 1988) proposed that jurors integrate the testimonies of witnesses by constructing a plausible story that reflects their interpretations of the evidence.

A recent study by Willis (1991) illustrates that even the order of presentation of questions after all the testimony can affect attributions of responsibility and guilt. She had subjects read a trial transcript based on the one used by Wiener et al. (1989). Afterward, subjects completed questionnaires that varied the order of questions about the culpability of the defendant and the victim. Statistically significant interactions were found between the sex of the subject and the ratings of the victim's truthfulness, the seriousness of the victim's suffering, the victim's responsibility, and the defendant's guilt. When judgments concerning the victim were made first, males thought the victim to be less truthful than when judgments about the defendant were made first. However, for females, the victim's truthfulness was greater if the victim judgments were made first than if defendant judgments were.

A similar interaction was found for the seriousness of the victim's suffering. When judgments concerning the victim were made first, males thought the victim's suffering was less serious than when judgments about the defendant were made first. The opposite effect occurred when females did the ratings.

Also, when judging the victim's responsibility, a trend existed for males to perceive the victim to be more responsible for the incident than did the females. The women believed that the defendant had greater responsibility when judgments of the victim were made before they rated the defendant. In contrast, males tended to believe the defendant to bear less responsibility when judgments of the victim were made first.

A similar pattern was found for the defendant's guilt. Males perceived the defendant's guilt to be less when they made judgments of the victim first than when they rated the defendant first. The trend in females was in the opposite direction.

Jury Deliberations

Accounts of the deliberations of the jury from "the inside" are rare—rarer still if the charge is rape. So the account by John C. Brigham (1989), a psychologist who is an expert on legal issues, of his experience as jury foreperson in a rape trial is truly unique.

Brigham was one of six jurors in a classic date rape case in Tallahassee, Florida, in October 1988 (the trial lasted 4 days). An 18-year-old woman testified that she went to a fraternity-house party and talked to a young man she liked a lot. Given a ride home, she went to his apartment. After they kissed once, she went to the bathroom. When she returned, all the lights were out, the man grabbed her, and forced her to have sexual intercourse.

The cross-examination of the young woman lasted for 3 hours, and Brigham described it as "savage." She was in tears quite often, and had to stop her testimony several times. Brigham, as a juror, felt that the defense attorney's strategy was wrong, to go after her "with fang and claws." The strong attack permitted the jury to discount small inconsistencies in her story.

A physician testified to the presence of a small vaginal tear that could have resulted from forced intercourse. The defendant testified that the young woman did not protest much. He said she did get "hysterical about getting pregnant." She was described as allegedly a virgin, who had had few dates.

The charge was a second-degree felony, "sexual battery with force or violence not likely to cause serious harm."

During jury deliberations, the majority of the jurors pushed for an early vote, despite Brigham's wishes, as foreperson, to have the jurors discuss the case first. The first vote was 3-3, with two males and one female voting guilty.

Thus, four issues emerged in the deliberations:

1. *Was this legally rape?* (Clearly intercourse took place.) The young woman had not fought violently against the man. Several of the jurors

did not like the law that stated, in effect, "if she's not hurt, he's not guilty."

2. *The issue of defining "force or violence not likely to cause serious physical harm."* The jury spent a great deal of time and energy discussing what violence or force is.

3. *The responsibility of the jurors.* A later vote was five jurors for guilt and one for acquittal. The holdout said "I don't want to be responsible for sending him to jail."

4. *The defendant's image.* His defense was, basically, that he had a good reputation and would not do the things with which he was charged. His attorney arranged for a counselor to give him a set of personality tests. The counselor testified that on the basis of the test results, "This man is not a rapist." His mother, his high school guidance counselor, and a priest all testified about his character.

But on cross-examination it was brought out that he had been convicted of assaulting a man who was then a companion of the defendant's former girlfriend, causing the other man $500 in medical bills.

The jury discussed the responsibilities of the victim, also. She did go to his apartment at 2 a.m. The holdout juror felt she was dressed like a "slut." They agreed her behavior was stupid and naive but that did not make her deserving of being raped.

Finally, the holdout juror relented, and voted guilty, along with the rest. "I want to get the hell out of here," she said.

Summary

The treatment of the victim of rape by those within the legal system—police officers, attorneys, judges, and juries—is truly unique. Rape is the only crime in which the credibility of the victim is considered relevant to the issue of whether the defendant's behavior constitutes rape. Prosecuting attorneys often use this information to determine if they will prosecute or not. Defense attorneys use this information to attempt to convince the jury that there is reasonable doubt in the case, and that their client should be acquitted. Juries, which are composed of individuals who bring with them their personal attitudes about rape, are often persuaded by the arguments of the defense attorney. The result of this process is too often a second victimization of the victim.

10 Rape and the Law

The Evolution of Rape Laws: A Brief History

Rape is not only an outrageous violation of selfhood; it is a major crime. The definition of *rape* the legal system provides affects whether prosecutors will bring a case to trial and whether a jury will find the defendant guilty. Because the specific legal definition of rape contributes greatly to the outcome of a rape trial, it is worthy of a detailed examination—one of the purposes of this chapter.

But definitions in the legal system are products of the values of the lawmakers who create them. Another purpose of the chapter is to examine the psychological determinants of both the origins and the shifts in the definitions of rape and the laws applying to this crime.

A contributing factor to the estimates that only 2% to 5% of all rapes lead to convictions (Bienen, 1983) may be, ironically enough, the very nature of those laws that outlaw rape. Often they have been ambiguous, allowing judges and juries freedom to interpret these laws in whatever manner they have seen fit. Only part of the problem with this ambiguity is that it has permitted the burden of

---

AUTHORS' NOTE: This chapter relies heavily on Susan Estrich's book, *Real Rape*, Harvard University Press, 1987.

195

proof to be effectively transferred to the victim, as we saw in Chapter 9.

Origins of Rape Laws

As is true of the legal system of the United States generally, the origins of our laws about rape can be traced back to medieval England. English tradition classifies crimes into two categories; first are those crimes (such as parking in a prohibited area) that are not intrinsically wrong but are deemed illegal by a legislative body. These were in the category *malum prohibitum*. The second type, called *malum per se*, consists of those crimes considered inherently evil by society.

In England, behavior that was *malum per se* was considered to be criminal under the common law (i.e., law that is "judge-made") even before any legislative body, through statutes, declare the act illegal. The crime of rape was considered *malum per se* and was, therefore, illegal before the English Parliament passed formal statutes declaring rape a felony.

The earliest law created on the topic of rape was included in the English First Statutes of Westminster, in A.D. 1275 (see *Black's Law Dictionary*, 1968, p. 1766). Although common law considered rape a felony, this statute made the crime of rape only a misdemeanor and declared that no man should "ravish a maiden within age, neither by her own consent, nor without consent, nor a wife or maiden of full age, nor other women against her will" (Inbau & Thompson, 1970, p. 258). Three decades later, in 1309, two significant changes were made in the statutes: first, rape was recategorized as a felonious crime. The second change involved defining rape only when the victim did *not* consent. "If a man should ravish a woman, married, maiden, or other woman, where she did not consent, neither before nor after . . ." (see also Box 10.1). As Borgida (1981, p. 211) notes, consent remains, in most circumstances, a sufficient defense to the charge of rape.

American Beginnings

The earliest statute in the American colonies concerning rape was passed in 1642, in Massachusetts (Inbau & Thompson, 1970). The legal definition declared that rape occurred if any man had "carnal copulation" with "any woman child under ten years of age, forcibly

BOX 10.1

Rape Laws
Protecting Injury to Men?

Although it has become increasingly clear that traditional laws required an in-depth analysis of both an alleged victim's behavior and thoughts before a man could be legally convicted of raping her, the specific sentences for rape were more likely to take the *men* active in the woman's life into account. Rape has long been viewed by some as an injury to men (Estrich, 1987). Indeed, the word *rape* comes form the Latin *rapere*, meaning to steal (Bohmer, 1991) and indeed the traditional sentences for a rape conviction focused on the marital status of the victim, or more explicitly, her status as a piece of property. For example, the first American statute, created in Massachusetts, imposed death for the crime of rape *except* in circumstances where the woman was single. As Goldstein (1976) points out, "If a woman belongs to no man, the damage seems to be not as great as when she is married or claimed by some man" (p. 3). Other sentences during that early time included payment by the rapist to the husband or father of the woman raped (Wyatt & Gold, 1978). Sometimes the female who had been raped was actually forced to marry her rapist!

But the idea that the rape of a female is more harmful to her husband or father than to herself—that women are essentially the property of men—is not, unfortunately, solely an ancient artifact. In 1952, an excerpt from the *Yale Law Journal* read:

> The consent standard in our society does more than protect a significant item of social currency for women; it fosters, and in turn is bolstered by, a masculine pride in the exclusive possession of a sexual object. The consent of a woman to sexual intercourse awards the man a privilege of bodily access, a personal "prize" whose value is enhanced by sole ownership. An additional reason for the man's condemnation of rape may be found in the threat to his status from a decrease in the value of his sex possession which would result from forcible violation. (Note, 1952, p. 72).

and without consent ravished any maid or woman that is lawfully married or contracted, or ravished any maid or single woman with her by force or against her will, that is above the age of ten."

Eventually the statutes came to define rape as "illicit carnal knowledge of a female by force and against her will." If we break this definition down into its individual components, we note that to convict a defendant of rape, five elements had to be proven beyond a reasonable doubt: (1) that the act was illicit, (2) that carnal knowledge (sexual intercourse) took place, (3) that the victim was female, (4) that force was used, and (5) that such force was against her will. Careful thought regarding this definition may lead one to consider this seemingly simple definition to be quite filled with ambiguities. For example, what is meant by "illicit"? What type of sexual activity does "carnal knowledge" include? How does one operationalize "force?" Perhaps most important of all, how does one determine that carnal knowledge was, indeed, "against her will"?

For better or worse, traditional common law in different jurisdictions in the United States eventually came to incorporate each of these issues into their own definitions of rape; for example, common law in the United States and the FBI criminal code define rape as the "carnal knowledge of a female forcibly and against her will." However, because rape is a personal crime that most often occurs in places over which the individual state has jurisdiction, the commission of a rape is governed not so much by federal laws but more often by state laws. (Federal rape laws would apply, however, to acts that occur on federal land, Indian reservations, and in federal prisons.)

These various laws generally offer four possible defenses to a charge of rape (LaFree, 1989). They are: (1) that "it wasn't me," (2) that no sex took place, (3) that the defendant isn't responsible for his behavior, and (4) that sexual intercourse did take place but was consensual (Bohmer, 1991).

Statutes in the 50 states vary, of course, as do attitudes about the appropriate roles for women and the seriousness of the crime. Indeed, statutes are written (or revised) to reflect such societal values (Loh, 1981). We will, later in this chapter, document recent rape-law changes that de-emphasize "resistance"; these have resulted from the increased awareness of implicit coercive behavior in our society in the 1980s. But even while recognizing variance between states with respect to the wording of their statutes, we emphasize that, until recently, laws in most states followed the same script: "A man commits rape when he engages in intercourse with a woman not his wife, by force or threat of force, against her will and without her consent" (Estrich, 1987, p. 8).

Stability and Change in Rape Laws

As we will see, the definition of any given law, as identified by statutes, may remain surprisingly stable. The interpretation of such statutes, or how the laws are applied, however, may reflect continuous changes. Once a crime has been defined by a legislature and has generated a statute, the final interpretation is up to the appellate courts. These courts review cases that have been decided by juries, local judges, or lower courts, in order to determine whether the statutes were appropriately applied to a particular case. Appellate courts are unique in that they are the only participants in the criminal justice system that must provide reasons (via written opinions) for their decisions. Such reasoning by the appellate-court judges serves two important functions. First, all written opinions are incorporated into the *corpus juris,* or body of law, and therefore they effectively become law—they are what is called the common law (see Box 10.2 for an elaboration).

A second important function involves setting the boundaries for the definitions provided by the statutes; they determine the limits of the law. Eventually, the appellate courts have to decide, for example, what "against her will" means. Both of these functions serve to guide any future decisions made by lower courts, as well as those made by other participants in the criminal justice system. Such decisions may help a prosecuting attorney decide whether to prosecute a case or not; they may also affect other future appellate decisions. Ultimately they may affect a rape victim's decision to report her victimization.

The Traditional Treatment of Rape
by the Criminal Justice System

In order for a defendant to be found guilty of the crime of rape, all the elements in the definition must be satisfied. By examining

BOX 10.2

Statutes and Common Law

Although most of us think of law as that which is created by a
legislature, this is only one of several sources of law. Laws that
are created by legislatures are known as *statutes*. The consequences of breaking the statutes become real only after a defendant accused of breaking that law enters the judicial system, or
the courts. If the defendant does not plead guilty, then he or she
is given a trial, either by a judge or a jury. It is either the judge
or the jury that decides whether the facts in the case constitute
breaking the law, as defined by the statute. It may be at this
point that a different source of law may develop. Because every
defendant has the right to appeal a conviction, an appeals court
may decide to hear the case. At this point, the written decision
of the appeals court becomes what is known as *common law*. It
is in this way that law is created by the judicial system, and it is
in this way that the judicial system has its greatest impact on
law. Any appeals court may decide, for example, that part of a
statute is unconstitutional and therefore effectively nullifies that
portion of the law. Or an appeals court may determine the
parameters of an element within the definition. As we will see
in this chapter, appellate decisions have ruled many times on
what constitutes *nonconsent* in a rape case, and have in this
way provided the boundaries for this part of the definition of
rape. As a practical matter, it does not matter whether law is
derived from a statute or from common law. In the final analysis, a defendant's guilt is determined.

the published decisions of appellate courts, however, we find that
certain aspects and issues are given more weight than others. The
fact that these issues—such as nonconsent and resistance or the need
for corroboration—are placed in a *legal* context makes their consequences for an act of rape even more important. In this section we
discuss several of these issues that have received attention by the
appellate courts.

The Nonconsent Requirement

The first issue, the nonconsent requirement, has proven significant for legal judgments in the past and remains an essential part of the definition of rape to this day. A second basic requirement, at least in earlier rape laws, is the need for corroboration. These two requirements—that the rape victim actually prove she adequately resisted her assailant, as well as that she present tangible proof that she was raped—led the courts to consider the psychology of the female. In doing so, the courts increasingly focused on the victim in order to determine if the defendant was guilty. As noted in Chapter 9, only in cases of rape and sexual assault was the burden of proof thus shifted to the victim.

Of the five elements used to determine whether or not a rape has, in fact, occurred, the issue of nonconsent has long been viewed as the definition's key element (Estrich, 1987). Although nonconsent is a required element in the definition of many crimes (e.g., theft, assault, and kidnapping), rape is uniquely different in one very important way. Appellate court decisions have traditionally made it clear that, in the case of rape, for a female to demonstrate that she did not consent, she must accordingly demonstrate that she did actively *resist* the alleged crime (LeGrand, 1973). As Estrich puts it: "The law of rape is striking in the extent to which nonconsent defined as resistance has become the rubric under which all of the issues in a close case are addressed and resolved" (1987, p. 29).

Resistance. Common law initially accepted resistance as an appropriate operationalization of nonconsent for several reasons (Gordon & Riger, 1989). First, resistance was considered the means by which the female behaviorally communicated her nonconsent. Second, resistance provides an apparently objective standard for nonwitnesses (e.g., jurors) to assess whether there was nonconsent. Finally, such a resistance standard was further deemed appropriate because it held the implicit assumption that those persons worthy of protection under the law would defend their virtue by undergoing a significant degree of other physical harm before submitting to sexual attack (Gordon & Riger, 1989). Unfortunately, the logical converse to this rationale includes an assumption that those who do not submit to other types of physical harm and hence are raped are not deserving of being protected by the law.

Interestingly, the requirement of "utmost resistance" was not universally applied in all rape cases. As Estrich (1987) points out, a selective application of the criterion prevailed; for example, when the accused was a stranger, or armed, or otherwise fit the characteristics of what society assumed to be the typical rapist, the victim was usually given the benefit of the doubt by the courts. Furthermore, when the victim was white *and* the defendant was black, credibility was bent on the side of the victim. Or when the victim was brutally beaten, the likelihood was good that she would be found credible. But any deviations from the stereotyped "typical" rape were more likely than not to require active resistance for credibility, and as pointed out earlier, such deviations are plentiful. The "utmost resistance" requirement, ironically enough, was applied in its strictest form to those cases that we now know are most common: the acquaintance rape.

Furthermore, as Bohmer points out, the legal system defined resistance in *male terms,* with the standard being a fight in which one's fists, elbows, or knees were used to fight back. This is "not the behavior of a reasonable *woman* at all," she concludes (Bohmer, 1991, p. 323, italics in original).

The Elusiveness of Nonconsent. A common understanding of what nonconsent specifically means has not been achieved. Exactly how much resistance is required in order for nonconsent to be present? In a 1973 Wisconsin decision, it became evident that the nonconsent requirement was strict (*Brown v. State,* 1973). In this case, the 16-year-old victim testified that:

> I tried as hard as I could to get away. I was trying all the time to get away just as hard as I could. I was trying to get up; I pulled at the grass; I screamed as hard as I could, and he told me to shut up, and I didn't, and then he held his hand on my mouth until I almost strangled. (Estrich, 1987, p. 30)

Upon hearing all the facts and testimony, a jury agreed that the victim had met the criterion of nonconsent and declared the defendant guilty of rape. On appeal, however, the Supreme Court of Wisconsin overturned the conviction of Brown, despite the fact that the appellate judges, in their reviews of convictions, are supposed to evaluate the evidence in a way most favorable to the prosecution (Estrich, 1987).

Interestingly, the Wisconsin Supreme Court decision was not based on any redeeming characteristics of the defendant. Indeed, it found that the defendant showed both criminal intent and sufficient force. Instead, the court based its reversal on the behavior of the *victim*, concluding that despite her struggling to get away, pulling at the grass, and screaming incessantly, she had not adequately demonstrated her nonconsent. Summarizing the court's requirement of resistance, the majority opinion stated that: "Not only must there be entire absence of mental consent or assent, but there must be the most vehement exercise of every physical means or faculty within the woman's power to resist the penetration of her person, and this must be shown to persist until the offense is communicated" (Estrich, 1987, p. 30). In this incredible decision, rendered only 20 years ago by the supreme court of one of our most liberal states, comments were made about the "inconsistency" between the absence of torn clothes or bruises and the "terrific resistance which the determined woman should make" (Estrich, 1987, p. 30).

Other courts agreed that an unyielding interpretation of nonconsent was appropriate. The Texas courts, for example, explained that if the alleged victim "does not put forth all the power of resistance which she was capable of exerting under the circumstances, it will not be rape" (*Perez v. State*, 1906, quoted in Estrich, 1987, p. 31). Other states' requirements included that "resistance [must] be to the uttermost" (*Reynolds v. State*, 1889; also *Moss v. State*, 1950) in Mississippi; "until exhausted or overpowered" (*People v. Dohring*, 1874) in New York; or "in every way possible and continued such resistance until she was overcome by force, was insensible through fright, or ceased resistance from exhaustion, fear of death, or great bodily harm" (*King v. State*, 1962) in Tennessee. Note that in almost all these cases, appellate courts overturned jury verdicts of guilt.

Such reasoning ultimately culminated in a widespread standard of "utmost resistance" by the victim in order for nonconsent to be determined. But the extreme standard was not applied in all cases, especially those with black defendants (see Estrich, 1987, pp. 33-36, for examples).

In order for it to be determined that a rape had indeed occurred, in most instances the victim must have demonstrated that she did everything possible—everything within her physical and psychological power—to prevent the rape from occurring. As LeGrand (1973) points out, rape was the only crime that required the victim's

active resistance *up to the point of severe injury,* as an indication
of nonconsent.

A clear result of such a strict resistance requirement is a low rate
of convictions in rape cases. As one district attorney put it, "Sometimes when a rape has obviously been committed, a guilty person
could just walk away because it couldn't be proved that the victim
had been physically overcome. . . . You had to demonstrate at the
trial that the victim had resisted almost to the point of death"
(Schultz, 1984, p. 1).

Furthermore, it should be noted that in traditional rape laws the
primary determining factor of whether or not a rape has occurred
was not the behavior of the alleged rapist, but rather the alleged
victim's behavior during the event. It was not until the 1950s
and 1960s that the "ultimate resistance" standard began to be replaced by one emphasizing reasonable resistance (see The Resistance Standard under Actual Reforms, below.

Evidentiary Distrust and the Need
for Corroboration

Just as certain criteria must be met before a judgment can be made
that rape has occurred, certain rules determine how one decides if,
indeed, adequate proof exists that such criteria are satisfied. Traditional common law imposed two strict requirements on the victim.
First, the rape had to be "properly" reported. If the victim waited
too long, the alleged rapist could not be tried. A second common
law requirement mandated that the testimony in a rape case be
corroborated. This corroboration requirement meant that the word
of the victim was not enough—she must have more tangible proof
that she was, indeed, raped before a defendant could be found guilty
of rape. It was considered an essential part of the rape laws primarily because of the fear of what would happen without it.

As late as the 1960s legal scholars were justifying the presence of
the corroboration rule: "Surely the simplest, and perhaps the most
important, reason not to permit conviction for rape on the uncorroborated word of the prosecutrix is that word is very often
false. . . . Since stories of rape are frequently lies or fantasies, it is
reasonable to provide that such a story, in itself, should not be
enough to convict a man of a crime" (Note, 1967, p. 1137). And this
corroboration requirement effectively eliminated many guilty verdicts that, without it, might have been sustained.

Placing the corroboration requirement on the rape victim quite likely means the attack will go unpunished. Usually the only persons present during a rape are the attacker and the victim. Jurors are especially influenced by eyewitnesses; their absence is a discouragement for conviction. Next to a confession, testimony by an objective eyewitness is considered to be the strongest evidence against a defendant (Kassin & Wrightsman, 1988).

Several other factors inhibit the availability of corroborating evidence. Recall that quite often a rapist encounters sexual problems during a rape, including impotency or the inability to ejaculate. In such cases, vital evidence is absent. Also, because rape victims often do not report the rape, other important evidence that could corroborate the victim's story—bruises, proof of penetration, traces of semen or blood—may be lost.

The Psychology of the Female

Perhaps it was because the courts felt a need to justify the validity of their distrust in the female who alleges rape that they found themselves compelled to delve into the psyche of the female. Indeed, determining the motivations of alleged rape victims for their accusations became quite popular in judicial decisions. In too many cases, the courts tried to determine if the victim "really wanted it." How else to determine the answer to such a question than to ascertain what was going on in the alleged victim's mind?

Several factors account for the court's willingness to analyze rape victims psychologically. First, the ubiquitous fear of falsely charging someone with rape clouded many judicial decisions. A second factor involved the emergence of psychoanalysis as an influence upon American society. Also, certain societal norms dictated appropriate behavior for males and females.

The Fear of False Accusations. As noted earlier, the *actual* frequency of false rape reports is estimated to be a low 2%—about the same percentage as in other major crimes. Still, fear of such a false accusation has permeated the court system (Katz & Mazur, 1979). Such a fear is not unique to the halls of justice, however. Anecdotes of false accusations of rape have been recorded in the Bible and in mythology. In the Old Testament, Potiphor's wife, angered at Joseph's refusal to sleep with her, took revenge by claiming to her husband that Joseph had tried to rape her (Gen. 39:10-20). In Greek mythology, Phaedra, scorned by Hippolytus, also retaliated by claiming rape (Graves, 1955, Vol. 1, p. 357). In Chapter 1 we described the more recent case of Cathleen Crowell Webb, who recanted her story of rape only after the defendant had been convicted of rape and imprisoned for 7 years. Although false reports of rape may provide sensational reading for the public, they also lead to the inaccurate conception that a woman "crying rape" is common. The actual problem with reporting rape is quite the contrary—an alarmingly low percentage of rape victims report their victimization (Warshaw, 1988).

Wrongly charging someone with rape, or any other crime, is inexcusable and should not be taken lightly. But fears of false reports have permeated the laws and judicial decisions regarding rape far beyond that of any other crime, including arson. Rape myths have been the basis for these for a long time. This point is illustrated by a statement of the 17th century English jurist Lord Chief Justice Matthew Hale (1680), who wrote:

> It is true, rape is a most detestable crime, and therefore ought severely and impartially to be punished with death, but it must be remembered that it is an accusation easily to be made and hard to be proved; and harder to be defended by party accused tho ever so innocent. (p. 635)

To this day, this statement is published in law-school textbooks, as well as quoted by some judges as they instruct juries in rape cases (Gordon & Riger, 1989). In 1904, a Georgia appellate court asserted that "every man is in danger of being prosecuted and convicted on the testimony of a base woman, in whose testimony there is no truth" (*Davis v. State*, 1904, p. 181).

Freudian Psychology and the Masochistic Personality. It was in 1924 that Freud identified femininity with masochism, or sexual arousal derived from experiencing pain (Hyde, 1986). The concept that females were innately masochistic (Scully & Marolla, 1985) gave the courts justification for the following interpretations of the victim's motivations: "If females are inherently masochistic, then they may be found at least partially responsible for being raped." As an article published in the *Stanford Law Review* put it, "a woman may note a man's brutal nature and be attracted to him rather than repulsed" (Note, 1966, p. 682).

The idea that women secretly enjoy brutality by men was used as a rationale for judicial decisions and legal scholarship. A Catch-22 for the rape victim was thus created. As the *Yale Law Journal* asserted in 1952:

> A woman's need for sexual satisfaction may lead to the unconscious desire for forceful penetration, the coercion serving neatly to avoid the guilt feeling that might arise after willing participation. . . . Where such an attitude of ambivalence exists, the woman may, nonetheless, exhibit behavior which would lead the fact finder to conclude that she opposed the act. To illustrate . . . the anxiety resulting from this conflict of needs may cause her to flee from the situation of discomfort, either physically by running away, or symbolically be retreating to such infantile behavior as crying. The scratches, flight, and crying constitute admissible and compelling evidence of nonconsent. But the conclusion of rape in this situation may be inconsistent with the meaning of the consent standard and unjust to the man. . . . Fairness to the male suggests a conclusion of not guilty, despite signs of aggression, if his act was not contrary to the woman's formulated wishes. (Estrich, 1987, p. 39)

Hence, we have the paradoxical situation in which evidence of resistance is sufficient enough to meet the *nonconsent* requirement, but such evidence is now used as proof that victim really desired the "forceful penetration." Evidence of resistance—supposedly needed for a conviction—can now be used against the victim.

Societal Norms. As we saw in Chapter 2, the norms of society, dictating what is appropriate behavior, have always had a significant impact on our lives. We have stringent rules to follow, especially when it comes to interacting with the other sex, and we face negative consequences for nonconformity.

Such social rules are hard to change; research confirms that what is considered appropriate behavior for males and females has changed very little over the past 30 years (Rose & Frieze, 1985). Males are advised to take the more dominant role in social interactions while females are supposed to be as pleasant and attractive as possible. In 1966, the *Stanford Law Review* acknowledged such roles, in another blatant display of finding reasons to doubt the word of the victim: "Although a woman may desire sexual intercourse, it is customary for her to say 'no, no, no' (Although meaning 'yes, yes, yes') and to expect the male to be the aggressor" (Estrich, 1987, p. 38).

On the Road to Rape Reform

Certainly, blatant distrust of a woman claiming rape has not altogether disappeared—as recently as 1990, women in certain jurisdictions of the United States who had claimed to be raped were asked to take a lie detector test before their charges of rape were taken seriously (Manhattan, KS Women's Crisis Center, personal communication, May 1990). But gradually things began to change when it came to the justice system's response to claims of rape. Active agents in the system began to take a long, hard look at previous decisions; these evaluations provided the impetus for changes in the rape laws and in the treatment of rape victims. Looking back, we find several factors that proved central to the call for rape-law reform and in the treatment of rape victims (Giacopassi & Wilkinson, 1985). First, the criminal justice system was becoming increasingly incapable of dealing effectively with offenders in rape cases. Furthermore, the public began to realize that the treatment of rape victims by the police and the courts was often cold and uncaring. Finally, the victims of rape themselves played a major role in hastening reform. Each of these is described in the following sections.

An Ineffective Court System

Several objective means can be used to assess the effectiveness of a court system. Among these are the clearance (arrest) and conviction rates for a given type of crime. By the 1970s it became increasingly clear that the court system was grossly inadequate in its ability to deal with cases of rape (Giacopassi & Wilkinson, 1985). For example, Hindelang and Davis (1973) reported that from 1960 to 1973 the clearance rate for forcible rape declined by 29%. This rate of decline in percentage of cases for which arrests were made was twice as steep as that of either homicide or aggravated assault. Furthermore, this disparity was expected to increase in the future (Largen, 1988).

Another source of dissatisfaction was the low conviction rate. LeGrand (1973) estimated that during 1970 a *reported* rape had only a one-in-eight chance of resulting in conviction. As one observer noted, "it is obvious that the chance of a sex offender continuing to roam the streets even after the crime is reported to be astonishingly large" (Hursh, 1973, p. 125).

The General Public

Just at the time that objective evaluations of the court's effectiveness were becoming known, the general public began to realize that something had to be done about the rape crisis. Horror stories about the treatment of rape victims by the court system became abundant (Giacopassi & Wilkinson, 1985). Awareness increased regarding the "second victimization" described in Chapter 9.

The feminist movement deserves much of the credit for increasing public awareness, as well as for putting pressure on legislatures to change laws. Furthermore, more women were becoming lawyers, as well as running for—and winning—seats in state legislatures. The impact of these women on rape-law reform was tremendous.

The Rape Victim

At the same time, the actual *reporting* rate of rape saw a dramatic increase; between 1960 and 1975 the number of reported rapes increased by 378% (McNamara & Sagarin, 1977). By reporting their rapes, victims were both demonstrating courage and demanding to be heard.

By 1980, as a result of these forces, every state had considered rape reform legislation and a majority of them—41 states—had passed significant reforms. In 1986 the Congress followed suit, unanimously passing a bill that would make the federal rape law conform with most state statutes.

The Objectives of Rape Law Reform

The ultimate goal of rape reform was shared, but conservatives and liberals often had different objectives for change (Largen, 1988). These specific goals are described in the following paragraphs.

Protecting Victims' Rights. Rape victims' advocates were greatly concerned with gaining respect for and better treatment of the rape victim by personnel in the criminal justice system—by the police, the attorney prosecuting the case, the defense attorney during cross-examination, the judge hearing the case, and the jury. Statutes were sought that protected the rights of victims and incorporated more humane rules affirming the existence of those rights without undermining the constitutional rights of defendants (Largen, 1988). Traditional laws were seen as denying to many the legal status of victim. For example, in no traditional statute was it considered criminal for a husband to rape his wife (see Chapter 5). Similarly, males were not considered possible victims of rape, according to the statutes. With this in mind, expanded definitions of the crime were sought in order to extend equal protection of the law to *all* victims.

Social Goals. It was becoming increasingly recognized in this period of advocated reform that the legal system was not the only institution responsible for the inadequate handling of rape charges. After all, the members of legislatures are chosen by private citizens and laws are presumed to represent the views of the constituency. Therefore, general public attitudes and social bias against women also become targets for change. Through rape-law reform, women's groups hoped to shed light on the long-held myths and misconceptions about the crime of rape and the harsh attitudes that existed toward women, so as to promote a higher level of equality between the sexes (Largen, 1988).

Law and Order. Not all advocates of reform shared the ideological goals of social change. In the early 1970s, when rape reform proposals were first gaining attention, societal concern was not centered so much on the treatment of the victim, but on the criminal justice system's coddling of criminals. The public was appalled by the rising crime rate (Largen, 1988); rape reform was seen as but one of the many changes needed in criminal law. The tremendous concern here was congenial with the interests of victims' advocacy groups. Perhaps most of the support for law reform came from those concerned with creating order in what was perceived as an increasingly disordered society.

Actual Reform

Exactly how does one go about changing the statutes—many of which had not been modified in three centuries—in a way that could meet the goals of such a diverse group of people? With no simple answer, several different reforms evolved. Most of the enacted changes fell under one of three categories: changes in the definition of rape and other sex offenses, changes in the penalty structure for those convicted of rape, and changes in the evidentiary rules for cases involving rape.

As we discuss the actual reforms that have taken place, keep in mind that all 50 states, as well as the federal government, have made their own decisions concerning what is appropriate reform for their jurisdiction. No two states have adopted exactly the same changes in all possible aspects of rape law reform. Some states have chosen to make radical changes, complying with the demands of both society at large and feminist groups. Other states have chosen not to disrupt the status quo, thus retaining most of the traditional statutes.

The Definition of Rape

Almost every state, as well as the federal government, has chosen to broaden its definition of the crime of rape (Largen, 1988). Traditional definitions legally eliminated half the population (females) from the possibility of being charged with rape; married people were denied status as victims. Much of the language in the new statutes is gender-neutral, making it possible for a female to rape or for a male to be raped. Efforts at rape reform made extraordinary progress in instituting spousal rape prohibitions, as described in Chapter 5.

Yet another significant change dealt with what types of sexual acts could constitute rape. Traditional laws considered rape to require the specific act of sexual intercourse. Through rape reform efforts, many jurisdictions changed the definition of rape to include other acts besides vaginal penetration by the penis. The intrusion of other objects, for example, could constitute rape under new laws. The trend-setting Michigan statute also includes "any other intrusion, however slight, of any part of a person's body or of any object into the genital or anal openings of another person's body" (Estrich,

1987, p. 83). Some states now include "sexual contact" as a misdemeanor or even a felony (i.e., any intentional touching of another's intimate parts or the clothing covering them).

Merely broadening the definition of rape was not, however, the only type of definitional change made. Some states, noting the negative emotional connotation automatically activated with the very words *rape* or *rapist*, opted to eliminate these terms altogether (Giacopassi & Wilkinson, 1985). Such statutes avoided the term by subsuming the act of rape under the crime of "assault." It was argued that such reclassification would serve two very important functions: to help promote the equality of all citizens, and to place emphasis on the violent, rather than the sexual, nature of the crime.

Levels of Crime

Another major change involved a *gradation* of the crime of rape; or dividing the crime into several levels depending on such variables as the amount of coercion, the extent of injury, and the age of the victim (Feild & Bienen, 1980). The new Washington state law, for example, divides rape into three degrees according to the extent of force or threat (Wrightsman, 1991):

1. First-degree rape: Sexual intercourse (with a nonspouse) by forcible compulsion under aggravated circumstances (e.g., use of a deadly weapon, kidnapping the victim). Punishable with a minimum sentence of 20 years and a minimum confinement period of 3 years.
2. Second-degree rape: Requires only sexual intercourse by forcible compulsion. Penalty: maximum of 10 years.
3. Third-degree rape: Defined as sexual intercourse without consent or with threat of substantial harm to property rights. Penalty: not more than 5 years.

The basic goal behind this reform was to increase the rate of convictions. Based on the presumption that juries are often hesitant to convict and thereby impose a heavy sentence on a rapist except under the most brutal of circumstances, reformers believe that by specifying degrees of rape, juries might be more inclined to convict without being excessively punitive. Some feminists do not agree with this rationale, and others are skeptical that the innovation is achieving its intended effect (MacKinnon, 1987; Tong, 1984).

The Resistance Standard

Beginning in the 1950s and 1960s, the "utmost resistance" standard was loosened in favor of a more lenient "reasonable" resistance standard (Estrich, 1987). Legal scholars were finally beginning to recognize that the physical and mental capabilities of a victim, while being attacked, might not enable her to resist to the "utmost." With the reasonable-resistance standard, courts are generally acknowledging that the circumstances of the rape must be taken into account. But the standard is being applied selectively. In cases involving acquaintances, for example, a more stringent resistance requirement is still often applied (Bohmer, 1991). Race of both the defendant and the victim also seem to be compelling factors that affect how the resistance of the victim is judged. In cases in which the alleged rapist is black and the victim white, the standard gets lax. As a California appellate court explained in *People v. Harris*, in 1951,

> when a young, white woman returning home from her work meets a strange male person of the Negro race in the dead of night in a quiet vicinity . . . [who] proceeds to remove her clothing, compels her to perform the nameless act to stimulate his own amorous impulses, it would border upon the stupid to find that she freely acquiesced in his acts as he ravished her body. While she made some resistance, it may be safely presumed that she would have rebelled with a vengeance but for her fear of bodily harm. (cited in Estrich, 1987, p. 37)

A Texas appellate court, however, also exercised its own interpretation of the reasonable resistance standard within a year of the California decision, but it came up with a different conclusion. The circumstances were similar in the Texas case, with one noteworthy exception: the victim was also black, and the defendant's conviction was overturned because of her "feigned and passive resistance" (*Killingworth v. State*, 1950).

The advent of rape-law reform efforts strengthened attacks on the resistance standard. Many states eventually changed their definition so as to place the emphasis on the alleged rapist's behavior as opposed to the victim's (Gordon & Riger, 1989). Some jurisdictions have reflected this change by eliminating the phrases *against her will* or *without her consent* and replacing them with a standard of force used by the alleged rapist. The authors of the Model Penal

Code, for example, redefined rape as sexual intercourse in which the man "compels her to submit by force or by threat of imminent death, serious bodily injury, extreme pain or kidnapping, to be inflicted on anyone" (Estrich, 1987, pp. 58-59).

Perhaps the greatest discrepancy in laws in different jurisdictions is in the resistance standard; some states have eliminated it but most have not (as of 1988, 38 states still imposed it). But many states have also expanded their definition of *force* to include coercion or intimidation by the alleged rapist. Thus the standard of resistance has been attenuated somewhat (Largen, 1988).

Changes in Sentencing Structures

Traditional rape laws were always accompanied by harsh sentences for those convicted of rape, including life imprisonment or death. The severity of such sentences has been cited as a major reason behind the long-held view that men are often falsely accused of rape (Largen, 1988). In 1971, 16 states and the federal government allowed capital punishment as a potential penalty for a rape conviction. After the *Furman v. Georgia* (1972) decision was handed down, however, and the states were forced to review their capital punishment provisions, only 3 of the 16 reinstituted the death penalty for the crime of rape (Giacopassi & Wilkinson, 1985).

In 1977, all of this changed when the Supreme Court of the United States ruled in *Coker v. Georgia.* The defendant in this case, Ehrlich Anthony Coker, was serving prison time for murder, rape, kidnapping, and assault, when he escaped. In the course of committing another armed robbery, Coker raped a woman. After he was apprehended, Coker was tried and convicted of rape and armed robbery; the jury sentenced him to death. Coker's appeal claimed that the sentence was a violation of the Eighth and Fourteenth Amendments prohibiting cruel and unusual punishment. The Supreme Court not only agreed, but also deemed capital punishment for raping an adult woman "grossly disproportionate and excessive." In its written decision, the Court noted that public attitudes had to be given attention, and the fact that "in no time in the last 50 years has a majority of the states authorized death as punishment for rape" (*Coker v. Georgia,* 1977, p. 584) indicated that the public did not sanction capital punishment in such cases.

Thus, at this time, it is justifiable to the Supreme Court to put mentally retarded or adolescent individuals to death for murder, but death is not justified by the Supreme Court, in any case, no matter how brutal, if a raped victim survives.

Abolishing the possibility of a death sentence for rape was not, however, viewed by all rape-reform advocates as a negative step. Some saw it as potentially positive, because—as mentioned earlier—jurors do seem reluctant to convict if they believe that the sentence to be imposed is too severe. Using this rationale, Weir (1991) has documented that the likelihood of obtaining a conviction of rape is increased if jurors are allowed to recommend a sentence in addition to rendering a verdict.

Just as the offense of rape itself was graded, so too were proposals made to tailor sentences to fit the circumstances of the crime (Largen, 1988). Instead of increased severity of punishments, some advocates of sentencing reform opted for increased certainty that a punishment would be given (Estrich, 1987). Along with decreasing the maximum possible sentence, some jurisdictions eliminated parole and probation for those convicted of rape (Polk, 1985). Such efforts effectively attenuated the great discretion previously allowed.

A survey in 1987 of 28 state court systems verified the need for revisions in sentencing. It found that 16% of the 3,100 people convicted of rape had been put on parole without receiving any prison sentence.

Evidentiary Reforms

Perhaps the most significant changes made in rape laws dealt with evidentiary issues, specifically what types of evidence a jury will or will not hear. Three of the most significant reforms were the following: first, the requirement that the report be made immediately was repealed. No longer did the victim's reluctance to come forth automatically exclude the opportunity for a conviction. Other evidentiary reforms included the abolishing of the corroboration requirement, the establishment of rape shield laws (see Chapter 9), changes in the resistance standard (previously described), and admissibility of testimony by expert witnesses regarding rape trauma syndrome (also described in Chapter 9).

Corroboration

The corroboration requirement imposed on victims of rape has been considered impractical, if not impossible, for years. In most states the requirement of supplementary objective evidence has been abolished and the word of the victim is now sufficient for a suspect to be charged with rape. Currently, courts are increasingly finding their cases to be "credibility contests" in which the word of the victim is pitted against that of the defendant.

Evaluating Rape Law Reforms: How Successful Are They?

To be sure, the multitude of changes made in the rape statutes are not insignificant. The adoption of rape shield laws, for example, has been extensive. To most advocates of rape reform, however, such changes were only the first step—not the final solution (Largen, 1988). Some warned of a "risk that the passage of the law will be viewed as a solution, will dull social sensibilities to unresolved problems, will slow the impetus for further reform" (Largen, 1988, p. 290).

The ultimate implementation and hence implicit interpretation of the written statutes comes from those active in the criminal justice system, including the police, prosecuting and defense attorneys, judges, and juries. These people decide exactly how far to take a charge of rape. We will look at the effects of changes on some of these specific aspects in subsequent paragraphs. But first it should be noted that efforts to assess the effects of these reforms empirically have led to conflicting conclusions (Goldberg-Ambrose, 1992; Loh, 1980; Polk, 1985). Bohmer (1991) concludes that "many of these reforms have had limited effect on the experience of the victim or the likelihood that there will be a conviction" (p. 326). For example, in one study the repeal of the corroboration requirement was perceived as increasing the likelihood that an uncorroborated case would be pursued further by the police, enabling the police to get more cases into the system (Largen, 1988). (This is important because, according to LaFree, 1989, police have believed that rape complaints are less valid than other complaints.) But in contrast, Polk (1985) concluded that in California between 1975 and 1982 no significant increase occurred in either the percentage of rape complaints that resulted in arrests or the percentage of felony complaints that led to convictions.

A recent and thorough review of the effects of rape law reforms by a law professor (Goldberg-Ambrose, 1992) finds the conclusions of individual studies range all the way from highly successful impact through little impact to conclusions that feminists' goals have been thwarted. Myths and false assumptions held by jurors remain an obstacle. Nonetheless, the legal reforms are a beginning. We have seen a trend toward increased reporting of rapes and a perception that legal reforms have encouraged this trend. The evidentiary reforms have especially been credited with influencing victims to remain in and cooperate with the criminal justice system. Changes in the laws that facilitate specific charges for specific acts as well as plea-bargaining have been credited with accelerating the resolution of a case and avoiding the unwanted publicity of a trial (Largen, 1988).

Yet it is easier to change laws than to change attitudes. Largen (1988) found no consensus in her study that private attitudes among those in the criminal justice system had greatly changed. Though there was some agreement that the conviction rate for those defendants accused of raping a stranger had increased, conviction rates for acquaintance rape were not seen as any different. As Largen notes, juries were described by her respondents as "having their own standards" for judging a case, most of which involved following the myths and stereotypes that had formed the earlier laws. One judge in her study commented, "Juries still think good women don't get raped and bad women deserve it," despite any changes in the law. And Estrich (1987), in reviewing recent appeals, finds that "judges in the 1980's continued to think about women and rape in the same way as the law-review writers of the 1950's and 1960's or even the judges of the 1940's" (p. 80). For example, she notes a 1977 Michigan opinion (*People v. Vaughan,* 1977) that claims it is so "natural" for a rape victim to file a complaint promptly that if "she did not, that . . . was in effect an assertion that nothing violent had been done" (Estrich, 1987, p. 90).

As Estrich wisely observes, changing the words of statutes is not nearly so important as changing the way we understand them (1987, p. 91).

Summary

Rape laws are a reflection of the attitudes of their representative society members. The history of rape laws indicates that alleged victims of rape have traditionally been met with suspicion by the legal system. Judicial interpretations of the traditional rape law incorporated standards, such as the "utmost resistance" standard, that resulted in overturned convictions and, in many cases, acquittals in legitimate rape cases. Since the 1970s, through the efforts of both the women's movement and those concerned about the treatment of criminals, virtually all jurisdictions in the United States have reformed their rape laws in some form. The definition of rape has been expanded or altered in many states. The resistance standard, although still present in the majority of states, has been loosened. Changes in the sentencing structure for the crime of rape have been implemented, and reforms in the evidentiary rules have occurred. Even though these changes are important steps, it appears that the effectiveness of these laws is equivocal. Ultimately, it is the individuals within society who will implement change.

11 The Treatment of Victims and Rapists

This chapter will focus on the treatment of both victims and rapists. Not until we validate through understanding the fact that those who are sexually assaulted are, indeed, victims, and those who assault are indeed, victimizers, can we even begin to address the problem adequately. For too long the line between the victims and the victimizers has been ill defined. Both, however, need and deserve adequate and concerned treatment.

Treatment of the Victims

Those who choose to report their victimization—either to the police, a rape crisis center, or even to a friend—face the unknown. How will they be treated? Recall from Chapter 8 that these victims are in an acute stage of trauma. They are frightened; they may be in shock. Some may be feeling angry or guilty or confused or sad and some may be feeling all of these emotions at once. These victims need compassion. But no matter how compassionate a friend, a police officer, or a victim advocate may (or may not) be, what rape victims will likely go through in the next few hours will not be a positive experience. According to Bard (1982), the actions of those individuals with whom the victim may interact immediately after being assaulted are critical to the victim's ultimate psychological health.

The Reactions of Loved Ones

The first recipient of disclosure for many victims will not be the police, or even a rape crisis center; more often a friend or family member is contacted, and the decision about telling this individual depends on how close the victim feels to this person, who is usually a female (Shore, 1979). How this person responds to the victim is of utmost importance. Bard (1982) stresses that a combination of tolerance, stability, and reassurance are essential. Similarly, Koss and Harvey (1991) focus on acceptance, empathy, and support. Acceptance includes attentiveness to everything the victim says, a calm facial expression, a restatement of what the victim has said, and communicating at a level that the victim's current status permits her to understand. Empathy includes seeing the matter from the victim's perspective without expressing personal vengeance. Support, according to Koss and Harvey (1991), means reassuring the victim that rape, though often not avoidable is survivable. The victim whose trust for humankind has just been shattered needs to be reassured that there are "good" people, and most of all, that she is *safe* with them.

Unfortunately, being a close friend or family member to a victim of rape does not guarantee that such an individual will be able to provide the support that the victim so desperately needs. Many of these individuals may believe some or even many of the rape myths that exist. The acceptance of rape myths by those closest to the victim can be devastating to the victim, who may sense that they are blaming her for what happened. In addition, because those who are usually contacted first by victims of rape closest to the victim, they are themselves sometimes unable to offer her the quality of assistance that is needed—these individuals are going through their own complex emotional reactions. Some experts have speculated that as many as three or four family members may seek psychological services for every victim who receives counseling (Foley, 1985).

Generally, the kinds of reactions of the significant others that may interfere with their ability to be empathetic are anger, guilt, and confusion (Frank, 1979). An important distinction to be made here is between the *feeling* of these emotions and the *expression* of these emotions. It is quite natural for someone to be angry and confused when they learn that someone close to them has been raped. But caution is always warranted in the expression of the anger. Anger that is directed at the victim is certainly harmful to any victim. Men whose partners have been raped often want revenge against the rapist; some may express their desire to "kill the bastard," or to "surgically castrate the S.O.B." (Foley, 1985). Actively to seek revenge against a perpetrator will only make matters worse.

Many significant others may also experience guilt about not having been there to "protect" their loved one. The confusion experienced by these individuals may be concerned with a number of issues. If the significant other is a boyfriend or husband, sexual overtones may come into play—feelings of insecurity and jealousy may lead the other to question what the victim's "real" feelings were. Others may not understand why the victim responded as she did, because *in hindsight* it is easy to conclude that whatever she did was not successful (this is also discussed in Chapter 7). The confusion and search for understanding, especially if combined with the acceptance of rape myths, result in blaming the victim. Such blaming will lead to a response from the victim, who is likely to distance herself from the very person she loves but who does not meet her expectations of support (Frank, 1979).

It is, in fact, the rape victim's relationship with her boyfriend or husband that suffers the most as a result of rape (Foley, 1985; Shore, 1980). Between 50% and 80% of victims' relationships will end as a consequence of the rape (see Chapter 8). Surprisingly, although mothers of victims are often told before the fathers—who often find out indirectly from someone other than the victim—research suggests that fathers are often more supportive (Shore, 1980). The way that a victim is responded to, however, has been found to be more important than the gender of the individual responding (Holmstrom & Burgess, 1978).

According to Gurley (1986), a cautious approach to someone who has just been raped is often the best approach—to rush frantically to her and throw your arms around her may be introducing a physical gesture that is not welcome. Rather, Gurley suggests that simply going to the victim with love and acceptance is the best approach. To be judgmental in any way will be destructive. To inquire about details of the event may be traumatizing. Rather, listening to the victim, if she chooses to talk, and acknowledging her pain is the best approach. Significant others should remember that the victim may be experiencing a number of different emotions, and it is important that the family accept these emotions. At least initially, to try to stop her from having these feelings may seem to the victim like a denial that what she has gone through was a traumatic experience. This may very well lead to alienation. Box 11.1 offers suggestions for both adaptive and maladaptive stress responses of friends and family members.

Treatment of the Victim at the Hospital

Not all victims go to the hospital following a rape. Some victims who were not badly beaten as well as raped may not believe that it is necessary. Others may not want to deal with the trauma in front of others. However, there are advantages to seeking medical treatment for rape victims (Grossman & Sutherland, 1991). An important reason is to determine if the victim has been injured in any way. Recall that often victims may be in a state of shock or denial immediately following a rape; they may not be aware of some injuries that they have sustained (Koss & Harvey, 1991). A second advantage is to deal with any fears that the rape victim may have about injuries, venereal disease, or pregnancy; testing can be done and options for preventing such occurrences can be discussed. Finally, medical evidence can be collected that could aid in future prosecution. Even if the victim does not believe that she wants to prosecute, this evidence could be used if, after she has carefully thought through her decision to prosecute, she chooses to change her mind. It is vital that evidence be collected as soon as possible for the sake of prosecution; it may be destroyed as time passes.

Despite the advantages of seeking medical treatment, if a rape victim does choose to seek medical treatment after being raped, she is not in for a pleasant experience. Both the psychological experience of discussing her experience with the medical staff and the physical experience of the examination provide opportunity for further traumatization. Generally, the assessment and care of a victim of rape in a hospital—usually in the emergency room—can be divided into three aspects: (a) treatment of physical and psychological trauma, (b) collection and processing of evidence, and (c) prevention of pregnancy and venereal disease.

Treatment of Physical and Psychological Trauma. The hospital staff can have a tremendous impact on a victim's recovery; the treatment that she receives has the potential to either aid in the recovery process or create further trauma (Burgess & Holmstrom, 1974a). In order to ensure adequate psychological treatment of the victim, it is imperative that hospital staff react to the victim with understanding and compassion (Ledray, 1990). In order to stress its importance, Symonds (1980) refers to this need as "psychological first aid." Before the actual physical examination, the rape victim may be approached by a social worker or medical advocate, with goals to listen to the needs and fears of the victim and to help in any way possible (Grossman & Sutherland, 1991). If the victim is required to wait before a physician can see her (and some do) then these individuals may be especially important. They are not there to force a victim to discuss her experience, but they are there to offer some assistance if the victim desires it.

Holmstrom and Burgess (1978) have studied the reactions that emergency ward personnel have had toward victims who sought treatment. They found that the majority (65%) of the physicians they observed were professionally polite; they concentrated on accomplishing the technical job at hand: treating any injuries that the victim may have incurred, or collecting the evidence necessary for potential prosecution. However, physicians generally fulfilled these duties with a pleasant smile and reassuring comments. The staff was neither extremely sympathetic, nor were they overly demeaning. Of the physicians examining victims, 14% were especially positive and 20% were either negative or indifferent to the victims, or engaged in conscientious harassment of the victim (for example, pressuring the victim to consent to certain medical procedures that the victim clearly did not want). Interestingly, characteristics of the victim were found to be associated with the treatment that they received. Those adults who were more attractive and articulate, or children who were victims of sexual assault, were most likely to be treated in an especially positive manner. Those victims who were treated negatively were generally less attractive, less articulate, and more likely to have "discrediting" backgrounds or circumstances of attack.

BOX 11.1

Adaptive and
Maladaptive Family Stress
Reactions to Rape

Adaptive Stress Reactions

Care and concern for the victim
Support of the victim
Feelings of shock, disbelief, dismay
Feelings of helplessness and disequilibrium
Physical revulsion that may parallel the victim's affective responses
Distraction tactics to keep the victim and themselves occupied
Reacting to rape as a violent act
Anger and rage directed at the rapist or society
Blame directed at the rapist
Thoughts (vs. actions) about violent retribution or active retaliation
Reaching out to extended family/significant others for support
Empathic with each other
Use of crisis counseling as needed
Supportive of victim's medical or gynecological care needs and follow-up care
Cooperation with criminal justice system to prosecute rapist
Participation in rape prevention programs
Supporting the victim's decisions and wishes
Reevaluating previous relationship with the victim

Despite the overwhelming response of "professional politeness" while dealing with victims of sexual assault, Holmstrom and Burgess (1978) note that there is also a personal reaction by medical staff. While most do well to hide their own personal feelings from the victim, the behind-the-scenes conversation of medical staff is often filled with judgmental statements. Consider the following conversation that took place between two professional workers while a rape victim waited in another room:

BOX 11.1 (Continued)

Maladaptive Stress Reactions

Concern primarily about how others will think of the family

Contested feelings over who was raped, hurt most, or victimized

Minimizing the victim's feelings or response

Feeling guilty or responsible for not having protected the victim

Rape Trauma Syndrome (see Chapter 8)

Patronizing or overprotecting the victim

Viewing rape as a sexually motivated act and the victim as "damaged goods"

Direct or indirect anger and resentment as seen in communication difficulties

Blame directed at the victim or family members

Acting out violent retribution toward assailant or victim

Emotional cut-offs with extended family/significant others

Absence of empathic responses with each other; emotional isolation or withdrawal

Failure to seek professional counseling when needed

Failure to seek medical or gynecological care and follow-up care

Inability to cooperate with criminal justice system

Belief in rape myths

Pressuring for action against victim's wishes, such as forced or pressured sexual relations with victim, informing others, dropping charges, or insisting that prosecution be carried out

Divorce/separation

Source: Foley & Davies, 1983.

A: I kind of doubt this one. What was she doing in a tavern alone, with her husband in Vietnam! I just can't believe some of these women.

B: It figures. You can't trust any of them, not even your own wife. If I caught 'em together, I'd kill him first—then her. All a woman has to do is scream "rape"—and a guy is ruined.

A: Well, what shall we do with this one?

B: How about the biggest speculum we've got without any lubricant! (Williams & Williams, 1977, p. 93)

Many professionals may dichotomize the rape as either legitimate or not, and most "legitimized" cases are those that do match the stereotype of a "real rape:" the victim is either very young or older, is visibly upset, has bruises or other physical manifestations of the rape, and reports that the assailant was a stranger. This offers the potential for many actual cases of rape that may not meet these criteria to be considered illegitimate by hospital professionals—as we discussed in Chapter 4, most cases of rape do not match this stereotype. One gynecologist who was examining a very upset, badly beaten woman who was raped by a complete stranger told the researchers, "We seldom get a really legitimate case, and this, unfortunately, is one" (Holmstrom & Burgess, 1978, p. 73).

Part of the problem that underlies medical professionals' reactions to rape victims is their lack of training in dealing with rape victims. Until recently, specialized training in this area was widely unavailable. In recent years, however, many in the medical profession have issued a call for more sympathetic treatment of rape victims. Some nurses have, in fact, sought out specialized training in the treatment of rape victims (Lenehan, 1991). These nurses, called sexual assault nurse examiners (SANEs), have been very helpful to rape victims who come into the emergency room. Instead of just having someone who, for the most part, works with emergencies of the body, victims will have someone caring for them who is specially trained in dealing with situations of rape. These nurses have chosen to take on the responsibility of caring for the rape victim during her stay at the hospital.

Collecting and Processing Evidence. Whereas the personal experience involved in the interaction between victim and hospital personnel may either facilitate or inhibit a rape victim's recovery, the rape victim's experience of the physical examination that is done to obtain evidence may be less variable. Although the nature of the physical examination may be determined by the extent of the patient's condition, most hospitals follow similar protocols—specifically the use of a rape kit—while collecting evidence.

A rape kit includes the materials and instructions necessary to obtain the minimum amount of evidence needed by a medical laboratory for a thorough examination. Informed consent is required before an examination for a rape kit may be performed. Such consent generally allows the medical doctor to collect and preserve all of the available evidence—including the clothes that the victim was wearing at the time of the assault. Victims seeking medical treatment do have the right to refuse the collection of medical evidence. As discussed earlier, however, to submit to the rape kit examination offers the advantage of an increased chance of prosecution, and ultimately, the conviction of the rapist. Box 11.2 discusses in detail the steps that are usually taken while the rape kit examination is being performed.

The procedure that is performed using the rape kit is a methodical and an affectively cold experience, and for the victim, can serve as a second source of victimization. Remember, perhaps only hours earlier the victim was sexually assaulted. Now, in a hospital setting, the victim must completely disrobe and tell about details of the assault to complete strangers; she must endure a vaginal examination—an event all too similar to what she experienced during her victimization—and she must give up the clothing that she wore during the assault. If bruises or lacerations are present, pictures may be taken. Although the experience itself is generally not physically painful, it can be a psychologically humiliating one.

Prevention of Pregnancy and Venereal Disease. Although the probabilities of either getting pregnant or developing a venereal disease are not high, they are possibilities. These possible consequences of being raped can be a riveting fear (Warshaw, 1988).

Prevention of Pregnancy. The risk of pregnancy as a result of the rape should be assessed by the physician and discussed with the victim. If the risks are considered high, the victim may choose to take the "morning after pill" (DES, or diethylstilbestrol). This medication is taken orally, and consists of a large dose of synthetic estrogen, which prevents implantation of a fertilized egg in the wall of the uterus (Warner, 1980). A full course must be taken twice a day for 5 days, and must begin within 24 hours of the sexual assault for it to be effective. Hazardous side effects to this drug may exist, however, and the victim needs to be aware of these before she may give her informed consent to take the drug. These include: (a) danger to the fetus if the victim is already pregnant at the time of the sexual assault, but is unaware of this, (b) danger to the fetus if the victim remains pregnant as a result of the rape, and (c) nausea and vomiting, possible vaginal spotting, breast tenderness, insomnia, and development of a rash while being treated. In addition, DES is known to be linked with a rare form of vaginal cancer in daughters

BOX 11.2

The Rape Kit

Although different hospitals may have different protocols for handling the collection of evidence, most follow similar standards. The following instructions are those provided by a crime lab in Missouri, for use after a victim has consented to the rape kit examination.

1. The attending nurse should individually bag each article of the victim's clothing to be submitted to the investigating police officer or directly to the crime laboratory. Place panties in the bag provided; use larger paper bags or containers for other clothing.

2. Comb the pubic hair region with the comb provided to recover any foreign hair which may have been deposited by the assailant. Place the comb in the envelope provided; seal and initial the envelope.

3. Examine the patient for visible blood or seminal stains; if such stains are observed, moisten one of the gauze pads with water and remove the stain onto the pad. *ALLOW THE PAD TO AIR DRY* and place it in one of the plastic bags provided. Document properly, including the area swabbed.

4. Obtain pubic hair control sample (10-15) from victim—*PREFERABLY PULLED*, otherwise cut very close to the skin.

5. During the normal vaginal exam (PLEASE DO NOT LUBRICATE), use one set of swabs to prepare two vaginal smears on the microscope slides provided. Spray the slides with a cytological fixative (if available) and allow the slides to *AIR DRY* for 3-5 minutes. When dry, place labeled slides in the mailer (LABEL THESE SWABS AS *VAGINAL SMEARS*).

   Obtain two additional swabs from each of the vaginal and cervical walls and label the swabs as *VAGINAL SWABS* AND *CERVICAL SWABS* respectively. PLEASE AIR DRY ALL SWABS BEFORE PLACING IN PROTECTIVE ENVELOPES.

of women who took DES from 1945 to 1970 in order to avoid miscarriages during their pregnancy.

To be sure, a victim who has not only been raped, but who also faces the possibility of pregnancy, is in a difficult situation. One

BOX 11.2 (Continued)

A sample from the vaginal pool should be submitted to your hospital laboratory for preparation of a wet mount and determination of mobile sperm. Cultures for GC or other clinical tests are to be obtained at the discretion of the hospital staff. (A plastic pipet is enclosed for collection of vaginal fluids).

6. Examine fingernails—if any blood, hair, or foreign tissue is observed. Scrape under the nails with the wooden splints provided (over a clean white paper; if blood is present, clip the nails).

7. Obtain oral samples by swabbing the mouth with two swabs (LABEL AS *ORAL SWABS*). Collect a second saliva control on the filter paper disk provided (spittle from patient onto disk is adequate); this would be used to determine secretor status. If oral-genital contact is indicated, please document.

8. If genital-anal contact is indicated, prepare anal smears (for spermatozoa) and submit an anal swab.

9. Obtain a blood sample from the victim for later typing. A second tube of blood should be collected and submitted to the hospital clinical laboratory for normal serology, pregnancy test, CBC, etc..

10. Obtain a representative head hair sample (10-15); *PREFERABLY PULLED*, otherwise cut very close to the scalp. Place in envelope provided.

PLACE ALL THE EVIDENCE COLLECTED ABOVE IN THE ORIGINAL BOX, SEAL THE BOX, AND PLACE AN EVIDENCE SEAL ON EACH SIDE. PROVIDE INFORMATION REQUESTED. SUBMIT THIS KIT IN PERSON TO THE INVESTIGATION OFFICER OR DIRECTLY TO THE CRIME LABORATORY.

victim, after choosing to be treated with DES, reported: "I took those awful pills for five days. It was utter agony. Although I was sick and nauseous the whole time, I did not want to be pregnant" (Warshaw, 1988, p. 71).

The Treatment of Venereal Disease. Another common fear of rape victims is that of contracting a venereal disease. Professionals generally recommend that the victim be advised to receive antibiotic therapy: the relief the victim experiences at not having to worry about contracting either syphilis or gonorrhea, they believe, far outweighs the discomfort of the multiple penicillin injections. Again, however, it should be emphasized that, ultimately, whether to receive treatment or not is the victim's choice. Any victim who chooses to "wait and see" before any treatment is received, however, will be given both an internal exam on the last day of her menses, as well as a blood test at that time. Sadly, the possibility exists that a rape victim may contract the HIV-virus, which causes AIDS, for which there is no cure.

The rape victim's experience in the emergency room leaves the possibility for a second victimization, but also leaves the possibility for a supportive atmosphere that could help the victim cope with her experiences. Supportive personnel—rape advocates, nurses, and physicians—should be aware of the victim's need to be supported and to be in an environment that is free of judgmental responses. It is not the role of the medical staff to determine whether rape has legally occurred. Kilpatrick (1983) has pointed out that sometimes the medical staff believes that they must conclude for themselves whether a "real" rape has occurred before they can provide "real" support. This reaction reflects a confusion of roles. Although a rape kit examination may be done to collect any legal evidence, their primary job is to treat the needs of the victim.

The Need for Long-Term Treatment. As we discussed in Chapter 8, the long-term consequences of rape can be devastating, lasting anywhere from a few months to several years. It is especially important that these victims get the help that they need to be able to cope with their victimization. Although talking to a close friend or relative who is sympathetic with the victim's experience and reactions to her experience can help immensely, many symptoms that develop as a result of rape may need special treatment from trained professionals. It is advisable for anyone who has been raped to seek professional help.

Some of the treatment approaches that have been found useful in treating victims of rape have also been used for other problems as well. These may include systematic desensitization, exposure-based treatment (also referred to as flooding or implosion therapy), writing about the trauma, stress inoculation training, assertion training, and both individual or group therapy to deal with depression (Calhoun & Atkeson, 1991).[1] Sexual dysfunctions may also need to be dealt with. Exactly which of these treatments is most useful will depend on what particular symptoms the victim is experiencing.

Treatment of the Rapist

In 1990, more than 85,000 sex offenders were in state and federal prisons, or more than 15% of all prisoners (Goleman, 1992). Society's major goal for convicted rapists is that they be punished for their acts. One purpose of this section is to describe the various prison sentences along with other types of punishments for rapists. For example, even ancient devices such as castration have recently been reconsidered.

But the question also exists: Are sex offenders capable of reform? Although new treatment procedures are reducing the recidivism rates of rapists, the vast majority of sex offenders in prison receive little or no treatment (Goleman, 1992). For example, California has 15,000 sex offenders in prison; only 46 are in an innovative treatment program. Nevertheless, this section also reviews what is being done.

Crime and Punishment

Is it possible to stop rapists from raping? Certainly processing those who rape through the criminal justice system is a beginning to at least temporary deterrence. Recent efforts have also been made by those in the U.S. Congress to confront the problem of those who commit violence against women (see Box 11.3). To send rapists to prison will prevent them from raping—at least those outside of prison. Unfortunately, most rapists are not in prison. In one study that followed 635 actual rape complaints in Seattle, WA, and Kansas City, MO, only 10 offenders—less than 2%—were convicted (Groth, 1979).

Of those individuals who are found guilty of rape, sentences can be entirely unpredictable, depending upon the judge who renders the sentence, the circumstances of the crime, and the laws of the

BOX 11.3

The "Violence Against Women Act"

In 1991, The "Violence Against Women Act" was introduced into Congress. Some of its provisions included: (1) doubling penalties for rape and aggravated rape, creating new penalties for repeat sex offenders, and increasing the restitution for victims of sex crimes; (2) aiding women in prosecuting their attackers by requiring states to pay for women's medical examinations; (3) authorizing $300 million for beefed-up law enforcement efforts to combat sex crimes, with $100 million targeted for the 40 metropolitan areas most dangerous for women; (4) defining gender-motivated crimes as "bias" or "hate" crimes that deprive victims of their civil rights, allowing them to bring civil rights suits against their assailants; and (5) creating a $20 million grant program for the neediest colleges to fund campus rape education and prevention programs and services.

Such Congressional action, although it has not been passed to date, at least acknowledges that there is a problem; that sexual violence is unacceptable and will be treated with the seriousness that is commands. However, such specific measures cannot directly stop rapists from raping. For example, increasing the potential penalties for rape may actually result in *fewer* rape convictions. Furthermore, even if a rapist does serve more time in prison, chances are that he will eventually be released. If attempts to treat the problem are not implemented, the chances that the rapist will again rape are high (Turkington, 1987b).

state in which the crime occurs (see also Box 11.4). Consider the following examples:

- In 1984, Cleophus Parker was sentenced to 880 years in prison for kidnapping, rape, and armed criminal action by a Clay County, MO, judge after already receiving a sentence of 525 years in prison for raping a woman in Jackson County, MO (Bocchetti, 1989).

BOX 11.4

Sentencing Disparity in the United States

Sentences for rape vary dramatically, depending upon in which state the crime of rape occurs. With the help of Timothy Harper, a writer for the Associated Press, Ann Landers (1984) provided readers with information about the sentences of each state. Each of the potential penalties may provide insight as to how each state views the crime of rape.

In one state, a rapist may receive the death penalty: Mississippi.

In 20 states, a rapist can receive a sentence of life in prison. These include: Alabama, Delaware, Florida, Georgia, Idaho, Iowa, Kansas, Louisiana, Michigan, Mississippi, Missouri, Nevada, North Carolina, Oklahoma, Pennsylvania, Tennessee, Utah, Virginia, Rhode Island, and Washington, DC.

In Alaska, Montana, Nevada, and South Carolina, the maximum penalty for rape is 40 years in prison.

In Indiana and Wyoming, the maximum penalty for rape is 50 years.

In Minnesota, a rapist may receive 20 years in prison, plus a fine of up to $35,000. In South Dakota, a rapist may receive 25 years in prison, plus a fine of $25,000.

Finally, in several states, the penalties may be more severe under certain circumstances. For example, Arizona increases the possible penalty from 14 years in prison to 21 years in prison if a weapon is used. In Illinois, the sentence structure changes from 4 to 15 years to 6 to 30 years if the victim is less than 13 years of age or older than 60. In Tennessee, the sentence is increased by 5 years if the rape results in venereal disease, pregnancy, or mental breakdown.

We find some of these "special circumstances" curious. Why, for example, should it matter how old the victim is? As we pointed out in Chapter 8, *all* victims of rape suffer.

- In 1989, in Jackson County, MO, of the 27 out of 547 rape convictions obtained, 9 men received 5-year sentences, the minimum for rape. One of these cases involved a man who had taken part in the gang rape of a 24-year-old pregnant woman. None received the maximum penalty (Snider, 1990).
- A habitual sex offender in Washington state who finishes serving his prison sentence is likely to be met by a prosecutor, ready to put him back on trial for what he might do in the future (London, 1991).

These are examples of the discretionary power that prosecutors and judges alike have and use when it comes to adjudicating rape cases. Recently, the possibility that a victim may contract AIDS has also become a legal issue. Prosecutors in one Manhattan case agreed to a reduced sentence for a defendant who pleaded guilty to rape if he promised to take an AIDS test and provide the results to his victim (Glaberson, 1990a).

Psychological Treatment

It is especially important that those who are convicted of rape receive treatment; not only does their involvement in the court system offer the opportunity to secure treatment, but these are the men who are more likely to have committed more acts more flagrantly (Turkington, 1987b). Unfortunately, the vast majority of rapists are unlikely ever to receive treatment. It is very rare for a rapist even to acknowledge the inappropriateness of his behavior, let alone seek treatment for it (Greer & Stuart, 1983).

The development of effective treatment programs for rapists is still in its early stages, and in many cases even the treatment outlook is not promising—on average, about 66% of sexual offenders will relapse (i.e., commit another offense) within 9 months of treatment (Turkington, 1987a). However, coordinating efforts are under way to implement more and more successful programs throughout the United States. In the 1980s there were more than 50 such treatment programs located in 25 states and provinces across the United States and Canada (Greer & Stuart, 1983).

Although the approaches used by each of the programs may differ from organization to organization, each of them has as its primary goal the discontinuance of the illegal behavior (Greer & Stuart, 1983). This goal to stop recidivism seems to us as both a massive undertaking and somewhat inadequate. Removing the propensity to rape would be a significant success. However, those who treat rapists are also concerned with the mental health of these individuals and providing them with skills that will enhance their ability to cope with everyday occurrences.

Greer and Stuart (1983, p. 166) describe a treatment Nicholas Groth heads at Somers State Prison in Connecticut that seeks to assist each incarcerated sex offender to achieve several goals:

1. To recognize and acknowledge that he does have a problem, through an understanding of his symptoms.
2. To accept responsibility for his actions.
3. To reevaluate his attitudes and values towards sexuality and aggression.
4. To realize that sexual assaultiveness is repetitive or compulsive behavior over which he must gain control.

As can be seen, essential to this treatment is the ability of the offender to take responsibility of his behavior, and to learn that he can and must control his actions. Key treatment components of this program include reeducation, resocialization, and counseling.

Reeducation. The goals of reeducation are to provide the sex offender with information about sexuality, to give him an understanding of sexual assault, and for him to gain a more personalized understanding about the consequences of sexual assault for rape victims.

Groth notes that the majority of sex offenders he has treated are either uninformed or misinformed about basic human sexuality. As we have already discussed, many tend to have sexually conservative attitudes and values, despite their sexual experiences.

For example, Groth describes the response of one sex offender after being asked about whether consensual sex between two members of the same sex or the rape of a woman was better behavior: "Raping a woman is better [behavior]—at least that's normal" (1983, p. 169). The sex education group that Groth provides includes frank discussions about the anatomy and physiology of sex, sex and gender roles, reproduction, variations in sexual behavior, and attitudes and values.

The education group targeted to provide the sex offender with an understanding of sexual assault aims at dispelling the myths and misconceptions so many rapists believe. These men have their own stereotypical beliefs about the rapist, and often do not see themselves as fitting this stereotypical category. Consequently, another aim of this group is to get the sex offender to stop justifying his behavior through self-deceptions and rationalizations, and to come to an understanding that his behavior constitutes rape and that he is responsible for it.

Because those who rape have little understanding of how the lives of those who are sexually assaulted are affected, efforts to personalize the victim are also included in the reeducation program. Sex offenders are informed about the consequences of their actions for the victims of their assaults—in both the short term and the long term.

Resocialization. The second component of Groth's program deals with attempts to resocialize sex offenders. Those who rape are violating another individual in an interpersonal situation. Almost all sex offenders have problems with interpersonal relationships. Groth therefore emphasizes the importance of training sex offenders to cope better with interpersonal relationships and to take responsibility for the quality of these relationships. Particular attention is given to concerns and problems experienced in relating to others—to both men and women, to attitudes about their relationships, to problems in communication, and to issues related to both forming and maintaining relationships based on equality and respect.

In addition to these general interpersonal relationship skills, two other more specific issues are addressed in Groth's program. One of these issues concerns how sex offenders manage their anger and aggression. By including discussions about the mismanagement of aggression by getting involved in high-risk situations or by exploiting others, they are offered techniques of dealing with frustration and stressful situations. Sex offenders must learn that although immediate aggression may be temporarily effective, the long-term consequences can be catastrophic.

A second specific issue that is addressed with regard to interpersonal relationships concerns parenting. Groth organized the second chapter of Parents Anonymous ever to be established for sex offender inmates. This chapter operates on the self-help model, with groups focusing on better recognizing and then responding appropriately to the needs of children.

Counseling. The third component of Groth's program deals specifically with counseling the sex offender. This component includes group therapy, personal victimization, and combating sexual assault. Group therapy focuses on the sexually assaultive behavior of the offender. Attention is given to the offense itself and the psychological factors that accompany the offense, including the precipitating factors and feelings along with their accompanying fantasies and feelings. In this way, the sex offender can better identify those factors, situations, or feelings that precede his sexual aggression. Identification of these components is essential before inhibitory or avoidance actions can be taken.

The sex offender is also expected to address his own issues of personal victimization. Recall in Chapter 2 that the majority of imprisoned sex offenders whom Groth has interviewed and worked with have themselves been abused as children: both sexual and physical abuse are common, as well as neglect, exploitation, or abandonment. The sex offender must address these early developmental years, which often reflects an unresolved conflict, and learn to deal with the abuse. To confront the trauma and come to an understanding of how these experiences have affected the different facets of his life can help the rapist not only to come to a better understanding of himself and his behavior, but can help him to reestablish his own control over his life.

Finally, a third element of the counseling process involves the sex offender becoming actively involved in combating sexual assault. Taking some responsibility for the safety of his community not only constitutes partial restitution for the damage that he has done in the past, but can also enhance the sex offender's self-esteem and sense of worth. This process involves meetings with persons from the community who deal with sexual assault, in which sex offenders may provide their own insights about sexual assault.

In addition to these three primary components of Groth's program, which utilize group sessions to a large extent, Groth advises that other additional treatment components may be necessary. For example, some offenders may be better suited—at least initially—to individual sessions. Biofeedback is encouraged as a way to help the sex offender learn how to reduce stress. Sex offenders can be encouraged to write their autobiography privately; such activities can be important for the offender in causing him to both reflect and come to a better understanding of his own life, as well as instill

UNIVERSITY OF WINCHESTER
LIBRARY

the need for him to work regularly on his own rehabilitation. Finally, role-playing, the use of demonstrations, and video feedback are also useful treatment procedures.

How successful is this particular program? Groth notes that in the second year of the program, the involvement rate of the incarcerated sex offenders jumped from 14% to 28%. In addition, of those who had participated in the program and were later released, 19% had later either violated parole or been rearrested. This percentage is lower than the 36% who had either violated their parole or been rearrested but had not been in the treatment program and were released. We believe that given the fact that this program has no operating budget and only two paid staff, Groth's work is to be highly commended and shows promise. Certainly, however, these statistics could improve. This program is also not the only one utilized by therapists treating sexually aggressive persons. Recently, a program known as Relapse Prevention has been showing great promise as a complementary program with other types of therapy. It is an especially valuable approach because incarcerated rapists often show good progress during confinement but after they are released, the stresses of the outside world contribute to their committing further rapes (Eisenman, 1991).

Relapse Prevention was first developed by Alan Marlatt, an alcoholism researcher, for individuals with addictive disorders. It is now believed by most researchers that there are commonalities underlying both the behavioral and cognitive components associated with relapse, regardless of the type of addiction (Turkington, 1987a). This assumption led psychologist William Pithers and his colleagues (Pithers, Marques, Gibat, & Marlatt, 1983) to develop a modified version of Marlatt's Relapse Prevention for use with sexual offenders.

The Relapse Prevention program is a cognitive-behavioral program of assessment and treatment designed to strengthen the maintenance of changes prompted by other therapies—to help the offender maintain control of his behavior over time and across different situations. Too many offenders may believe that once their therapy is over, they are "cured." Such is not the case and offenders must realize that at some point in the future the same feelings (e.g, moodiness or brooding) or deviant fantasies that preceded their past assault may occur again.

At the heart of the offender's ability to maintain control over his actions is the ability of the offender to recognize the preceding feelings, fantasies, situations, or actions that could ultimately lead the offender to relapse. He is taught to consider such feelings or fantasies—called lapses—as learning opportunities instead of failures. Relapse, then, can be avoided if the offender can learn to expect and detect such precursors, to spot risky situations, and to avoid or cope with them. For example, a "former rapist, still angry over an argument, may face such a situation while driving by a woman who is hitchhiking. In relapse prevention, men are trained to deal with such moments without progressing through the cycle that led to the crime" (Goleman, 1992, p. B8). Pithers believes that the men who are the most successful candidates for treatment are those "who have no other criminal record, have an established network of family and friends, hold a job and who are not so preoccupied with sex fantasies that they think of them hours a day" (Goleman, 1992, p. B8). In one evaluation of this approach, California sex offenders who completed this type of program were matched with comparable sex offenders in regard to their age, background, and type of crimes. Of the 26 rapists in the program, only one was rearrested for rape within 3 years of his release from prison; in contrast, of 26 in the control group, 7 were rearrested for rape during this period (Goleman, 1992).

Pithers believes that relapses should not necessarily be blamed on ineffective treatment. Rather, he identifies ineffective goals as a culprit, noting that even therapists experienced with sexual offenders may have doubts about whether sex offenders are curable because of the likely recurrences of preceding fantasies (Turkington, 1987a). Such doubt could serve as a prophetic factor and actually decrease chances of success before the program begins.

What About Chemical Treatment?

In recent years the use of an experimental drug called Depo-Provera to treat sex offenders has been receiving widespread attention. Depo-Provera (medroxyprogesterone acetate) is a female hormone (antiandrogen) that reportedly lowers the sex drive in males by reducing their level of serum testosterone. Some convicted rapists have, in fact, been offered freedom from imprisonment if they agree to undergo the once-a-week injections of Depo-Provera. In 1983, Joseph Frank Smith, 30, of San Antonio, TX, became the first convicted rapist actually to receive such injections as a condition of his 10-year probation.

In response to such options, both feminists, on the one side, and defense attorneys, on the other, have raised a number of questions and criticisms of this procedure. Its effectiveness has yet to be fully assessed, even though one of its advocates, Dr. Fred Berlin of Johns Hopkins Hospital in Baltimore, claims an 85% success rate in reducing sex drive in more than 100 men who have received it since the experimental program began in 1979 (Thompson, 1984). In addition, its effects are immediate, its administration is simple, and it is a reversible procedure (Groth, 1979). At least 50 men are currently being treated with Depo-Provera; they report that they feel better and are less sexually aggressive.

But the drug has side effects, including gaining up to 30 pounds, fatigue, loss of hair, itching, backache, and symptoms like those of menopause. Furthermore, men receiving Depo-Provera need to come in for weekly injections.

Most important, critics raise the question of the appropriateness of this drug for treatment of what are seen as violent acts rather than sexual ones. Even if Depo-Provera inhibits sexual appetites, it may not control violent outbursts (Thompson, 1984). Hence it does not truly rehabilitate. But as Susan Estrich, a law school professor, has said, "There is a sense that judges continue to view rape in some large respects as different from other crimes. They have to deal with the fact it is not crime of sexual desire but brutal violence of the worst sort short of murder" (Goodman, 1983). Not even judges are immune to misunderstanding the crime of rape.

Ironically, the great-grandson of the founder of the Upjohn Company, the distributor of Depo-Provera, is one of the sexual abusers ordered to take the drug. Roger A. Gauntlett, age 41 at the time of his sentencing, pleaded no contest to a charge of sexually abusing his 14-year-old stepdaughter (Standish, 1984).

Summary

The treatment of both victims of rape and of rapists is an extremely important issue of concern. Without proper treatment, the consequences can be devastating. Both friends and family members of the victim, as well as professional personnel, have the power to either aid or inhibit both the short-term and the long-term recovery of the victim. It is important that the victim receive compassionate and nonjudgmental care.

The development of successful programs that can reduce or even end recidivism among rapists is also extremely important, yet still in its early stages. To date, there is no single method or program of treatment that has been found to be totally effective, and more research is needed to determine the utility of the programs that have been developed (Groth, 1979). This research is extremely important, however, to the future of sexual violence in our society. At the very least, it places the responsibility for change in the hands of those who rape, where it belongs.

Note

1. We suggest that the reader review Karen S. Calhoun & Beverly M. Atkeson's book, *Treatment of Rape Victims: Facilitating Psychosocial Adjustment* (Pergamon Press, 1991), for a clear and thorough review of the long-term treatment possibilities for victims of rape.

12 Preventing Rape

A woman from Edinburgh, Scotland, tells an interviewer:

> Over the years, my awareness of the possibility of rape has dawned
> on me so much that I'm a lot more fearful of going out at night on my
> own. Sometimes, I won't even go out in the day if I know its [sic] an
> isolated place. It seems crazy that it's only dawned on me now and
> not in my teens or early twenties. I haven't been raped, but now I live
> in fear, and it drains me to even think about it. The realization that it
> can happen almost anywhere is crucifying. In the past, I've hitched
> alone, lived alone in quiet places, and gone to isolated places alone.
> Now I do none of these things. I feel my sense of freedom to be
> crushed, while men do not experience this fear. Their allowance of
> freedom sickens me. (Dowdeswell, 1986, p. 51)

How does one avoid being raped? Is the above strategy the only
solution? Certainly these are important questions for both the
public and researchers to ask. Unlike the questions, which seem so
straightforward and simple, there is no one simple answer. Many
aspects are involved and must be considered, and even after such
review, any answer must come in qualified form. For example,
when someone asks, "How can I avoid being raped?" is she asking
how to avoid being attacked, or how to avoid being raped, once an
attack begins?

242

"Preventing" rape is a broad umbrella, and—as Koss and Harvey (1991) observe—the aims of specific rape prevention strategies can include any number of diverse goals, including the following:

1. to eliminate the act of rape by scrutinizing those beliefs, values, and myths of our society that perpetuate and condone sexual assault;
2. to deter attempted rapes by educating potential victims about avoiding risks and defending themselves;
3. to attempt to reduce the trauma of rape by appropriate responses to the needs of victims; and
4. to prevent recurrence of rapes by incarceration and/or treatment of offenders. (Koss & Harvey, 1991)

Previous chapters have assessed the last two of the goals. The purpose of this chapter is to examine approaches that seek to achieve the first two of these goals.

Research motivated to answer potential victims' questions has been multifaceted in an effort to reflect the importance of many determinants in preventing rape. This chapter will be organized around three approaches: the individual's response in preventing rape, the role of the situation, and society's place in the instigation and discouragement of rape. Although each of these is discussed separately, in real life these aspects cannot be disentangled.

The individualistic approach to avoiding rape examines aspects of the potential rape victim, including what she or he may do in order to secure personal safety. Research that has used this level of analysis has, as an example, looked at personal factors of rape victims and the behaviors that potential rape victims could employ to avoid rape. This approach, on occasion, places the responsibility for avoiding victimization solely on the potential victim, and therefore runs the risk of creating an environment conducive to blaming the victim. For some, the following is a logical development: if there are actions one can take to avoid being raped, then if one *is* raped, one is responsible. It is therefore extremely important to remember that often one only knows in hindsight whether a particular response was successful. And a successful response used by one individual may prove to be futile for another.

In considering the prevention of sexual assault, Koss and Harvey (1991) distinguish between a medical model and a public health model. The individualistic approach is more congruent with the medical model, in that its primary concern is with individual patients and the application of diagnostic and treatment skills to them.

In contrast, the situational approach to avoiding rape focuses on identifying situations that may place individuals at a higher risk of being raped. For example, is rape more likely to be avoided when an attack takes place in the open, as opposed to an attack within the confines of four walls? Does alcohol play a role in the risk of rape? Certain situations place an individual at a higher risk of being raped. Like the individual approach, however, the fact that there are identifiable situations that may be more "rape-prone" does not mean that if an individual is raped in this particular situation, the victim somehow deserved to be raped because of being in the situation.

Finally, the third conceptual approach to avoiding rape treats rape as a societal problem that can be effectively treated only by community awareness and involvement. This approach considers rape as a human issue, rather than just a women's issue or a men's issue. The Central Park "wilding" incident in Manhattan and the gang rape in New Bedford, MA, make us aware that rape is a community concern. The goals of this approach include educating society in an attempt to nullify the existence of rape myths, as well as altering the imbalanced power structure between men and women. To use Koss and Harvey's (1991) analogy, this approach emulates a public health model in that it seeks "to eliminate the environmental conditions that promote disease and to inoculate all or all at-risk members of the population against disease" (p. 250).

The Individualistic Approach

As stated earlier, the individualistic approach to avoiding rape seeks to identify strategies that particular persons may employ to reduce their chances of being a victim. To identify one universally successful strategy for avoiding rape is an impossible task. Marcia Morgan (1986) conducted an extensive review of 50 books, articles, and pamphlets written during the past 15 years by experts; she concluded that "the most striking feature of rape prevention and self-defense advice is the lack of agreement among the experts . . . as a group they provide few clear messages about what to do" (p. 160). These 50 publications generated more than 400 different prevention and self-defense strategies. Among these, not only was there *confusing* advice, but often *conflicting* advice concerning what women, as individuals, can do to prevent being raped. Box 12.1 provides examples of the inconsistent messages given to the layperson.

The Traditional Approach

Interestingly, the type of advice that was given depended on the type of approach advocated by the specific experts (Morgan, 1986). In the *traditional* approach, the responsibility for avoiding rape is placed solely on the woman. Experts who adhere to this approach emphasize that women should restrict their behavior—and therefore reduce their freedom and independence—in order to secure their own protection. Koss and Harvey (1991) call it a *deficit-oriented approach* to rape prevention. Golda Meir, former prime minister of Israel, tells the story of the time when rape and sexual assault increased and the government leaders sought a solution to the problem. Their solution: to establish a curfew—for women! (Meir asked: Why not a curfew for men?) This approach thus identifies "good" (day) and "bad" (night) times for a woman to be out alone. Women are advised not to hitchhike, or go on blind dates, or invite men into their homes, or wear short dresses or skirts. An example of this approach is given by Frederic Storaska (1975), whose book has the catchy title, "How to Say No to a Rapist and Survive." He advised women faced with the imminent possibility of sexual assault to avoid angering or upsetting their potential assailant unless they were certain the perpetrator intended to kill them or they knew they could incapacitate him and flee. The message to remain passive in the face of attack was for a time popular among police and law-enforcement agencies but it has been severely criticized by researchers and rape crisis center activists. In 1983 the National Coalition Against Sexual Assault condemned Storaska's advice (Koss & Harvey, 1991). To restrict women's behavior so drastically that they are essentially "prisoners in their own home" may be an effective (but not foolproof) rape deterrent, but the consequences are not healthy for women. Critics argue that the traditional view is necessarily oppressive, renders women powerless, and therefore serves to increase the differential power structure between men and women. Furthermore, such advice builds fear and encourages women to see themselves as helpless (Koss & Harvey, 1991); all these make for a situation more conducive to rape.

BOX 12.1

The Experts:
Not of One Mind on Prevention

It is no wonder that women are confused about how to respond to an attacker, given the abundance of conflicting advice from the experts that can be found. The following are just a few examples of the conflicting advice that Morgan found. The advice reflects the empowered individual approach, and the traditional approach, respectively.

1. Make direct eye contact with strangers or suspicious people (so you look strong and confident and not easily frightened or manipulated) vs. do not look strangers in the eye (they might misinterpret your intentions).
2. Fight immediately vs. exhaust less violent resources first.
3. Scream (so others will hear you and it will scare him off) vs. do not scream (he will hurt you more or kill you).
4. Do not be passive (if he is going to hurt/kill you, being passive does not make any difference) vs. be passive, go along with him sexually (this will turn him off or at least not antagonize him further).
5. Joke and be sarcastic (show the attacker you are not an easy person to control) vs. do not antagonize the attacker, do not put him down or hurt his ego.
6. Do not cry or appear weak (so you do not look like an easy target) vs. cry (appeal to his sympathy).
7. Harass the rapist, become angry with the audacity of him to treat you in such an animalistic way vs. treat the rapist as a human being.

SOURCE: Morgan, 1986.

The effects of such advice are often subtle. For example, a provocative review by White and Farmer (1992) notes how use of particular research methodologies can lead to distorted views of sexual assault. The traditional approach, by leaving situational and societal factors unexplored, implies that they are unimportant.

The Empowered Individual Approach

A more moderate approach, the *empowered individual* approach, still recognizes a woman's responsibility for avoiding rape, but argues that this should be done by *increasing* women's power, not by curtailing it. Instead of setting limits on what women should do, this approach proposes that women should have the same freedoms as men to live their lives as they wish. The empowered individual approach advises women to be constantly aware of their surroundings, not afraid of them. If a woman does find herself confronted by an attacker, she is advised to defend herself aggressively and not give in to her attacker. Although this approach restores the freedom and power to women in society, critics argue that it is not realistic for those women who are not psychologically or physically able to overcome an attacker (Morgan, 1986).

Such inconsistent advice from the experts may result in real confusion in the minds of women about what to do if they are attacked. Indeed, one study (Fischhoff & Furby, 1987) has found that the average woman generated only nine different strategies, with many women overlooking strategies that were very high on other women's lists of possibilities. Box 12.2 reflects a sample of the possibilities and how they were produced.

Empirical Assessments of Strategies by Potential Victims

Unfortunately, many of those who give advice to women about how to avoid rape do not offer evidence that their strategies will work (Morgan, 1986). Indeed, much of it is based on biased perceptions and experiences. A handful of studies exist, however, that have empirically investigated the effectiveness of various self-protection strategies. These studies are valuable because they include women who actually have been attacked. Some of these women were successful in avoiding; some were not. These studies, therefore, help to shed light on which of the strategies have actually succeeded.

Each of the studies that have included women who were actually attacked found that action was more successful than inaction. Sanders (1980) surveyed 481 women in Southern California (of

(text continued on page 250)

BOX 12.2

Strategies for Response

The decision about how to respond to an attack is a very personal one. And no one can second guess the final decision that any individual makes. What seems to be very important is that women think about what they would do if they were confronted with an attack (Bart & O'Brien, 1985). Of course this necessarily means that a woman must acknowledge the possibility that she could be attacked—an event that many do not wish to acknowledge. However, to think about how one would respond offers one a kind of cognitive preparation that may prove very useful in the long run. According to Fischhoff and Furby (1987), for a woman to choose the best strategy for her personal situation, she should do the following things:

1. Identify strategies that she could use for self-defense.
2. Identify the consequences that might follow from using these strategies.
3. Estimate the probability of each consequence actually occurring.
4. Decide what to do, in a way that reflects how much she cares about each consequence and how likely she thinks it is.

The approach used here is unique because it considers not only the possible ways to respond, but what the consequences of particular responses may be. To be sure, a woman who is primarily concerned with saving her life may respond quite differently from one who is determined to avoid being raped. The following is a sample—only 33 of a total of 268 possibilities produced—of the rape self-defense strategies collected by Fischhoff and Furby. Note that the particular strategy chosen depends on its perceived consequences or intended effect.

1. Manage yourself in ways that maximize agility to implement self-defense measures successfully.
    A. Control own thoughts/emotions/actions
        (1) know/believe that you do not have to be a rape victim
        (2) do not faint or pass out

    B. Assess the situation
       (1) Evaluate rapist
          (a) consider attacker's strength
          (b) assess attacker's personality
       (2) Evaluate surroundings
          (a) mentally assess the situation for alternatives
    C. Wait/stall/use guile until good self-defense opportunity
       (1) go along until you can safely react
       (2) use something as a distraction, then react
2. Reduce/minimize assailant's propensity to rape.
    A. Avoid antagonizing assailant
       (1) do not fight back
       (2) pretend you are asleep
    B. Don't miscommunicate intentions
       (1) state clearly you like him as a person but do not want a
          physical relationship
    C. create bizarre/unattractive impression
       (1) feign a seizure
       (2) do crude, unfeminine things
    D. Appeal to assailant's sympathy, morals
       (1) plead or beg
       (2) make him see you as human
    E. Reason with assailant
       (1) tell attacker your friendship might be ruined
       (2) talk your way out of the situation
3. Increase perceived ability to cope with assailant.
    A. assume a karate stance
    B. make it known you have a weapon
    C. give clear verbal resistance
4. Increase perceived chances of outside intervention.
    A. fake arrival of others
5. Increase actual chances of outside intervention.
    A. General appeal (to anyone who might be aware of it)
       (1) yell "fire"
       (2) use whistle
    B. Directed appeal (to specific individuals)
       (1) call the police
       (2) summon nearest male

(Continued)

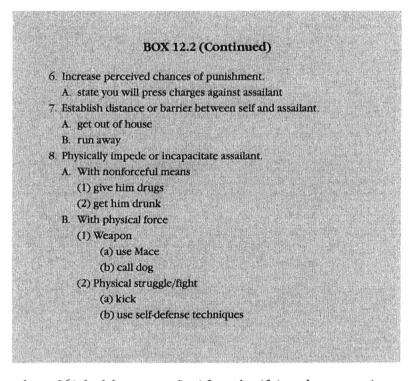

BOX 12.2 (Continued)

6. Increase perceived chances of punishment.
   A. state you will press charges against assailant
7. Establish distance or barrier between self and assailant.
   A. get out of house
   B. run away
8. Physically impede or incapacitate assailant.
   A. With nonforceful means
      (1) give him drugs
      (2) get him drunk
   B. With physical force
      (1) Weapon
         (a) use Mace
         (b) call dog
      (2) Physical struggle/fight
         (a) kick
         (b) use self-defense techniques

whom 261 had been raped). After classifying the women's responses to assault into categories, he concluded that just about any form of resistance had some degree of effectiveness. In this survey, the women who did nothing were more likely to be raped.

Another study, the Queens Bench Foundation study (1975), included 108 women (of whom 68 had been raped and 40 had successfully resisted). The researchers found that women who avoided rape were more likely to use more types of resistance measures, to respond both physically and verbally, to be more suspicious and hostile, and to resist immediately.

McIntyre (1980) also found that women who were aggressive—and aggressive early—were more effective in avoiding rape. Hesitation, in this study, was associated with the likelihood that the rape would be completed. Block and Skogan (1982), investigating 550 stranger rapes, also found that women who responded by physically attacking in return were less likely to be raped, whereas those who were less forceful (defined here as reasoning, verbally threatening, yelling for help, or running away) were more likely to be raped.

Finally, Bart and O'Brien (1985) found that the more active the strategies used by women, the more likely they were to avoid rape. In fact, the more different strategies that a woman used in addition to physical force, the more likely she was to avoid rape. They state: "We know that advice about how to behave when attacked, advice telling women to act in traditionally feminine ways, is wrong." (p. 1), and conclude that their best advice to avoiding rape is: "Don't be a nice girl."

We have, then, five different studies that have empirically investigated the success of various response strategies to attack. Each of these studies points to the same conclusion: Doing something is better than doing nothing. Whether the attacker is a complete stranger or an acquaintance, active response strategies are positively associated with rape avoidance (Levine-MacCombie & Koss, 1986). Furthermore, immediate physical responses seem to be an especially important deterrent to rape. Not only is this in direct conflict with much of the traditional advice offered to women, it is in direct conflict with much of the advice that police departments currently offer. Tacie Dejanikus (1981), after interviewing police rape prevention units in six areas of the United States, found that almost all of the departments encouraged women to use passive resistance before or instead of active resistance. Rape avoidance programs are, however, beginning to teach women how to respond aggressively in attack situations (see Box 12.3 for an example).

Despite the fact that the research clearly shows a relationship between physical resistance and rape avoidance, a note of caution is warranted. Although physical and active strategies have certainly been found to be more successful than passive strategies, it must be emphasized again that there is no magical formula for avoiding rape. There have been, and will continue to be, women who fight vehemently and still get raped. The fact that a relationship exists between action and rape avoidance does not mean that physical action *causes* rape avoidance. There are too many other factors involved to make such a confident statement. A rapist who is absolutely determined to rape will probably succeed. And a woman who is only concerned with surviving the event may decide to choose other responses. As stated earlier, it depends on what effect one wishes to produce as to what particular responses will be chosen (Furby & Fischhoff, 1987). Situational factors, which will be discussed later, have also been found to play a role. After a thoughtful review, Koss and Harvey (1991) conclude that "the data do not

---

BOX 12.3

Model Mugging

Model Mugging is a nationwide program designed to teach
women self-defense techniques. Since it began in 1973, more
than 6,000 women from ages 11 to 73, from all walks of life and
physical capabilities, have taken the Model Mugging course.
This program is unique because it emphasizes the practice of
full-force resistance techniques using simulated attack scenarios. Because rape victims invariably end up on the ground,
women are taught to fight from the ground. Also emphasized is
personal growth and the empowerment of women. Similar
courses exist at the local level, including Alternatives to Fear, a
self-defense, feminist karate program in Seattle, WA, and Illusion Theater, housed in Minneapolis, that focuses on sexual
assault of children.

---

warrant a recommendation that all women in all circumstances
attempt active resistance" (p. 260).

The above discussion emphasized a *behavioral* approach to individual rape prevention. An important psychological component
must also be considered. Several studies have examined characteristic differences between women who have been attacked and
raped, and women who were attacked but successfully avoided
rape. Although such intrapsychic variables are not the determining
factors of whether an individual will avoid rape or not, they have
sometimes been found to play a role. For example, Selkin (1978)
examined personality differences between rape victims and rape
avoiders and found that women who successfully avoided being
raped scored higher on the dominance, Social Presence, Sociability,
and Communality scales of the California Psychological Inventory,
compared to women who were raped. Myers, Templer, and Brown
(1984) report similar findings, but a study with broadened methodology and sampling by Koss (1985) did not find that personality
characteristics distinguished between victims and nonvictims.

Background variables related to independence have also been found to predict successful avoidance by females who were attacked (Bart, 1981). And it appears that childhood experiences as well as adult experiences may play an indirect role in one's ability to avoid rape.

In another study on this issue, Bart and O'Brien (1985) found that individuals with parents who advised them to fight back as children, who encouraged them to play football, and who encouraged nontraditional future images were more likely to avoid rape than those who had parents who punished their physical aggressions, discouraged them from fighting back, and emphasized the traditional expectations of future life (e.g., marriage, children, and domesticity). As adults, women who knew first aid and self-defense, engaged in sports regularly, were larger in size, and were in control of their emotions—particularly anger—were more likely to avoid rape. In addition, recent research had found a relationship between childhood sexual abuse and sexual victimization in adulthood (Koss & Dinero, 1989; Miller et al., 1978; Murphy, 1987; Russell, 1986). For example, childhood victims may be more likely to experience depression, very low self-esteem, feelings of isolation, interpersonal problems, and substance abuse (Browne & Finkelhor, 1986). These factors may serve to increase a person's vulnerability to abuse in adulthood (Browne & Finkelhor, 1986; Harney & Muehlenhard, 1989).

As noted earlier, it is important for women cognitively to prepare themselves for the possibility of being attacked, and to think about how they would respond. One study that actually asked about women's expectations of submitting to sexual intercourse under various circumstances, found that some women do indeed report that under certain circumstances where force or the threat of force is present, they would be at least somewhat likely to submit (Allison & Branscombe, 1992). In this study, 42% of females asked indicated at least some likelihood that they would have sex under threat of force. This research showed that as unique predictors, these women were less likely to date frequently and reported less self-esteem in both their general abilities and their public selves. When these two predictors were combined with other theoretically relevant variables for statistical analysis, it was found that dating frequency and aspects of self-esteem *in combination* with the intensity of general affect experienced, Machiavellianism, anger, and age successfully

discriminated between those women who acknowledged a willingness to submit from those who did not.

The Situational Approach

The situational approach to avoiding rape focuses on those social
or environmental conditions that may increase the possibility for an
individual to commit rape, and hence for other persons to be
potential rape victims. As Koss and Harvey observe: "It is likely that
situational factors beyond the victim's control (e.g., locale, lighting,
nearness of others) have much to do with the success or failure of
any rape-avoidance strategy she might employ" (1991, p. 258).
Given that college campuses are environments in which rape occurs, prevention strategies based upon the situational approach
include increased lighting on campus walkways and the development of skills workshops for university staff.

Both psychological and practical explanations may explain why
the very dating behaviors that are considered appropriate in our
society are conducive to rape. Psychologically, a man might feel
entitled to sex if he spends his time and money on his date. Or he
may believe that if a woman allows her date to pay for her expenses
that this indicates a willingness to have sex (Muehlenhard & Linton,
1987; see also Chapter 4). On a practical level, allowing the man to
initiate the date, which may involve deciding where the couple may
go (location, you will see, is also important to victimization likelihood), or to drive on the date may render a women powerless to
leave a situation that may be dangerous.

Research has shown that rapes are more likely to take place in
particular locations than others. In the case of date rape, assaults
are more likely to occur in areas that are either enclosed or isolated
and therefore serve to reduce the possibility of escape (Amick &
Calhoun, 1987; Harney & Muehlenhard, 1990; Muehlenhard &
Linton, 1987). Rape attempts are more likely to occur, in fact,
indoors than outdoors (Bart & O'Brien, 1985). In addition, Bart and
O'Brien (1985, p. 108) have identified several factors that were
positively associated with being raped:

1. The time of the attack was between midnight and 6:00 a.m.
2. Another crime in addition to the sexual assault was committed or
   attempted (e.g., robbery).

3. The rape attack was a sudden, intense "blitz" rather than part of a more elaborate "con," and the rapist used force (including a weapon) to obtain compliance.
4. The rapist choked the victim (this was coded separately from the degree of force or beating).
5. No observer was present.
6. The woman lived alone.
7. The woman lived on the first floor.
8. The assault took place inside rather than outside.

If one combines all of these factors, a general picture emerges of a premeditated attack. As stated earlier, if a rapist is determined to rape and takes action that may preclude a woman from escaping, then the rapist is likely to be successful.

Another important factor that seems both to promote the assaultive actions of a rapist and to inhibit a victim's ability to resist is the use of alcohol. In one study whose sample consisted of more than 6,000 men and women in higher education settings, it was found that about 75% of the men were under the influence of alcohol when they assaulted their acquaintances. In addition, of the acquaintance rape victims in this study, about 55% of the women reported having drunk alcohol before the incident took place (Warshaw, 1988). The high prevalence rate of alcohol in rape situations has also been found by others (Amir, 1971; Koss & Dinero, 1989; Rada, 1975; Russell, 1984). Clearly, alcohol use serves to increase the chances that a rape will occur.

The Societal Approach

Chapter 1 argued that the United States *might* be considered a rape-prone society. Traditional attitudes and values, as well as the alarming amount of violence in general, and sexual violence specifically, all point to this conclusion. To be considered a potentially rape-prone society, however, does not mean that this must be a permanent status. To address the problem of rape on a societal level, one must examine the power differential between women and men, the attitudes traditionally held in society that perpetuate the myths about rape, and the education programs that have recently begun.

Until recently, little attention has been given to the societal approach, partly because it is difficult to demonstrate the effects of such factors on behavior (George, Winfield, & Blazer, 1992). But in the last few years, more systematic analyses have emerged. For example, Burkhart and Fromuth (1991) have identified three specific societal mechanisms that affect rape incidence and hence inhibit its prevention:

1. gender role socialization patterns and power differentials that normalize rape by advancing rape-supportive beliefs
2. sexually coercive cognitive schemata and beliefs that encourage the tendency to blame the victim, and reduce society's capacity to empathize, and
3. social-sexual interaction scripts that prescribe norms about courtship.

According to Doyle (1983), no evidence has been produced that a truly egalitarian society exists—one in which men and women are considered equal. And there is not, nor has there ever been, a matriarchal society, where women controlled the resources of society (Tavris & Wade, 1984). Hence, the only possibility for true equality between the sexes—and the removal of the differential power structure—rests in its potential in the future. Because research suggests that ascribing more power to males in society increases the risk of rape for women (Sanday, 1981), removing such barriers to power for women should decrease such a risk. It is up to society—and those who hold positions of power—to take responsibility for removing such barriers.

Some progress has been made on this area. Fraternities, for example, are beginning to respond to the problem of gang rape, which has been found to occur all too often on college campuses—especially in fraternities (Ehrhart & Sandler, 1985).

The Supreme Court, in *New York State Club Association, Inc. v. City of New York* (1988), recently ruled unanimously that a city may bar sex and race discrimination in large clubs where members make important business and professional contacts. And some large corporations, such as IBM, are increasing their employee benefit options that allow up to 3 years of unpaid leave for such purposes as caring for a new baby, sick child, or elderly relative, without the threat of losing one's employment status.

Some have suggested that the power differential between women and men in nearly all societies, which has been documented for centuries, created sex-role stereotypes as a justification for treating women differently (Tavris & Wade, 1984). As long as traditional sex-role stereotypes and attitudes remain, so probably will rape. We documented in earlier chapters the large role that attitudes may play in both the likelihood to rape and the condoning of aggression between the sexes. Social change takes time, and such beliefs or behaviors are not expected to change overnight. Indeed—such efforts to change began with the women's movement in the early 1970s. We believe that stronger acceptance of truly egalitarian values is not an impossible goal and would lead to less sexual violence committed against women.

White and Sorenson (1992) describe how pervasive sex-role stereotypes have even influenced the study of rape itself. Until the advent of the women's movement, research on rape was primarily done by male investigators from a clinical perspective rather than one reflecting an awareness of societal forces (see Chapter 2). The emphasis was on the diagnosis of rapists; as White and Sorenson note, the experiences of victims were almost irrelevant in the early stage. More recently, the emphasis has shifted to the experiences of women and victims, as exemplified by the chapters in the last half of this book.

But as we have noted earlier, this more recent focus runs the risk of perpetuating concepts of victim blame. White and Sorenson (1992, p. 190) urge that research focus on the context of sexual assault; that is, greater analysis of societal contributions to the prevention of rape.

All of these changes must be made through education and awareness in order ultimately to prevent rape. Linz, Wilson, and Donnerstein (1992), for example, call for educational interventions specifically designed to change beliefs about rape and sexual violence. Some of this is going on—in the media, in popular magazines, and through the efforts of crisis centers and schools.

Koss and Harvey (1991) distinguish between two types of societal response. Approaches that employ *environmental action* include community education programs, "Take Back the Night" marches, and school-based or university-based awareness programs (see Box 12.4). Approaches focusing on *citizen inoculation* seek to develop both self-defense competencies in those at risk and values and beliefs incompatible with rape in others. It is too early to establish the effectiveness of such initiatives but at the very least they should reduce the status of rape as a misunderstood crime.

BOX 12.4

What Can Colleges and Universities Do
to Prevent Rape?

In two recent book chapters Andrea Parrot (1991a, 1991b) has detailed some policies and procedures that college and university administrators can follow to prevent acquaintance rape on campus. These include:

1. Acknowledge that sexual assaults occur on campus and then develop policies that define such acts, condemn them, and specify how they will be punished. Be explicit that such rules apply to visitors to the campus, as well as to students, faculty, and staff.

2. Disseminate information about the policies in a variety of ways (not only through newspapers, pamphlets, and posters but also through films, a speaker's bureau, and campus radio broadcasts).

3. Recognize that alcohol consumption is usually linked with campus rapes and develop college-sponsored nonalcoholic activities. Parrot (1991b) proposes that enforcing alcohol prohibition on campus "is crucial to reducing the incidence of acquaintance rape" (p. 371).

4. Train faculty and staff to know what behaviors constitute acquaintance rape and to respond appropriately when it occurs. Provide victim support but do not pressure a victim to pursue a particular course of action.

5. Develop educational programs addressed to men as well as to women. Because a disproportionate number of campus gang rapes and acquaintance rapes are committed by members of fraternities or by athletes, these groups of men should be involved in the planning and implementation of educational interventions (Parrot, 1991a, p. 361).

Summary

There is no easy solution to preventing rape. The experts are unclear about the "best" strategy to use to prevent rape because there is no best strategy. However, research that has studied victims who have been attacked have found that those who used more active strategies were generally more likely to avoid being raped.

Still, this does not solve the problem of preventing the possibility of attack. To do that requires focusing our attention not on potential victims, but on the situations that create vulnerabilities for rape, on potential rapists, and on society in general.

General Conclusions

Ultimately, if we as a society are going to prevent rape, we have to understand it. Even though it is possible to come to an understanding of rape, we do not see that rape is justifiable. Rape is a crime, it is an act of violence, and its consequences are dramatic. To attempt to prevent rape by focusing on the behavior of the victim serves to perpetuate the myths and misconceptions about rape that we have discussed throughout this book. Ultimately, we need to hold all individuals responsible for their own behavior. It must be recognized that rape is a behavior for which rapists must be held accountable. Society as a whole must recognize that all violence, including rape, is unacceptable behavior.

References

Abbey, A. (1982). Sex differences in attributions for friendly behavior: Do males misperceive females' friendliness? *Journal of Personality and Social Psychology, 42,* 830-838.

Abbey, A. (1987). Misperceptions of friendly behavior as sexual interest: A survey of naturally occurring incidents. *Psychology of Women Quarterly, 11,* 173-194.

Abbey, A. (1991). Misperception as an antecedent of acquaintance rape: A consequence of ambiguity in communication between women and men. In A. Parrot & L. Bechhofer (Eds.), *Acquaintance rape: The hidden crime* (pp. 96-111). New York: John Wiley.

Abbey, A., Cozzarelli, C., McLaughlin, K., & Harnish, R. J. (1987). The effects of clothing and dyad sex composition on perceptions of sexual intent: Do women and men evaluate these cues differently? *Journal of Applied Social Psychology, 17,* 108-126.

Abel, G. G., Blanchard, E. B., & Becker, J. V. (1978). An integrated treatment program for rapists. In R. T. Rada (Ed.), *Clinical aspects of the rapist* (pp. 161-214). New York: Grune & Stratton.

Acock, A. C., & Ireland, N. K. (1983). Attribution of blame in rape cases: The impact of norm violation, gender, and sex-role attitudes. *Sex Roles: A Journal of Research, 9,* 179-193.

Adorno, T., Frenkel-Brunswik, E., Levinson, D. J., & Sanford, N. (1950). *The authoritarian personality.* New York: Harper & Row.

Albin, R. (1977). Psychological studies of rape. *Signs: Journal of Women in Culture and Society, 3,* 423-435.

Allison, J. A., & Branscombe, N. R. (1992). *The influence of affective and general personality factors on the likelihood of sexual aggression.* Unpublished manuscript, Pittsburg State University, Pittsburg, KS.

Allison, J. A., Adams, D. L., Bunce, L. W., Gilkerson, T., & Nelson, K. (1992, November). *The rapist: Aggressive, dangerous, power hungry, and manipulative.* Paper presented at the annual meeting of Psychological and Educational Research, Emporia, KS.

Allport, G. W. (1935). Attitudes. In C. M. Murchison (Ed.), *Handbook of social psychology* (pp. 798-844). Worcester, MA: Clark University Press.

American Psychiatric Association (APA). (1987). *Diagnostic and statistical manual of mental disorders* (3rd ed.). Washington, DC: Author.

Amick, A., & Calhoun, K. (1989). Resistance to sexual aggression: Personality, attitudinal, and situational factors. *Archives of Sexual Behavior, 19,* 153-163.

Amir, M. (1971). *Patterns in forcible rape.* Chicago: University of Chicago Press.

Associated Press. (1990, January 14). South Dakota astir over rape case. *Kansas City Star,* p. A-12.

Associated Press. (1991, January 14). Rape attempts drop 46% over 14 years. *Kansas City Star,* p. A-3.

Associated Press. (1992a, March 5). Illinois boy is found guilty of rape committed at age 7. *The New York Times,* p. A8.

Associated Press. (1992b, April 24). National rape statistics released. *Lawrence Journal-World,* p. 10B.

Attorney General's Commission on Pornography: Final Report. (1986). Vols. I and II. Washington, DC: U.S. Department of Justice.

Bamberger, P. S. (1990, March 9). Never underestimate the injury in rape. *The New York Times,* p. A12.

Bandura, A. (1973). *Aggression: A social learning process.* Englewood Cliffs, NJ: Prentice-Hall.

Bandura, A. (1978). Social learning theory of aggression. *Journal of Communication, 28,* 12-29.

Barbaree, H. E., Marshall, W. L., & Lanthier, R. D. (1979). Deviant sexual arousal in rapists. *Behavior Research and Therapy, 17,* 215-222.

Barber, R. (1974). Judge and jury attitude toward rape. *Australia and New Zealand Journal of Criminology, 7,* 157-172.

Bard, M. (1982). [Testimony presented at a public hearing of the President's Task Force on Victims of Crime.] Washington, DC, September, 1982.

Bard, M., & Sangrey, D. (1979). *The crime victim's book.* New York: Basic Books.

Barnett, N., & Feild, H. S. (1977). Sex differences in attitudes toward rape. *Journal of College Student Personnel, 18,* 93-96.

Barr, J. (1979). *Within a dark wood.* Garden City, NY: Doubleday.

Bart, P. B. (1981). Women who both were raped and avoided being raped. *Journal of Social Issues, 37*(4), 123-137.

Bart, P. B., & O'Brien, P. H. (1984). Stopping rape: Effective avoidance strategies. *Signs: Journal of Women in Culture and Society, 10,* 83-101.

Bart, P. B., & O'Brien, P. H. (1985). *Stopping rape: Successful survival strategies.* Elmsford, NY: Pergamon.

Basow, S. A. (1986). *Gender stereotypes: Traditions and alternatives* (2nd ed.). Pacific Grove, CA: Brooks/Cole.

Bassuk, E. (1980). The crisis theory perspective on rape: In S. L. McCombie (Ed.), *The rape crisis intervention handbook.* New York: Plenum.

Baumgardner, S. R., Becker, C. S., Beaulieu, D., & Kenniston, A. (1988, August). *Cause, responsibility, blame for rape: Do we blame the victim?* Paper presented at the meetings of the American Psychological Association, Atlanta.

Baumgardner, S. R., Kenniston, A., Becker, C. S., & Beaulieu, D. (1989). *Two approaches to measuring cause, responsibility, and blame*. Unpublished manuscript, University of Wisconsin at Eau Claire.

Bayles, F. (1984, March 25). Contradictions mark testimony during New Bedford rape trial. *Lawrence Journal-World*, p. 3.

Bechhofer, L., & Parrot, A. (1991). What is acquaintance rape? In A. Parrot & L. Bechhofer (Eds.), *Acquaintance rape: The hidden crime* (pp. 9-25). New York: John Wiley.

Beck, A., Ward, C., Mendelsohn, M., Mock, J., & Erbaugh, J. (1961). An inventory for measuring depression. *Archives of General Psychiatry, 4*, 53-63.

Beck, M., & Zabarsky, M. (1984, April 2). Rape trial: "Justice crucified?" *Newsweek*, p. 39.

Becker, J. V., Abel, G. G., Blanchard, E. B., Murphy, W. D., & Coleman, E. (1978). Evaluating social skills of sexually aggressives. *Criminal Justice and Behavior, 5*, 357-368.

Becker, J. V., Skinner, L. J., Abel, G. G., Axelrod, R., & Treacy, E. C. (1984). Depressive symptoms associated with sexual assault. *Journal of Sex and Marital Therapy, 10*, 185-192.

Becker, J., Skinner, L., Abel, G., Howell, J., & Bruce, K. (1982). The effects of sexual assault on rape and attempted rape victims. *Victimology: An International Journal, 7*(1-4), 106-113.

Beneke, T. (1982). *Men on rape*. New York: St. Martin's.

Berger, R. J., Searles, P., & Neuman, W. L. (1988). The dimensions of rape reform legislation. *Law and Society Review, 22*, 329-357.

Best, J. B., & Demmin, H. S. (1982). Victim's provocativeness and victim's attractiveness as determinants of blame in rape. *Psychological Reports, 51*, 255-258.

Bienen, L. (1980). Rape III: Natural developments in rape reform legislation. *Women's Rights Law Reporter, 6*, 184-189.

Bienen, L. (1983). Rape reform legislation in the United States: A look at some practical effects. *Victimology: An International Journal, 8*, 139-151.

Black, H. C. (1968). *Black's law dictionary* (rev. 4th ed.). St Paul, MN: West.

Blanck, P. D. (1991). What empirical research tells us: Studying judges' and juries' behavior. *American University Law Review, 40*, 775-804.

Blanck, P. D., Rosenthal, R., Hart, A. J., & Bernieri, F. (1990). The measure of a judge: An empirically-based framework for exploring trial judges' behavior. *Iowa Law Review, 75*, 653-684.

Block, R., & Skogan, W. G. (1982). *Resistance and outcome in robbery and rape: Nonfatal stranger to stranger violence*. Unpublished paper, Center for Urban Affairs and Policy Research, Northwestern University.

Bocchetti, M. (1989, July 14). Rapist's latest sentence should keep him in prison. *Kansas City Star*, p. B-4.

Bohmer, C. (1991). Acquaintance rape and the law. In A. Parrot & L. Bechhofer (Eds.), *Acquaintance rape: The hidden crime* (pp. 317-333). New York: John Wiley.

Bond, S. B., & Mosher, D. L. (1986). Guided imagery of rape: Fantasy, reality, and the willing victim myth. *Journal of Sex Research, 22,* 162-183.

Borek, N., & Shaver, K. G. (1988, April). *Effects of attributions for parental conflict on intimacy.* Paper presented at the meetings of the Eastern Psychological Association, Buffalo, NY.

Borgida, E. (1980). Evidentiary reform of rape laws: A psychological approach. In P. D. Lipsitt & B. D. Sales (Eds.), *New directions in psychological research* (pp. 171-197). New York: Litton.

Borgida, E. (1981). Legal reform of rape laws. In L. Bickman (Ed.), *Applied social psychology annual* (pp. 211-242). Beverly Hills, CA: Sage.

Borgida, E., & White, P. (1978). Social perception of rape victims: The impact of legal reform. *Law and Human Behavior, 2,* 339-351.

Bouton, K. (1990, February 25). Linda Fairstein vs. rape. *The New York Times Magazine,* pp. 20-23, 58-60.

Braito, R., Dean, D., Powers, E., & Bruton, B. (1981). The inferiority games: Perceptions and behavior. *Sex Roles: A Journal of Research, 7,* 65-72.

Branscombe, N. R., & Weir, J. A. (1992). Resistance as stereotype-inconsistency: Consequences for judgments of rape victims. *Journal of Social and Clinical Psychology, 11,* 1-23.

Bridges, J. S., & McGrail, C. A. (1989). Attributions of responsibility for date and stranger rape. *Sex Roles: A Journal of Research, 21,* 273-286.

Brigham, J. C. (1989, August). *Discussant's comments for symposium "Rape on trial: Juror cognitions and the 'victim blame' phenomenon."* Paper presented at the meetings of the American Psychological Association, New Orleans.

Brown, G. W. (1974). Life events and the onset of depressive and schizophrenic conditions. In E. K. Gunderson & R. Rahe (Eds.), *Life stress and illness.* Springfield, IL: Charles C Thomas.

Brown v. State, 59 Wis. 2d 200. (1973).

Browne, A., & Finkelhor, D. (1986). Impact of child sexual abuse: A review of the research. *Psychological Bulletin, 99,* 66-77.

Brownmiller, S. (1975). *Against our will: Men, women, and rape.* New York: Simon & Schuster.

Bulman, R. J., & Wortman, C. B. (1977). Attributions of blame and coping in the "real world": Severe accident victims react to their lot. *Journal of Personality and Social Psychology, 35,* 351-363.

Bureau of Justice Statistics. (1984). *Criminal victimization in the United States, 1982* (Publication No. NCJ-92820). Washington, DC: U.S. Department of Justice.

Burger, J. M. (1981). Motivational biases in the attribution of responsibility for an accident: A meta-analysis of the defensive attribution hypothesis. *Psychological Bulletin, 90,* 496-512.

Burgess, A. W., & Holmstrom, L. L. (1974a). Rape trauma syndrome. *American Journal of Psychiatry, 131,* 981-999.

Burgess, A. W., & Holmstrom, L. L. (1974b). *Rape: Victims of crisis.* Bowie, MD: Robert J. Brady.

Burgess, A. W., & Holmstrom, L. L. (1985). Rape trauma syndrome and post-traumatic stress response. In A. W. Burgess (Ed.), *Research handbook on rape and sexual assault* (pp. 46-61). New York: Garland.

Burkhart, B. R., & Fromuth, M. E. (1991). Individual and social psychological understanding of sexual coercion. In E. Gruerholz & M. A. Koralewski (Eds.), *Sexual coercion: A sourcebook on its nature, causes, and prevention* (pp. 75-89). Lexington, MA: Lexington.

Burkhart, B. R., & Stanton, A. L. (1988). Sexual aggression in acquaintance relationships. In G. Russell (Ed.), *Violence and intimate relationships* (pp. 43-65). Great Neck, NY: PMA.

Burt, M. R. (1980). Cultural myths and supports for rape. *Journal of Personality and Social Psychology, 38,* 217-230.

Burt, M. R., & Albin, R. S. (1981). Rape myths, rape definitions, and probability of conviction. *Journal of Applied Social Psychology, 11,* 212-230.

Calderwood, D. (1987, May). The male rape victim. *Medical Aspects of Human Sexuality,* pp. 53-55.

Calhoun, K. S., & Atkeson, B. M. (1991). *Treatment of rape victims: Facilitating psychosocial adjustment.* Elmsford, NY: Pergamon.

Calhoun, K. S., Atkeson, B., & Resick, P. (1982). A longitudinal examination of fear reactions in victims of rape. *Journal of Counseling Psychology, 29,* 656-661.

Calhoun, K. S., Kelley, S. P., Amick, A., & Gardner, R. (1986). *Research on rape.* Paper presented at the Southeastern Psychological Association, Orlando, FL.

Calhoun, K. S., & Townsley, R. M. (1991). Attributions of responsibility for acquaintance rape. In A. Parrot & L. Bechhofer (Eds.), *Acquaintance rape: The hidden crime* (pp. 57-69). New York: John Wiley.

Calhoun, L. G., Selby, J. W., Cann, A., & Keller, G. T. (1978). The effect of victim physical attractiveness and sex of respondent on social reactions to victims of rape. *British Journal of Social and Clinical Psychology, 17,* 191-192.

Calhoun, L. G., Selby, J. W., & Warring, L. J. (1976). Social perception of the victim's causal role in rape: An exploratory examination of four factors. *Human Relations, 32,* 57-67.

Camp v. State, 3 Ga. 417 (1847).

Campbell, M. (1990, July 3). Mayor assailed over rape "joke." *Kansas City Star,* pp. B-1, B-2.

Cann, A., Calhoun, L. G., & Selby, J. W. (1979). Attributing responsibility to the victim of rape: Influence of information regarding past sexual experience. *Human Relations, 32,* 57-67.

Canon, S., & Brandon, K. (1990, March 31). Survivor of rape tells ugly details. *Kansas City Star,* pp. A-1, A-13.

Caplan, G. (1964). *Principles of preventive psychiatry.* New York: Basic Books.

Caplan, P. J. (1987). The myth of women's masochism. In M. R. Walsh (Ed.), *The psychology of women* (pp. 78-96). New Haven, CT: Yale University Press.

Carlson, M. (1991, April 29). The Kennedy boys' night out. *Time,* p. 38.

Carroll, J. (1991, June 24). The end of the dream. *New Republic,* pp. 22-25.

Carroll, J. S., & Wiener, R. L. (1982). Cognitive social psychology in court and beyond. In A. Hastorf & A. Isen (Eds.), *Cognitive social psychology* (pp. 213-253). New York: Elsevier-North Holland.

Chancer, L. S. (1987). New Bedford, Massachusetts, March 6, 1983-March 22, 1984: The "before and after" of a group rape. *Gender and Society, 1,* 239-260.

Chappell, D., Geis, G., & Fogarty, F. (1974). Forcible rape: Bibliography. *Journal of Criminal Law and Criminology, 65,* 248-263.

Check, J. V. P., & Malamuth, N. M. (1983). Sex role stereotyping and reactions to depictions of stranger versus acquaintance rape. *Journal of Personality and Social Psychology, 45,* 344-356.

Christie, R., & Geis, F. L. (1970). *Studies in Machiavellianism.* New York: Academic Press.

Clark, L., & Lewis, D. J. (1977). *Rape: The price of coercive sexuality.* Toronto: Women's Press.

Cohen, L. J., & Roth, S. (1987). The psychological aftermath of rape: Long-term effects and individual differences in recovery. *Journal of Social and Clinical Psychology, 5,* 525-534.

Cohen, M. L. (1976). *Patterns of conflict in the rapist.* Paper presented at the Butler Hospital Conference, Providence, RI.

Coker v. Georgia, 433 U.S. 584 (1977).

Coleman, J., & Branscombe, N. R. (1991, May). *Imagining alternative behaviors and outcomes: Effects on judgments of rape victims and assailants.* Paper presented at the meetings of the Midwestern Psychological Association, Chicago.

Costin, F. (1985). Beliefs about rape and women's social roles. *Archives of Sexual Behavior, 14,* 319-325.

Critchlow, B. (1985). The blame in the bottle: Attributions about drunken behavior. *Personality and Social Psychology Bulletin, 11,* 258-274.

Davis, R. C., & Friedman, L. N. (1985). The emotional aftermath of crime and violence. In C. R. Figley (Ed.), *Trauma and its wake: The study and treatment of post-traumatic stress disorder* (pp. 90-111). New York: Brunner/Mazel.

Davis v. State, 120 Ga. 433, 48 S.E. 180 (1904).

Dawkins, R. (1976). *The selfish gene.* New York: Oxford University Press.

Dean, C., & de Bruyn-Kops, M. (1982). *The crime and consequences of rape.* Springfield, IL: Charles C Thomas.

Deaux, K., & Wrightsman, L. S. (1988). *Social psychology* (5th ed.). Pacific Grove, CA: Brooks/Cole.

Deitz, S. R. (1980, Fall). Double jeopardy: The rape victim in court. *Rocky Mountain Psychologist,* pp. 1-17.

Deitz, S. R., Blackwell, K. T., Daley, P. C., & Bentley, B. J. (1982). Measurement of empathy toward rape victims and rapists. *Journal of Personality and Social Psychology, 43,* 372-384.

Deitz, S. R., & Byrnes, L. E. (1981). Attribution of responsibility for sexual assault: The influence of observer empathy and defendant occupation and attractiveness. *Journal of Psychology, 108,* 17-29.

Deitz, S. R., Littman, M., & Bentley, B. J. (1984). Attribution of responsibility for rape: The influence of observer empathy, victim resistance, and victim attractiveness. *Sex Roles: A Journal of Research, 10,* 261-280.

Deitz, S. R., Russell, S. A., & Hammes, K. M. (1989, August). *Who's on trial?: Information processing by jurors in rape cases.* Paper presented at the meetings of the American Psychological Association, New Orleans.

Dejanikus, T. (1981, February). New studies support active resistance to rape. *Off Our Backs,* pp. 9-23.

Deming, M., & Eppy, A. (1981). The sociology of rape. *Sociology and Social Research, 65,* 357-380.

Dion, K., Berscheid, E., & Walster, E. (1972). What is beautiful is good. *Journal of Personality and Social Psychology, 24,* 285-290.

Dohrenwend, B. S. (1973). Life events as stressors: A methodological inquiry. *Journal of Health and Social Behavior, 14,* 167-175.

Donahue, D. (1991, January 11). In '90 magazine readers devoured celebs, gossip. *USA Today*, p. 5D.

Donahue, D. (1992, January 6). Magazines reap sales from war and notoriety. *USA Today*, p. 1D.

Donnerstein, E. (1982). Erotica and human aggression. In R. G. Geen & E. Donnerstein (Eds.), *Aggression: Theoretical and empirical views* (Vol. 2, pp. 127-154). Orlando, FL: Academic Press.

Donnerstein, E., & Berkowitz, L. (1981). Victim reactions in aggressive erotic films as a factor in violence against women. *Journal of Personality and Social Psychology, 41,* 710-724.

Donnerstein, E., Berkowitz, L., & Linz, D. (1986). *Role of aggressive and sexual images in violent pornography.* Unpublished manuscript, University of Wisconsin-Madison.

Dowd, M. (1983, September 5). Rape: The sexual weapon. *Time,* pp. 27-29.

Dowdeswell, J. (1986). *Women on rape.* Wellingborough, UK: Thorsons Publishing Group.

Doyle, J. A. (1983). *The male experience.* Dubuque, IA: William C. Brown.

Dworkin, A. (1981). *Pornography: Men possessing women.* New York: Perigee.

Dworkin, A. (1989). *Letters from a war zone: Writings 1976-1989.* New York: E. P. Dutton.

Ehrhart, J. K., & Sandler, B. R. (1985). *Campus gang rape: Party games?* Washington, DC: Association of American Colleges.

Eisenman, R. (1991). Monitoring and post-confinement treatment of sex offenders: An urgent need. *Psychological Reports, 69,* 1089-1090.

Ellis, L. (1989). *Theories of rape: Inquiries into the causes of sexual aggression.* New York: Hemisphere.

Ellison, K., & Buckhout, R. (1981). *Psychology and criminal justice.* New York: Harper & Row.

Erickson, B., Lind, E. A., Johnson, B. C., & O'Barr, W. M. (1978). Speech style and impression formation in a court setting: The effects of "powerful" and "powerless" speech. *Journal of Experimental Social Psychology, 14,* 266-279.

Estrich, S. (1987). *Real rape.* Cambridge, MA: Harvard University Press.

Federal Bureau of Investigation (FBI). (1988). *Uniform Crime Reports-1987.* Washington, DC: Government Printing Office.

Feild, H. S. (1978). Attitudes toward rape: A comparative analysis of police, rapists, crisis counselor, and citizens. *Journal of Personality and Social Psychology, 36,* 156-179.

Feild, H. S. (1979). Rape trials and jurors' decisions: A psycholegal analysis of the effects of victim, defendant, and case characteristics. *Law and Human Behavior, 3,* 261-284.

Feild, H. S., & Barnett, N. J. (1978). Simulated jury trials: Students vs. "real" people as jurors. *Journal of Social Psychology, 104,* 287-293.

Feild, H. S., & Bienen, L. B. (1980). *Jurors and rape: A study in psychology and law.* Lexington, MA: D. C. Heath.

Feldman-Summers, S., & Ashworth, C. D. (1981). Factors related to intentions to report a rape. *Journal of Social Issues, 37*(4), 71-92.

Feldman-Summers, S., Gordon, P. E., & Meagher, J. R. (1979). The impact of rape on sexual satisfaction. *Journal of Abnormal Psychology, 88,* 101-105.

Feldman-Summers, S., & Lindner, K. (1976). Perceptions of victims and defendants in the criminal assault cases. *Criminal Justice and Behavior, 3*(2), 73-93.

Feldman-Summers, S., & Palmer, G. (1980). Rape: A view from judges, prosecutors, and police officers. *Criminal Justice and Behavior, 7,* 19-40.

Feshbach, S., & Malamuth, N. (1978, November). Sex and aggression: Proving the link. *Psychology Today, 12,* pp. 110-112.

Fincham, F. D., & Jaspers, J. M. (1980). Attribution of responsibility: From man the scientist to man as lawyer. In L. Berkowitz (Ed.), *Advances in experimental social psychology* (Vol. 13, pp. 81-138). Orlando, FL: Academic Press.

Finkelhor, D. (1984). *Child sexual abuse: New theory and practice.* New York: Free Press.

Finkelhor, D., & Yllö, K. (1985). *License to rape: Sexual abuse of wives.* New York: Holt, Rinehart & Winston.

Fischer, G. J. (1987). Hispanic and majority student attitudes toward forcible date rape as a function of differences in attitudes toward women. *Sex Roles: A Journal of Research, 17,* 93-101.

Fischhoff, B. (1975). Hindsight does not equal foresight: The effects of outcome knowledge on judgment under uncertainty. *Journal of Experimental Psychology: Human Perception and Performance, 1,* 288-299.

Fischhoff, B. (1980). For those condemned to study the past: Reflections on historical judgment. In R. A. Shweder (Ed.), *New directions for methodology of social and behavioral science* (Vol. 4). San Francisco: Jossey-Bass.

Fischhoff, B. (1982). For those condemned to study the past: Heuristics and biases in hindsight. In D. Kahneman, P. Slovic, & A. Tversky (Eds.), *Judgment under uncertainty: Heuristics and biases* (Vol. 4, pp. 79-93). New York: Cambridge University Press.

Fischhoff, B., & Beyth, R. (1975). "I knew it would happen"—Remembered probabilities of once-future things. *Organizational Behavior and Human Performance, 13,* 1-16.

Fischhoff, B., & Furby, L. (1987). *Fighting back: How should a woman decide?* Unpublished manuscript.

Fischhoff, B., Slovic, P., & Lichtenstein, S. (1977). Knowing with certainty: The appropriateness of extreme confidences. *Journal of Experimental Psychology: Human Perception and Performance, 3,* 552-564.

Fishbein, M. (1980). A theory of reasoned action: Some applications and implications. In H. E. Howe & M. M. Page (Eds.), *Nebraska Symposium on Motivation* (Vol. 27, pp. 65-116). Lincoln: University of Nebraska Press.

Fishbein, M., & Ajzen, I. (1973). Attribution of responsibility: A theoretical note. *Journal of Experimental Social Psychology, 9,* 148-153.

Fishbein, M., & Ajzen, I. (1975). *Belief, attitude, intention, and behavior: An introduction to theory and research.* Reading, MA: Addison-Wesley.

Fiske, S. T., & Taylor, S. E. (1984). *Social cognition.* New York: Random House.

Flynn, L. (1974). Women and rape. *Medical Aspects of Human Sexuality, 8,* 183-197.

Foley, T., & Davies, M. (1983). *Rape: Nursing care of victims.* St. Louis: C. V. Mosby.

Foley, T. S. (1985). Family response to rape and sexual assault. In A. W. Burgess (Ed.), *Rape and sexual assault: A research handbook* (pp. 159-188). New York: Garland.

Forrester, J. (1986). Rape, seduction, and psychoanalysis. In S. Tomaselli & R. Porter (Eds.), *Rape* (pp. 57-83). Oxford, UK: Basil Blackwell.

Frank, E. (1979). *Psychological response to rape: An analysis of response patterns.* Unpublished doctoral dissertation, University of Pittsburgh.

Frank, E., Turner, S. M., & Stewart, B. D. (1980). Initial response to rape: The impact of factors within the rape situation. *Journal of Behavioral Assessment, 2,* 39-53.

Frank, E., Turner, S. M., Stewart, B. D., Jacob, M., & West, D. (1981). Past psychiatric symptoms and the response to sexual assault. *Comprehensive Psychiatry, 22,* 479-487.

Frazier, P., & Borgida, E. (1985). Rape trauma syndrome evidence in court. *American Psychologist, 40,* 984-993.

Frazier, P., & Borgida, E. (1988). Juror common understanding and the admissibility of rape trauma syndrome evidence in court. *Law and Human Behavior, 12,* 101-122.

Frazier, P. A. (1989, August). *Coping strategies among rape victims.* Paper presented at the meetings of the American Psychological Association, New Orleans.

Frazier, P. A. (in press). Victim attributions and postrape trauma. *Journal of Personality and Social Psychology.*

Freeman, P. (1990, December 17). Silent no more. *People,* pp. 94-104.

Freiberg, P. (1990, November). APA testifies: Rape estimates far too low. *APA Monitor,* p. 25.

Freivogel, W. H. (1990, July 26). Quiet tone of Souter's opinions reflect quiet life. *Kansas City Star,* p. C-7.

Freud, S. (1924). The economic problem of masochism. In J. Strachey (Ed.), *The standard edition of the complete psychological works of Sigmund Freud.* London: Hogarth.

Fulero, S. M., & DeLara, C. (1976). Rape victims and attributed responsibility: A defensive attribution approach. *Victimology: An International Journal, 1*(4), 551-563.

Furby, L., & Fischhoff, B. (in press). Rape self-defense strategies: A review of their effectiveness. *Victimology: An International Journal.*

Furman v. Georgia, 4087 U.S. 238 (1972).

Gager, N., & Schurr, C. (1976). *Sexual assault: Confronting rape in America.* New York: Grosset & Dunlap.

Geis, G. (1979). Rape in marriage: Law and law reform in England, U.S., and Sweden. *Adelaide Law Review, 6,* 284-303.

Gelman, D. (1990, July 23). The mind of the rapist. *Newsweek,* pp. 46-52.

George, L. K., Winfield, I., & Blazer, D. G. (1992). Sociocultural factors in sexual assault: Comparison of two representative samples of women. *Journal of Social Issues, 48*(1), 105-125.

Giacopassi, D. J., & Wilkinson, K. R. (1985). Rape and the devalued victim. *Law and Human Behavior, 9*(4), 367-383.

Giarrusso, R., Johnson, P. B., Goodchilds, J. D., & Zellman, G. (1979, April). *Adolescent cues and signals: Sex and assault.* Paper presented at the meetings of the Western Psychological Association, San Diego.

Gibson, L., Linden, R., & Johnson, S. (1980). A situational theory of rape. *Canadian Journal of Criminology, 22,* 51-63.

Gidycz, C. A., & Koss, M. P. (1991). The effects of acquaintance rape on the female victim. In A. Parrot & L. Bechhofer (Eds.), *Acquaintance rape: The hidden crime* (pp. 270-283). New York: John Wiley.

Glaberson, W. (1990a, July 8). Rape and the fear of AIDS: How one case was affected. *The New York Times,* p. 13.

Glaberson, W. (1990b, July 13). Jogger rape: A scattershot defense. *The New York Times,* p. A14.

Gleicher, F., Kost, K. A., Baker, S. M., Strathman, A. J., Richman, S. A., & Sherman, S. J. (1990). The role of counterfactual thinking in judgments of affect. *Personality and Social Psychology Bulletin, 16,* 284-295.

Glueck, S. S. (1925). *Mental disorders and the criminal law.* Boston: Little, Brown.

Goldberg-Ambrose, C. (1992). Unfinished business in rape law reform. *Journal of Social Issues, 48,* 173-186.

Goldstein, C. (1976). The dilemma of the rape victim: A descriptive analysis. *Criminal Justice Monographs, 3*(2).

Goleman, D. (1989, August 29). When the rapist is not a stranger. *The New York Times,* pp. 13, 21.

Goleman, D. (1992, April 14). Therapies offer hope for sex offenders. *The New York Times,* pp. B5, B8.

Goodchilds, J. D., Zellman, G., Johnson, P. B., & Giarrusso, R. (1988). Adolescents and their perceptions of sexual interaction outcomes. In A. W. Burgess (Ed.), *Sexual assault* (Vol. 2, pp. 245-270). New York: Garland.

Goodman, E. (1983, October 18). Real men may be the only ones to cry. *Lawrence Journal-World,* p. 5.

Goodman, E. (1987, September 29). Jessica Hahn story has ring of truth. *Lawrence Journal-World,* p. 5A.

Goodman, E. (1990, July 29). The Brawley battlefield. *The New York Times Book Review,* p. 7.

Gordon, M. T., & Riger, S. (1989). *The female fear.* New York: Free Press.

Gore, T. (1990, January 22-28). Hate, rape, and rap. *Washington Post National Weekly Edition,* p. 29.

Graves, R. (1955). *The Greek myths.* Baltimore, MD: Pelican.

Green, S. K., & Sandos, P. (1983). Perceptions of male and female imitations of relationships. *Sex Roles: A Journal of Research, 9,* 849-852.

Greenberg, M. S., & Ruback, R. B. (1984). *Social psychology of the criminal justice system.* Pacific Grove, CA: Brooks/Cole.

Greenhouse, L. (1990, November 27). Justices to hear retirement age case. *The New York Times,* p. A12.

Greer, J. G., & Stuart, I. R. (1983). *The sexual aggressor: Current perspectives on treatment.* New York: Van Nostrand Reinhold.

Griffin, M. K. (1980). In 44 states, it's legal to rape your wife. *Student Lawyer, 9,* 21-23, 58-61.

Griffin, S. (1971). The all-American crime. *Ramparts, 10,* 26-35.

Gross, J. (1991, May 28). Even the victim can be slow to recognize rape. *The New York Times,* p. A8.

Grossman, R., & Sutherland, J. (1991). *Surviving sexual assault.* New York: Congdon & Weed.

Groth, A. N. (1983). Treatment of the sexual offender in a correctional institution. In J. G. Greer & I. R. Stuart (Eds.), *The sexual aggressor: Current perspectives on treatment.* New York: Van Nostrand Reinhold.

Groth, A. N., & Burgess, A. W. (1980). Male rape: Offenders and victims. *American Journal of Psychiatry, 137,* 806-810.

Groth, A. N., Burgess, A. W., & Holmstrom, L. L. (1977). Rape: Power, anger, and sexuality. *American Journal of Psychiatry, 134,* 1239-1243.

Groth, A. N. (1979). *Men who rape.* New York: Plenum.

Gurley, G. (1986). Counseling the rape victim's loved ones. *Response, 9,* 8-9.

Hagen, R. (1979). *The bio-sexual factor.* Garden City, NY: Doubleday.

Hale, M. (1680). *History of the pleas of the crown (Vol. I).* (Emlyn ed., 1847).

Hall, G. C. N. (1990). Prediction of sexual aggression. *Clinical Psychology Review, 10,* 229-245.

Hanley, R. (1989, May 26). New Jersey town shattered by sex assault on girl, 17. *The New York Times,* p. 11.

Harney, P. A., & Muehlenhard, C. L. (1991). Factors that increase the likelihood of victimization. In A. Parrot & L. Bechhofer (Eds.), *Acquaintance rape: The hidden crime* (pp. 159-175). New York: John Wiley.

Harris, D. M., & Guten, S. (1979). Health-protective behavior: An explanatory study. *Journal of Health and Social Behavior, 20,* 17-29.

Hart, H. L. A. (1968). *Punishment and responsibility.* New York: Oxford University Press.

Hazelwood, R. R., & Burgess, A. W. (1987). *An introduction to the serial rapist: Research by the FBI.* Washington, DC: Federal Bureau of Investigation, Department of Justice.

Hazelwood, R. R., Reboussin, R., & Warren, J. I. (1989). Serial rape: Correlates of increased aggression and the relationship of offender pleasure to victim resistance. *Journal of Interpersonal Violence, 4,* 65-78.

Hazelwood, R. R., & Warren, J. (1989). *The serial rapist: His characteristics and victims (Part I).* Washington, DC: Federal Bureau of Investigation, Department of Justice.

Heider, F. (1958). *The psychology of interpersonal relations.* New York: John Wiley.

Heilbrun, A. B., & Loftus, M. P. (1986). The role of sadism and peer pressure in the sexual aggression of male college students. *Journal of Sex Research, 22,* 320-332.

Heilbrun, A. B., & Seif, D. T. (1988). Erotic value of female distress in sexually explicit photographs. *Journal of Sex Research, 24,* 47-57.

Hemsley, G. D., & Doob, A. M. (1978). The effect of looking behavior on perceptions of a communicator's credibility. *Journal of Applied Social Psychology, 8,* 136-144.

Hennessee, J. A. (1989, June 4). All that mattered was the 6 p.m. news. *The New York Times Book Review,* p. 9.

Herzog, A. R., Bachman, J. G., & Johnston, L. D. (1983). Paid work, child care, and housework: A national survey of high school seniors' preferences for sharing responsibilities between husband and wife. *Sex Roles: A Journal of Research, 9,* 109-135.

Hindelang, M. J., & Davis, B. (1977). Forcible rape in the United States: A statistical profile. In D. Chappell, R. Geis, & G. Geis (Eds.), *Forcible rape* (pp. 87-114). New York: Columbia University Press.

Hindelang, M. J., Gottfredson, M. R., & Garofalo, J. (1978). *Victims of personal crime.* Cambridge, MA: Ballinger.

Holmstrom, L. L., & Burgess, A. W. (1978). *The victim of rape: Institutional reactions.* New York: John Wiley.

Hood, J. C. (1989, May 16). Why our society is rape-prone. *The New York Times,* p. 23.

Horney, K. (1973). The problems of feminine masochism. In J. Miller (Ed.), *Psychoanalysis and women*. Baltimore, MD: Penguin.

Horowitz, M. J., Wilner, N., & Alvarez, W. (1979). Impact of event scale: A measure of subjective stress. *Psychosomatic Medicine, 41*, 209-218.

Horowitz, M. J., Wilner, N., Marmar, C., & Krupnick, J. (1980). Pathological grief and the activation of latent self-images. *American Journal of Psychiatry, 137*, 1137-1162.

Howells, K., Shaw, F., Greasley, M., Robertson, J., Gloster, D., & Metcalfe, N. (1984). Perceptions of rape in a British sample: Effects of relationship, victim status, sex, and attitudes to women. *British Journal of Social Psychology, 23*, 35-50.

Hunter, B. A., & Shotland, R. L. (1990, August). *Token resistance to sex: Confusion about sexual intent*. Paper presented at meetings of the American Psychological Association, Boston.

Hursh, C. (1977). *The trouble with rape*. Chicago: Nelson-Hall.

Hyde, J. S. (1986). *Understanding human sexuality*. New York: McGraw-Hill.

Inbau, F. E., & Thompson, J. R. (1970). *Criminal law and its administration*. New York: Foundation Press.

Izard, C. E. (1977). *Human emotion*. New York: Plenum.

Janoff-Bulman, R. (1979). Characterological versus behavioral self-blame: Inquiries into depression and blame. *Journal of Personality and Social Psychology, 37*, 1798-1809.

Janoff-Bulman, R. (1985a). The aftermath of victimization: Rebuilding shattered assumptions. In C. R. Figley (Ed.), *Trauma and its wake: The study and treatment of post-traumatic stress disorder* (pp. 15-35). New York: Brunner/Mazel.

Janoff-Bulman, R. (1985b). Criminal vs. non-criminal victimization: Victims' reactions. *Victimology: An International Journal, 10*, 498-511.

Janoff-Bulman, R., & Frieze, I. H. (1983). A theoretical perspective for understanding reactions to victimization. *Journal of Social Issues, 39*(2), 1-17.

Janoff-Bulman, R., & Lang-Gunn, L. (1985). Coping with disease, crime, and accidents: The role of self-blame attributions. In L. Y. Abramson (Ed.), *Social cognition and clinical psychology: A synthesis*. New York: Guilford Press.

Janoff-Bulman, R., Timko, C., & Carli, L. L. (1985). Cognitive biases in blaming the victim. *Journal of Experimental Social Psychology, 21*, 161-177.

Jenkins, M. J., & Dambrot, F. H. (1987). The attribution of date rape: Observer's attitudes and sexual experiences and the dating situation. *Journal of Applied Social Psychology, 17*, 875-895.

Johnson, A. G. (1980). On the prevalence of rape in the United States. *Signs: Journal of Women in Culture and Society, 6*, 136-146.

Johnson, C. B., Freshnock, N., & Saal, F. E. (in press). Friendliness or sexual come-on: A clue to understanding sexual harassment? *Psychology of Women Quarterly*.

Johnson, J. D., & Jackson, L. A., Jr. (1988). Assessing the effects of factors that might underlie the differential perception of acquaintance and stranger rape. *Sex Roles: A Journal of Research, 19*, 37-45.

Jones, A. (1989, June 18). The whole town was molested. *The New York Times Book Review*, pp. 12-13.

Jones, C., & Aronson, E. (1973). Attribution of fault to a rape victim as a function of respectability of the victim. *Journal of Personality and Social Psychology, 26*, 415-419.

Kahn, A., Gilbert, L. A., Latta, M., Deutsch, C., Hagen, R., Hill, M., McGaughey, T., Ryen, A. H., & Wilson, D. W. (1977). Attribution of fault to a rape victim as a function of respectability of the victim: A failure to replicate or extend. *Representative Research in Social Psychology, 8,* 98-107.

Kahneman, D., & Miller, D. T. (1986). Norm theory: Comparing reality to its alternatives. *Psychological Review, 93,* 136-153.

Kalish, C. B. (1974). *Crimes and victims: A report of the Dayton–San Jose pilot study of victimization.* Washington, DC: National Crime Justice Information and Statistics Service.

Kalven, H., & Zeisel, H. (1966). *The American jury.* Boston: Little, Brown.

Kanekar, S., & Kolsawalla, N. B. (1977). Responsibility in relation to respectability. *Journal of Social Psychology, 102,* 183-188.

Kanekar, S., & Vaz, L. (1983). Determinants of perceived likelihood of rape and victim's fault. *Journal of Social Psychology, 120,* 147-148.

Kanin, E. J. (1957). Male aggression in dating-courtship relations. *American Journal of Sociology, 63,* 197-204.

Kanin, E. J. (1967). Reference groups and sex conduct norm violations. *Sociological Quarterly, 8,* 495-504.

Kanin, E. J. (1984). Date rape: Unofficial criminals and victims. *Victimology: An International Journal, 9,* 95-108.

Kanin, E. J., & Parcell, S. R. (1977). Sexual aggression: A second look at the offended female. *Archives of Sexual Behavior, 6,* 67-76.

Karmen, A. (1984). *Crime victims: An introduction to victimology.* Pacific Grove, CA: Brooks/Cole.

Karpman, B. (1951). The sexual psychopath. *Journal of Criminal Law and Criminology, 42,* 184-198.

Karuza, J., & Carey, T. O. (1984). Relative preference and adaptiveness of behavioral blame for observers of rape victims. *Journal of Personality, 52,* 249-260.

Kassin, S. M., & Wrightsman, L. S. (1983). The construction and validation of a juror bias scale. *Journal of Research in Personality, 17,* 423-441.

Kassin, S. M., & Wrightsman, L. S. (1988). *The American jury on trial: Psychological perspectives.* New York: Hemisphere.

Katz, B. L. (1987). *Prerape victim-rapist familiarity and recovery from rape: Psychological consequences.* Unpublished doctoral dissertation, Boston University.

Katz, B. L. (1991). The psychological impact of stranger versus nonstranger rape on victims' recovery. In A. Parrot & L. Bechhofer (Eds.), *Acquaintance rape: The hidden crime* (pp. 251-269). New York: John Wiley.

Katz, L. M. (1991, March 22). Rapes reach "epidemic" rate in 1990. *USA Today,* p. 1A.

Katz, S., & Mazur, M. A. (1979). *Understanding the rape victim: Synthesis of research findings.* New York: John Wiley.

Kauffman, R. A., & Ryckman, R. M. (1979). Effects of locus-of-control, outcome severity, and attitudinal similarity of defendant on attributions of criminal responsibility. *Personality and Social Psychology Bulletin, 5,* 340-343.

Kaul, D. (1989, May 4). Young woman jogger in Central Park was not behaving bravely. *Kansas City Times,* p. A-15.

Kayle, H. S. (1989, January). Jude Deveraux: Velvet author. *Inside Books,* pp. 67-69.

Kelley, H. H. (1972). *Causal schemata and the attribution process.* Morristown, NJ: General Learning Press.

Kelley, H. H. (1973). The processes of causal attribution. *American Psychologist, 28,* 107-128.

Kerr, N. L., & Kurtz, S. T. (1977). Effects of a victim's suffering and respectability on mock juror judgments: Further evidence on the just world theory. *Representative Research in Social Psychology, 8,* 42-56.

Killingworth v. State. 226 S.W. 2d 456, 457 Tex. Crim App. (1950).

Kilpatrick, D. G. (1983, Summer). Rape victims: Detection, assessment and treatment. *Clinical Psychologist,* pp. 92-95.

Kilpatrick, D. G. (1988). Rape aftermath symptom test. In M. Hersen & A. S. Bellack (Eds.), *Dictionary of behavioral assessment techniques* (pp. 366-367). Elmsford, NY: Pergamon.

Kilpatrick, D. G., Best, C. L., Veronen, L. J., Amick, A. E., Villeponteaux, L. A., & Ruff, G. A. (1985). Mental health correlates of criminal victimization: A random community survey. *Journal of Consulting and Clinical Psychology, 53,* 866-873.

Kilpatrick, D. G., Resick. P., & Veronen, L. (1981). Effects of a rape experience: A longitudinal study. *Journal of Social Issues, 37*(4), 105-112.

Kilpatrick, D. G., & Veronen, L. J. (1984). *Treatment of fear and anxiety in victims of rape* (Final report, NIMH Grant No. HMH 29602). Rockville, MD: National Institute of Mental Health.

Kilpatrick, D. G., Veronen, L. J., & Best, C. L. (1985). Factors predicting psychological distress among rape victims. In C. R. Figley (Ed.), *Trauma and its wake* (pp. 113-141). New York: Brunner/Mazel.

King v. State. 210 Tenn. 120 (1962).

Kirkpatrick, C., & Kanin, E. J. (1957). Male sexual aggression on a university campus. *American Sociological Review, 22,* 52-58.

Kirscht, J. P., Haefner, D. P., Kegeles, S. S., & Rosenstock, I. M. (1966). A national study of health beliefs. *Journal of Health and Human Behavior, 7,* 248-254.

Kleck, R. E., & Nuessle, W. (1968). Congruence between the indicative and communicative functions of eye-contact in interpersonal relations. *British Journal of Social and Clinical Psychology, 7,* 305-306.

Kleinberg, H. (1989, January 29). It's tough to have sympathy for Bundy. *Lawrence Journal-World,* p. 5A.

Knapp, M. L. (1980). *Essentials of nonverbal communication.* New York: Holt, Rinehart & Winston.

Koop, C. E. (1987). Report of the Surgeon General's Workshop on Pornography and Public Health. *American Psychologist, 42,* 944-945.

Korman, S. K., & Leslie, G. R. (1982). The relationship of feminist ideology and date expense sharing to perceptions of sexual aggression in dating. *Journal of Sex Research, 18,* 114-129.

Koss, M. P. (1985). The hidden rape victim: Personality, attitudinal, and situational characteristics. *Psychology of Women Quarterly, 9,* 193-212.

Koss, M. P. (1988a, August). *Criminal victimization among women. Impact on health status and medical services usage.* Paper presented at the annual meeting of the American Psychological Association, Atlanta, GA.

Koss, M. P. (1988b). Hidden rape: Incidence, prevalence, and descriptive characteristics of sexual aggression and victimization in a national sample of college students. In A. W. Burgess (Ed.), *Sexual assault* (Vol. II, pp. 3-25). New York: Garland.

Koss, M. P., & Dinero, T. E. (1989). Discriminant analysis of risk factors for sexual victimization among a national sample of college women. *Journal of Consulting and Clinical Psychology, 57,* 242-250.

Koss, M. P., Dinero, T. E., Seibel, C. A., & Cox, S. (1988). Stranger and acquaintance rape: Are there differences in the victim's experience? *Psychology of Women Quarterly, 12,* 1-24.

Koss, M. P., Gidycz, C. A., & Wisniewski, N. (1987). The scope of rape: Incidence and prevalence of sexual aggression and victimization in a national sample of higher education students. *Journal of Consulting and Clinical Psychology, 55,* 162-170.

Koss, M. P., & Harvey, M. R. (1991). *The rape victim: Clinical and community interventions* (2nd ed.). Newbury Park, CA: Sage.

Koss, M. P., & Leonard, K. E. (1984). Sexually aggressive men: Empirical findings and theoretical implications. In N. Malamuth & E. Donnerstein (Eds.), *Pornography and sexual aggression* (pp. 213-232). New York: Academic Press.

Koss, M. P., Leonard, K. E., Beezley, D. A., & Oros, C. J. (1985). Nonstranger sexual aggression: A discriminant analysis of the psychological characteristics of undetected offenders. *Sex Roles: A Journal of Research, 12,* 981-992.

Koss, M. P., & Oros, C. (1982). Sexual Experiences Survey: A research instrument investigating aggression and victimization. *Journal of Consulting and Clinical Psychology, 50,* 445-457.

Krahe, B. (1988). Victim and observer characteristics as determinants of responsibility attributions to victims of rape. *Journal of Applied Social Psychology, 18,* 50-58.

Krulewitz, J. E. (1981). Sex differences in evaluations of female and male victims' responses to assault. *Journal of Applied Social Psychology, 11,* 460-474.

Krulewitz, J. E., & Nash, J. E. (1979). Effects of rape victim resistance, assault outcome, and sex of observer on attributions about rape. *Journal of Personality, 47,* 557-574.

Krulewitz, J. E., & Payne, E. J. (1978). Attributions about rape: Effects of rapist force, observer sex and sex role attitudes. *Journal of Applied Social Psychology, 8,* 291-305.

Kutchinski, B. (1988, June). *Pornography and sexual violence: The criminological evidence from aggregated data in several countries.* Paper presented at the Fourteenth International Congress on Law and Mental Health, Montreal.

LaFree, G. (1980). The effect of sexual stratification by race on official reactions to rape. *American Sociological Review, 45,* 842-854.

LaFree, G. D. (1989). *Rape and criminal justice.* Belmont, CA: Wadsworth.

LaFree, G. D., Reskin, B., & Visher, C. (1985). Jurors' responses to victim's behavior and legal issues in sexual assault trials. *Social Problems, 32,* 389-402.

Lamar, J. V. (1989, February 6). "I deserve punishment." *Time,* p. 34.

Landers, A. (1984, September 30). Death penalty doesn't seem rape deterrent. *Lawrence Journal-World,* p. 5.

Landers, A. (1985, July 29). Date rape issue: Another view. *Lawrence Journal-World,* p. 5.

Landers, A. (1987, October 8). "Horsing around" was prelude to date rape. *Kansas City Times,* p. B-8.

Landers, A. (1988, April 24). Woman shares insight on dating married men. *Lawrence Journal-World,* p. 5A.

Largen, M. A. (1988). Rape-law reform: An analysis. In A. W. Burgess (Ed.), *Rape and sexual assault* (Vol. 2, pp. 271-292). New York: Garland.

L'Armand, K., & Pepitone, A. (1982). Judgments of rape: A study of victim-rapist relationship and victim sexual history. *Personality and Social Psychology, 8,* 134-139.

Larsen, R. M. (1984). Theory and measurement of affect intensity as an individual difference characteristic. *Dissertation Abstracts International, 5,* 2297B (University Microfilms No. 84-22112).

Law Enforcement Assistance Administration. (1977). *Forcible rape: A national survey of the response by prosecutors* (Vol. 1). Washington, DC: Government Printing Office.

Lawrence, R. (1984). Checking the allure of increased conviction rates: The admissibility of expert testimony on rape trauma syndrome in criminal proceedings. *University of Virginia Law Review, 70,* 1657-1704.

Layman, C. A., & Labott, S. M. (1992, August). *Attitudes toward rape victims: The roles of affect and gender.* Paper presented at the annual meetings of the American Psychological Association, Washington, DC.

Leak, G. K., Masciotra, T., Panza, S., & Unruh, K. (1992, August). *Personality, attitudinal, and familial correlates of rape myth acceptance.* Paper presented at the annual meetings of the American Psychological Association, Washington, DC.

Ledray, L. E. (1990). Counseling rape victims: The nursing challenge. *Perspectives in Psychiatric Care, 26,* 21-27.

LeGrand, C. E. (1973). Rape and rape laws: Sexism in society and law. *California Law Review, 61,* 919-941.

Lenehan, G. P. (1991). Sexual assault nurse examiners: A sane way to care for rape victims [Editorial]. *Journal of Emergency Nursing, 17,* 1-2.

Leo, J. (1987, March 23). When the date turns into rape. *Time,* p. 77.

Lerner, M. J. (1970). The desire for justice and reactions to victims. In J. Macaulay & L. Berkowitz (Eds.), *Altruism and helping behavior* (pp. 205-229). Orlando, FL: Academic Press.

Lerner, M. J., & Matthews, P. (1967). Reactions to suffering of others under conditions of indirect responsibility. *Journal of Personality and Social Psychology, 5,* 319-325.

Lerner, M. J., & Miller, D. T. (1978). Just world research and the attribution process: Looking back and ahead. *Psychological Bulletin, 85,* 1030-1051.

Lerner, M. J., & Simmons, C. (1966). Observer's reaction to the "innocent victim": Compassion or rejection? *Journal of Personality and Social Psychology, 4,* 203-210.

LeVine, R. (1959). Gusii sex offenses: A study in social control. *American Anthropologist, 61,* 965-990.

Levine-MacCombie, J., & Koss, M. P. (1986). Acquaintance rape: Effective avoidance strategies. *Psychology of Women Quarterly, 10,* 311-320.

Lewin, T. (1991, May 27). Tougher laws mean more cases are called rape. *The New York Times,* p. 9.

Linz, D., Donnerstein, E., & Penrod, S. (1984). The effects of multiple exposures to filmed violence against women. *Journal of Communications, 34,* 130-147.

Linz, D., Donnerstein, E., & Penrod, S. (1987a). The findings and recommendations of the Attorney General's Commission on Pornography: Do the psychological facts fit the political fury? *American Psychologist, 42,* 946-953.

Linz, D., Donnerstein, E., & Penrod, S. (1987b). Sexual violence in the mass media: Social psychological implications. In P. Shaver & C. Hendrick (Eds.), *Sex and gender* (pp. 135-175). Newbury Park, CA: Sage.

Linz, D., Donnerstein, E., & Penrod, S. (1988). Effects of long-term exposure to violent and sexually degrading depictions of women. *Journal of Personality and Social Psychology, 55,* 758-768.

Linz, D., Penrod, S. D., & Donnerstein, E. (1987). The Attorney General's Commission on Pornography: The gaps between "findings" and facts. *American Bar Foundation Research Journal, 1987,* 713-736.

Linz, D., Wilson, B. J., & Donnerstein, E. (1992). Sexual violence in the mass media: Legal solutions, warnings, and mitigation through education. *Journal of Social Issues, 48*(1), 145-172.

Lipton, D. N., McDonel, E. C., & McFall, R. M. (1987). Heterosocial perception in rapists. *Journal of Consulting and Clinical Psychology, 55,* 17-21.

Lisak, D., & Roth, S. (1988). Motivational factors in nonincarcerated sexually aggressive men. *Journal of Personality and Social Psychology, 55,* 17-21.

Littner, N. (1973). Psychology of the sex offender: Causes, treatment, prognosis. *Police Law Quarterly, 3,* 5-31.

Loh, W. (1980). The impact of common law and reform rape statutes on prosecutions: An empirical study. *Washington Law Review,* 552-613.

Loh, W. D. (1981). Q: What has reform of rape legislation wrought? A: Truth in criminal labeling. *Journal of Social Issues, 37*(4), 28-52.

London, R. (1991, February 8). Strategy on sex crimes in prison, then prison. *The New York Times,* p. B10.

Longino, H. E. (1980). Pornography, oppression, and freedom: A closer look. In L. Lederer (Ed.), *Take back the night: Women on pornography.* New York: William Morrow.

Lottes, I. L. (1988). Sexual socialization and attitudes toward rape. In A. W. Burgess (Ed.), *Rape and sexual assault* (Vol. 2, pp. 193-220). New York: Garland.

Lowe, C. A., Medway, F. J., & Beers, S. E. (1978). *Individual differences in causal attribution: The personal-environmental causal attribution (PECA) scale.* Paper presented at the meetings of the American Psychological Association, Toronto.

Luginbuhl, J., & Mullin, C. (1981). Rape and responsibility: How and how much is the victim blamed? *Sex Roles: A Journal of Research, 7,* 547-559.

MacKinnon, C. (1987). *Feminism unmodified.* Cambridge, MA: Harvard University Press.

Mahoney, E. R., Shively, M. D., & Traw, M. (1986). Sexual coercion and assault: Male socialization and female risk. *Sexual Coercion and Assault, 1,* 2-8.

Malamuth, N. M. (1981). Rape proclivity among males. *Journal of Social Issues, 37*(4), 138-157.

Malamuth, N. M. (1986). Predictors of naturalistic sexual aggression. *Journal of Personality and Social Psychology, 50,* 953-962.

Malamuth, N. M. (1988). Predicting laboratory aggression against female and male targets: Implications for sexual aggression. *Journal of Research in Personality, 22,* 474-495.

Malamuth, N. M. (1989). Distinguishing between the Surgeon General's personal views and the consensus reached at his workshop on pornography. *American Psychologist, 44,* 580.

Malamuth, N. M., & Briere, J. (1986). Sexual violence in the media: Indirect effects on aggression against women. *Journal of Social Issues, 42*(3), 75-92.

Malamuth, N. M., & Ceniti, J. (1986). Repeated exposure to violent and nonviolent pornography: Likelihood of raping ratings and laboratory aggression against women. *Aggressive Behavior, 12,* 129-137.

Malamuth, N. M., & Check, J. V. P. (1981). The effects of mass media exposure on acceptance of violence against women: A field experiment. *Journal of Research in Personality, 16,* 436-446.

Malamuth, N. M., & Donnerstein, E. (1982). The effects of aggressive-pornographic mass media stimuli. In L. Berkowitz (Ed.), *Advances in experimental social psychology* (Vol. 15, pp. 103-136). Orlando, FL: Academic Press.

Malamuth, N. M., Sockloskie, R., Koss, M. P., & Tanaka, J. S. (1991). Characteristics of aggressors against women: Testing a model using a national sample of college students. *Journal of Consulting and Clinical Psychology, 59* (5), 670-681.

Markush, R. E., & Favero, R. V. (1974). Epidemiologic assessment of stressful life events, depressed mood, and psychophysiological symptoms—A preliminary report. In B. S. Dohrenwend & B. P. Dohrenwend (Eds.), *Stressful life events: Their nature and effects* (pp. 171-190). New York: John Wiley.

McArthur, L. Z. (1981). What grabs you? The role of attention in impression formation and causal attribution. In E. T. Higgins, C. P. Herman, & M. P. Zanna (Eds.), *Social cognition: The Ontario Symposium* (Vol. I, pp. 201-246). Hillsdale, NJ: Lawrence Erlbaum.

McCahill, T. W., Meyer, L. C., & Fischman, A. M. (1979). *The aftermath of rape.* Lexington, MA: Lexington.

McCaul, K. D., Veltum, L. G., Boyechko, V., & Crawford, J. J. (1990). Understanding attributions of victim blame for rape: Sex, violence, and foreseeability. *Journal of Applied Social Psychology, 20,* 1-26.

McFadden, R. D., Blumenthal, R., Farber, M. A., Shipp, E. R., Strum, C., & Wolff, C. (1990). *Outrage: The story behind the Tawana Brawley hoax.* New York: Bantam.

McIntyre, J. (1980). *Victim response to rape: Alternative outcomes* (Final report of Grant MH 29045). Rockville, MD: National Institute of Mental Health.

McKenzie-Mohr, D., & Zanna, M. P. (1990). Treating women as sexual objects: Look to the (gender schematic) male who has viewed pornography. *Personality and Social Psychology Bulletin, 16,* 296-308.

McNamara, D., & Sagarin, E. (1977). *Sex, crime, and the law.* New York: Free Press.

Mead, M. (1935). *Sex and temperament in three primitive societies.* New York: Dell.

Medea, A., & Thompson, K. (1974). *Against rape.* New York: Farrar, Straus, & Giroux.

Mehrabian, A., & Williams, M. (1969). Nonverbal concomitants of perceived and intended persuasiveness. *Journal of Personality and Social Psychology, 13,* 37-58.

Melani, L., & Fodaski, L. (1974). The psychology of the rapist and his victim. In New York Radical Feminists (Eds.), *Rape: The first sourcebook for women* (pp. 82-93). New York: New American Library.

Mellen, S. L. (1981). *The evolution of love.* San Francisco: Freeman.

Meyer, C., & Taylor, S. (1986). Adjustment to rape. *Journal of Personality and Social Psychology, 50,* 1226-1234.

Miller, D. T., & McFarland, C. (1986). Counterfactual thinking and victim compensation: A test of norm theory. *Personality and Social Psychology Bulletin, 12,* 513-519.

Miller, D. T., & Ross, M. (1975). Self-serving biases in attribution of causality: Fact or fiction? *Psychological Bulletin, 82,* 213-225.

Miller, F. D., Smith, E. R., Ferree, M. M., & Taylor, S. E. (1976). Predicting perceptions of victimization. *Journal of Applied Social Psychology, 6,* 352-359.

Miller, J., Moeller, D., Kaufman, A., Divasto, P., Pathak, D., & Christy, J. (1978). Recidivism among sex assault victims. *American Journal of Psychiatry, 135,* 1103-1104.

Morelli, P. H. (1981, March). *Comparison of the psychological recovery of black and white victims of rape.* Paper presented at the meetings of the Association of Women in Psychology, Boston.

Morgan, M. (1986). Conflict and confusion: What rape prevention reports are telling women. *Sexual Coercion and Assault, 1,* 160-168.

Mosher, D. L., & Anderson, R. D. (1986). Macho personality, sexual aggression, and reactions to guided imagery of realistic rape. *Journal of Research in Personality, 20,* 77-94.

Mosher, D. L., & Sirkin, M. (1984). Measuring a macho personality constellation. *Journal of Research on Personality, 20,* 77-94.

Moss v. State, 208 Miss. 531, 536, 45 So. 2d 125, 126 (1950).

Muehlenhard, C. L. (1987, October). Date rape: The familiar perpetrator. In *Our sexuality newsletter,* supplement to R. Crooks & K. Baur, *Our sexuality* (3rd ed.). Menlo Park, CA: Benjamin/Cummings.

Muehlenhard, C. L. (1988). Misinterpreted dating behaviors and the risk of date rape. *Journal of Social and Clinical Psychology, 6,* 20-37.

Muehlenhard, C. L., & Cook, S. W. (1988). Men's self-reports of unwanted sexual activity. *Journal of Sex Research, 24,* 58-72.

Muehlenhard, C. L., & Felts, A. S. (1987). [An analysis of causal factors for men's attitudes about the justifiability of date rape.] Unpublished raw data.

Muehlenhard, C. L., Friedman, D. E., & Thomas, C. M. (1985). Is date rape justifiable: The effects of dating activity, who initiated, who paid, and men's attitudes towards women. *Psychology of Women Quarterly, 9,* 297-310.

Muehlenhard, C. L., & Hollabaugh, L. C. (1988). Do women sometimes say no when they mean yes? The prevalence and correlates of women's token resistance to sex. *Journal of Personality and Social Psychology, 54,* 872-879.

Muehlenhard, C. L., & Linton, M. A. (1987). Date rape and sexual aggression in dating situations: Incidence and risk factors. *Journal of Counseling and Psychology, 34,* 186-196.

Muehlenhard, C. L., & Schrag, J. L. (1991). Nonviolent sexual coercion. In A. Parrot & L. Bechhofer (Eds.), *Acquaintance rape: The hidden crime* (pp. 115-128). New York: John Wiley.

Mulvehill, D., Tumin, M., & Curtis, L. (1969). *Crimes of violence* (Vols. 11-13) (Staff report submitted to the National Commission on The Causes and Prevention of Violence). Washington, DC: Government Printing Office.

Murphy, J. E. (1987). *Prevalence of child sexual abuse and consequent experience of date rape and marital rape in the general population.* Paper presented at the meetings of the National Council on Family Relations, Atlanta, GA.

Murphy, W. D., Coleman, E. M, & Haynes, M. R. (1986). Factors related to coercive sexual behavior in a nonclinical sample of males. *Victims and Violence, 1*(4), 255-278.

Myers, M. F. (1989). Men sexually assaulted as adults and sexually abused as boys. *Archives of Sexual Behavior, 18,* 103-215.

Myers, M. P., Templer, D. L., & Brown, R. (1984). Coping ability of women who become rape victims. *Journal of Consulting and Clinical Psychology, 52,* 73-78.

New York State Club Association, Inc. v. City of New York, 108 S. Ct. 2225 (1988).

Nietzel, M. T. (1979). *Crime and its modification: A social learning perspective.* Elmsford, NY: Pergamon.

Nisbett, R. E., & Ross, L. (1980). *Human inference: Strategies and shortcomings of social judgment.* Englewood Cliffs, NJ: Prentice-Hall.

Nobile, P. (1989, July). The making of a monster. *Playboy,* pp. 41-45.

Nordheimer, J. (1989, January 25). Bundy is put to death in Florida, closing murder cases across U.S. *The New York Times,* pp. 1, 11.

Norris, J. (1989, August). *Acquaintance rape: Effects of victim's and assailant's alcohol consumption.* Paper presented at the meetings of the American Psychological Association, New Orleans.

Note. (1952). Forcible and statutory rape: An exploration of the operation and objectives of the current standard. *Yale Law Journal, 62,* 55-73.

Note. (1966). The resistance standard in rape legislation. *Stanford Law Review, 18,* 682.

Note. (1967). Corroborating charges of rape. *Columbia Law Review, 67,* 1137-1138.

Notman, M., & Nadelson, C. (1976). The rape victim: Psychodynamic considerations. *American Journal of Psychiatry, 133,* 408-413.

Olsen, J. (1989). *"Doc": The rape of the town of Lovell.* New York: Atheneum.

Olsen-Fulero, L., Fulero, S. M., & Wulff, K. (1989, August). *Who did what to whom? Modeling rape jurors' cognitive processes.* Paper presented at the meetings of the American Psychological Association, New Orleans.

O'Reilly, J. (1983, September 5). Wife beating: The silent crime. *Time,* pp. 23-26.

Owen, S. (1989). *Understanding men who rape.* Unpublished manuscript, University of Kansas.

Page, S. (1989). Misrepresentation of pornography research: Psychology's role. *American Psychologist, 44,* 578-580.

Pagel, M. D., Becker, J., & Coppel, D. B. (1985). Loss of control, self-blame, and depression: An investigation of spouse caregivers of Alzheimer's disease patients. *Journal of Abnormal Psychology, 94,* 169-182.

Parrot, A. (1991a). Institutional response: How can acquaintance rape be prevented? In A. Parrot & L. Bechhofer (Eds.), *Acquaintance rape: The hidden crime* (pp. 355-367). New York: John Wiley.

Parrot, A. (1991b). Recommendations for college policies and procedures to deal with acquaintance rape. In A. Parrot & L. Bechhofer (Eds.), *Acquaintance rape: The hidden crime* (pp. 368-380). New York: John Wiley.

Parrot, A., & Bechhofer, L. (Eds.). (1991). *Acquaintance rape: The hidden crime.* New York: John Wiley.

Paulsen, K. (1979). Attribution of fault to a rape victim as a function of locus of control. *Journal of Social Psychology, 107,* 131-132.

Paykel, E. S. (1974). Life stress and psychiatric disorder: Applications of the clinical approach. In B. S. Dohrenwend & B. P. Dohrenwend (Eds.), *Stressful life events: Their nature and effects* (pp. 135-149). New York: John Wiley.

Pederson, R. (1989, June 2). "Extraordinary" rape stories are becoming commonplace. *Kansas City Star,* p. A-16.

Pennington, N., & Hastie, R. (1986). Evidence evaluation in complex decision making. *Journal of Personality and Social Psychology, 51,* 242-258.

Pennington, N., & Hastie, R. (1988). Explanation-based decision making: Effects of memory structure on judgment. *Journal of Experimental Psychology: Learning, Memory, and Cognition, 14,* 521-533.

People v. Dohring, 59 N.Y. 374 (1874).

People v. Harris, 238 P. 2d. 158, 160, 161, Cal. Dist. Ct. App. (1951).

People v. Liberta, 64 N.Y. 2d 152, 474 N.E. 2d 567 (1984).

People v. Vaughan, 255 N.W. 2d 677, Mich. App. (1977).

Peplau, L. A., & Campbell, S. M. (1989). The balance of power in dating and marriage. In J. Freeman (Ed.), *Women: A feminist perspective* (pp. 121-137). Mountain View, CA: Mayfield.

Peplau, L. A., Rubin, Z., & Hill, C. T. (1977). Sexual intimacy in dating relationships. *Journal of Social Issues, 33*(2), 86-109.

Perez v. State, 94 S.W. 1036, Texas Crim. App. (1906).

Pesce, C., & Blais, J. (1992, April 23). Rape called "enormous" problem. *USA Today,* p. 3A.

Phares, E. J., & Wilson, K. G. (1972). Responsibility attributions: Role of outcome severity, situational ambiguity, and internal-external control. *Journal of Personality, 40,* 392-406.

Pithers, W. D., Marques, J. K., Gibat, C. C., & Marlatt, G. A. (1983). Relapse prevention with sexual aggressives: A self-control model of treatment and maintenance of change. In J. G. Greer & I. R. Stuart (Eds.), *The sexual aggressor: Current perspectives on treatment* (pp. 214-239). New York: Van Nostrand Reinhold.

Polk, K. (1985). Rape reform and criminal justice processing. *Crime and Delinquency, 31,* 191-205.

Pugh, M. D. (1983). Contributory fault and rape convictions: Loglinear models for blaming the victim. *Social Psychology Quarterly, 46,* 233-242.

Queens Bench Foundation. (1975). *Rape victimization study: Final report.* San Francisco: Author.

Quinsey, V. L. (1984). Sexual aggression: Studies of offenders against women. In D. Weisstub (Ed.), *Law and mental health: International perspectives* (Vol 1, pp. 84-121). Elmsford, NY: Pergamon.

Rada, T. (1975). Alcohol and rape. *Medical Aspects of Human Sexuality, 9,* 48-65.

Rapaport, K., & Burkhart, B. R. (1984). Personality and attitudinal characteristics of sexually coercive college males. *Journal of Abnormal Psychology, 93,* 216-221.

Regina v. Clarence, 22 Q.B.D. 23 (1888).

Reiss, I. L. (1986). *Journey into sexuality: An explanatory voyage.* Englewood Cliffs, NJ: Prentice-Hall.

Reynolds v. State, 27 Neb. 90, 91, 42, N.W. 903, 904 (1889).

Richardson, D., & Campbell, J. L. (1982). Alcohol and rape: The effect of alcohol on attributions of blame for rape. *Personality and Social Psychology Bulletin, 8,* 468-476.

Robbins, G. E. (1975). Dogmatism and information gathering in personality impression formation. *Journal of Research in Personality, 9,* 74-84.

Rogers, L. C. (1984). *Sexual victimization: Social and psychological effects in college women.* Unpublished doctoral dissertation, Auburn University.

Rokeach, M. (1960). *The open and closed mind.* New York: Basic Books.

Rose, D. (1986). "Worse than death": Psychodynamics of rape victims and the need for psychotherapy. *American Journal of Psychiatry, 143,* 817-824.

Rose, S., & Frieze, I. H. (1985, March). *The first date script.* Unpublished paper presented at the Feminist Psychology Research Conference, New York City.

Rosenthal, R., Hall, J. A., Di Matteo, M. R., Rogers, P. L., & Archer, D. (1979). *Sensitivity to nonverbal communication.* Baltimore, MD: Johns Hopkins University Press.

Ross, J. (1983). The overlooked expert in rape prosecutions. *Toledo Law Review, 14,* 707-734.

Ross, M., & Fletcher, G. J. O. (1985). Attribution and social perception. In G. Lindzey & E. Aronson (Eds.), *The handbook of social psychology* (3rd ed., Vol. 2, pp. 73-122). New York: Random House.

Rossi, P., Waite, E., Bose, C., & Berk, R. (1974). The seriousness of crimes: Normative structures and individual differences. *American Sociological Review, 39,* 224-237.

Rotter, J. B. (1966). Generalized expectancies for internal versus external control of reinforcement. *Psychological Monographs, 80*(1, Whole No. 609).

Rowland, J. (1985). *The ultimate violation.* Garden City, NY: Doubleday.

Rozée, P. D., Bateman, P., & Gilmore, T. (1991). The personal perspective of acquaintance rape prevention: A three-tier approach. In A. Parrot & L. Bechhofer (Eds.), *Acquaintance rape: The hidden crime* (pp. 337-354). New York: John Wiley.

Rubin, Z., & Peplau, L. A. (1975). Who believes in a just world? *Journal of Social Issues, 31*(3), 65-90.

Ruch, L. O., & Chandler, S. M. (1983). Sexual assault trauma during the acute phase: An exploratory model and multivariate analysis. *Journal of Health and Social Behavior, 24,* 174-185.

Ruch, L. O., Chandler, S. M., & Harter, R. A. (1980). Life change and rape impact. *Journal of Health and Social Behavior, 21,* 248-260.

Russell, D. E. H. (1975). *The politics of rape: The victim's perspective.* New York: Stein & Day.

Russell, D. E. H. (1984). *Sexual exploitation: Rape, child sexual abuse, and workplace harassment.* Beverly Hills, CA: Sage.

Russell, D. E. H. (1986). *The secret trauma: Incest in the lives of girls and women.* New York: Basic Books.

Russell, D. E. H. (1988). Pornography and rape: A causal model. *Political Psychology, 9,* 41-73.

Russell, D. E. H. (1990). *Rape in marriage* (rev. ed.). Bloomington: Indiana University Press.

Russell, D. E. H. (1991). Wife rape. In A. Parrot & L. Bechhofer (Eds.), *Acquaintance rape: The hidden crime* (pp. 129-139). New York: John Wiley.

Sack, K. (1991, July 31). New York limits trial talk on sex. *The New York Times,* p. A9.

Sanday, P. R. (1990). *Fraternity gang rape: Sex, brotherhood, and privilege on campus.* New York: New York University Press.

Sanday, P. R. (1981). The socio-cultural context of rape: A cross-cultural study. *Journal of Social Issues, 37*(4), 5-27.

Sanders, W. B. (1980). *Rape and woman's identity.* Beverly Hills, CA: Sage.

Schafran, L. H. (1991, February 14). Violence against women. *The New York Times Book Review,* p. 37.

Scheppele, K. L., & Bart, P. B. (1983). Through women's eyes: Defining dangers in the wake of sexual assault. *Journal of Social Issues, 39*(2), 63-81.

Scher, D. (1984). Sex-role contradictions: Self-perceptions and ideal perceptions. *Sex Roles: A Journal of Research, 10,* 651-656.

Schultz, L. (1984, October 2). Supreme Court upholds rape law; ruling praised. *Lawrence Journal-World,* p. 1.

Schwendinger, J. R., & Schwendinger, H. (1983). *Rape and inequality.* Beverly Hills, CA: Sage.

Scroggs, J. R. (1976). Penalties for rape as a function of victim provocativeness, damage, and resistance. *Crime and Social Justice, 1,* 18-26.

Scully, D. (1990). *Understanding sexual violence: A study of convicted rapists.* Boston: Unwin Hyman.

Scully, D., & Marolla, J. (1984a). Convicted rapists' vocabulary of motive: Excuses and justifications. *Social Problems, 31,* 530-544.

Scully, D., & Marolla, J. (1984b). Rape and psychiatric vocabularies of motive: Alternative perspectives. In A. W. Burgess (Ed.), *Rape and sexual assault: A research handbook.* New York: Garland.

Seligman, C., Brickman, J., & Koulack, D. (1977). Rape and physical attractiveness: Assigning responsibility to victims. *Journal of Personality, 45,* 554-563.

Seligmann, J. (1984, April 9). The date who rapes. *Newsweek,* pp. 91-92.

Selkin, J. (1978). Protecting personal space: Victim and resister reactions to assaultive rape. *Journal of Community Psychology, 6,* 263-268.

Shaver, K. G. (1970). Defensive attribution: Effects of severity and relevance on the responsibility assigned for an accident. *Journal of Personality and Social Psychology, 14,* 101-113.

Shaver, K. G. (1975). *An introduction to attribution processes.* Cambridge, MA: Winthrop.

Shaver, K. G. (1985). *The attribution of blame: Causality, responsibility, and blameworthiness.* New York: Springer.

Shaver, K. G. (1989). *Attribution of blameworthiness: A rational standard for the evaluation of victims.* Paper presented at the First International Conference on "Crisis and Loss in the Adult Years," University of Trier, Federal Republic of Germany.

Shaver, K. G., & Drown, D. G. (1986). On causality, responsibility, and self-blame: A theoretical note. *Journal of Personality and Social Psychology, 50,* 697-702.

Shore, B. (1980). *An examination of critical process and outcome factors in rape* (Final report). National Institute for Mental Health Grant #171-14-8194.

Shotland, R. L. (1989). A model of the causes of date rape in developing and close relationships. In C. Hendrick (Ed.), *Close relationships* (pp. 247-270). Newbury Park, CA: Sage.

Shotland, R. L., & Goodstein, L. (1983). Just because she doesn't want to doesn't mean it's rape: An experimentally-based causal model of perception of rape in a dating situation. *Social Psychology Quarterly, 46,* 220-232.

Shotland, R. L., & Strau, M. (1976). Bystander response to an assault: When a man attacks a woman. *Journal of Personality and Social Psychology, 34,* 990-999.

Shultz, T. R., & Schleifer, M. (1983). Towards a refinement of attribution concepts. In J. Jaspars, F. D. Fincham, & M. Hewstone (Eds.), *Attribution theory and research: Conceptual, developmental and social dimensions* (pp. 37-62). Orlando, FL: Academic Press.

Sigall, H., & Ostrove, N. (1975). Beautiful but dangerous: Effects of offender attractiveness and nature of the crime on juridic judgment. *Journal of Personality and Social Psychology, 31,* 410-414.

Skelton, C. A. (1982). *Situational and personological correlates of sexual victimization in college women.* Unpublished doctoral dissertation, Auburn University.

Skogan, W. G., & Maxfield, M. G. (1981). *Coping with crime.* Beverly Hills, CA: Sage.

Slade, J. (1984). Violence in the hard-core pornography film: An historical survey. *Journal of Communications, 34,* 148-156.

Slind-Flor, V. (1990, September 17). Prosecutor gets to see other side. *National Law Journal,* p. 8.

Smeal, E. (1991, April 15). Violence and women. *USA Today,* p. 13A.

Smith, R. E., Keating, J. P., Hester, R. K., & Mitchell, H. E. (1976). Role and justice considerations in the attribution of responsibility to a rape victim. *Journal of Research in Personality, 10,* 346-357.

Snider, A. (1990, May 5). Rapists in Kansas City rarely get punishment they deserve. *Kansas City Star,* p. A-1.

Snyder, C. R. (1978). The "illusion" of uniqueness. *Journal of Humanistic Psychology, 18,* 33-41.

Sorenson, S. B., Stein, J. A., Siegel, J. M., Golding, J. M., & Burnam, M. A. (1987). The prevalence of adult sexual assault: The Los Angeles Epidemiologic Catchment Area Project. *American Journal of Epidemiology, 126,* 1154-1164.

Sosis, R. H. (1974). Internal-external control and the perception of responsibility of another for an accident. *Journal of Personality and Social Psychology, 30,* 393-399.

Sperling, D. (1985, March 1). Trauma of rape continues without therapy. *USA Today,* p. 13A.

Standish, F. (1984, January 31). Child abuser sentenced to treatment. *Lawrence Journal-World,* p. 8.

Stanko, E. A. (1988). Fear of crime and the myth of the safe home. In K. Yllö & M. Bograd (Eds.), *Feminist perspectives on wife abuse* (pp. 75-88). Newbury Park, CA: Sage.

State v. Saldana, Minn. 234 N.W. 2d 227 (1982).

State v. Wood, 59 Ariz. 48, 122 P. 2d 416 (1942).

Stead, D. (1990, December 28). In Britain, a move to make marital rape a crime. *The New York Times,* p. B9.

Stecich, M. (1977). Note: The marital rape exemption. *New York University Law Review, 52,* 306-323.

Stewart, A. J. (1982). The course of individual adaptation to life changes. *Journal of Personality and Social Psychology, 42,* 1110-1113.

Stokols, D., & Schopler, J. (1973). Reactions to victims under conditions of situational detachment: The effects of responsibility, severity, and expected future interaction. *Journal of Personality and Social Psychology, 25,* 199-209.

Storaska, F. (1975). *How to say no to a rapist and survive*. New York: Random House.

Struckman-Johnson, C. (1991). Male victims of acquaintance rape. In A. Parrot & L. Bechhofer (Eds.), *Acquaintance rape: The hidden crime* (pp. 192-213). New York: John Wiley.

Sullivan, J. P., & Mosher, D. L. (1990). Acceptance of guided imagery of marital rape as a function of macho personality. *Violence and Victims, 5*(4), 275-286.

Sussman, L., & Bordwell, S. (1981). *The rapist file*. New York: Chelsea House.

Sutherland, S., & Scherl, D. J. (1970). Patterns of response among victims of rape. *American Journal of Orthopsychiatry, 40*, 503-511.

Symons, D. (1979). *The evolution of human sexuality*. Oxford, UK: Oxford University Press.

Symonds, M. (1980). The second injury. *Evaluation and change* (In Services to Survivors [Special Issue]). Minneapolis: Minnesota Medical Research Foundation.

Taibbi, M., & Sims-Phillips, A. (1989). *Unholy alliances: Working the Tawana Brawley Story*. San Diego: Harcourt Brace Jovanovich.

Tavris, C., & Wade, C. (1985). *The longest war: Sex differences in perspective*. San Diego, CA: Harcourt Brace Jovanovich.

Taylor, G. (1990, September 17). Jury views videotaped sex attack. *National Law Journal*, p. 22.

Taylor, S., & Brown, J. D. (1988). Illusion and well-being: A social psychological perspective on mental health. *Psychological Bulletin, 103*, 193-210.

Taylor, S. E., & Fiske, S. T. (1975). Point-of-view and perceptions of causality. *Journal of Personality and Social Psychology, 32*, 439-445.

Taylor, S. E., & Fiske, S. T. (1978). Salience, attention, and attribution: Top of the head phenomena. In L. Berkowitz (Ed.), *Advances in experimental social psychology* (Vol. 2, pp. 249-288). Orlando, FL: Academic Press.

Taylor, S. E., Lichtman, R. R., & Wood, J. V. (1984). Attributions, beliefs about control, and adjustment to breast cancer. *Journal of Personality and Social Psychology, 46*, 489-502.

Tetreault, P. A., & Barnett, M. A. (1987). Reactions to stranger and acquaintance rape. *Psychology of Women Quarterly, 11*, 353-358.

Thompson, J. (1984, February 2). Case thrusts Wichita into national debate over drug for rapists. *Kansas City Times*, pp. A1, A14.

Thornhill, R., Thornhill, N., & Dizinno, G. A. (1986). The biology of rape. In S. Tomaselli & R. Porter (Eds.), *Rape* (pp. 102-121). New York: Basil Blackwell.

Thornton, B. (1977). Effect of rape victim's attractiveness in a jury simulation. *Personality and Social Psychology Bulletin, 3*, 666-669.

Thornton, B. (1984). Defensive attribution of responsibility: Evidence for an arousal-based motivational bias. *Journal of Personality and Social Psychology, 46*, 721-734.

Thornton, B., Robbins, M. A., & Johnson, J. A. (1981). Social perception of the rape victim's culpability: The influence of respondents' personal-environmental causal attribution tendencies. *Human Relations, 34*, 225-237.

Thornton, B., & Ryckman, R. M. (1983). The influence of a rape victim's physical attractiveness on observer's attributions of responsibility. *Human Relations, 36*, 549-562.

Thornton, B., Ryckman, R. M., & Robbins, M. A. (1982). The relationships of observer characteristics to beliefs in the causal responsibility of victims of sexual assault. *Human Relations, 35,* 321-330.

Tong, R. (1984). *Women, sex, and the law.* Totowa, NJ: Rowman & Allanheld.

Turkington, C. (1987a, March). New focus on preventing relapse. *APA Monitor,* p. 15.

Turkington, C. (1987b, March). Sexual aggression "widespread." *APA Monitor,* p. 15.

U.S. Department of Justice, Bureau of Justice Statistics. (1988). *Sourcebook of criminal justice statistics—1987.* Washington, DC: Government Printing Office.

Veronen, L. J., Kilpatrick, D. G., & Resick, P. A. (1979). Treatment of fear and anxiety in rape victims: Implications for the criminal justice system. In W. H. Parsonage (Ed.), *Perspectives on victimology* (pp. 148-159). Beverly Hills, CA: Sage.

Vidmar, N., & Crinklaw, L. D. (1974). Attributing responsibility for an accident: A methodological and conceptual critique. *Canadian Journal of Behavioral Science, 6,* 112-130.

Villemur, N. K., & Hyde, J. S. (1983). Effects of sex of defense attorney, sex of juror, and age and attractiveness of the victim on mock juror decision making. *Sex Roles, 9,* 879-889.

Waggett, G. J. (1989, May 27). Let's stop turning rapists into heroes. *TV Guide,* pp. 10-11.

Warner, C. G. (1980). *Rape and sexual assault: Management and intervention.* Germantown, MD: Aspen.

Warshaw, R. (1988). *I never called it rape.* New York: Harper & Row.

Warshaw, R., & Parrot, A. (1991). The contribution of sex-role socialization to acquaintance rape. In A. Parrot & L. Bechhofer (Eds.), *Acquaintance rape: The hidden crime* (pp. 73-82). New York: John Wiley.

Waterman, C. K., Dawson, J. L., & Bologna, M. J. (1989). Sexual coercion in gay male and lesbian relationships: Predictors and implications for support services. *Journal of Sex Research, 26,* 118-124.

Weigel, R. H., Vernon, D. T. A., & Tognacci, L. N. (1974). The specificity of the attitude as a determinant of attitude-behavior congruence. *Journal of Personality and Social Psychology, 30,* 724-728.

Weinstein, N. D. (1980). Unrealistic optimism about future life events. *Journal of Personality and Social Psychology, 39,* 73-79.

Weir, J. A. (1991). *The effects of focus of attention, legal procedures, and individual differences on judgments in a rape case.* Unpublished doctoral dissertation, University of Kansas.

Weir, J. A., & Wrightsman, L. S. (1990). The determinants of mock jurors' verdicts in a rape case. *Journal of Applied Social Psychology, 20,* 901-919.

Weis, K., & Borges, S. S. (1973). Victimology and rape: The case of the legitimate victim. *Issues in Criminology, 8,* 71-115.

Wells, G. L. (1980). Asymmetric attributes for compliance: Reward vs. punishment. *Journal of Experimental Social Psychology, 16,* 47-60.

Wells, G. L., & Murray, D. M. (1984). Eyewitness confidence. In G. L. Wells & E. F. Loftus (Eds.), *Eyewitness testimony: Psychological perspectives* (pp. 155-170). New York: Cambridge University Press.

White, J. W., & Farmer, R. (1992). Research methods: How they shape views of sexual violence. *Journal of Social Issues, 48*(1), 45-60.

White, J. W., & Sorenson, S. B. (1992). A sociocultural view of sexual assault: From discrepancy to diversity. *Journal of Social Issues, 48*(1), 187-195.

Wiener, R. L., Feldman-Wiener, A. T., & Grisso, T. (1989). Empathy and biased assimilation of testimonies in cases of alleged rape. *Law and Human Behavior, 13,* 343-355.

Wiener, R. L., & Rinehart, N. (1986). Psychological causality in the attribution of responsibility for rape. *Sex Roles: A Journal of Research, 14,* 369-382.

Wiener, R. L., & Vodanovich, S. J. (1986). The evaluation of culpability in rape situations: A model of legal decision making. *Journal of Psychology, 120,* 489-500.

Wilcox, B. (1987). Pornography, social science, and politics: When research and ideology collide. *American Psychologist, 42,* 941-943.

Will, G. (1989, May 1). What the boys did in Central Park was evil, pure and simple. *Kansas City Times,* p. A11.

Williams, C. C., & Williams, R. A. (1977). Rape: A plea for help in the hospital emergency room. In D. R. Nass (Ed.), *The rape victim* (pp. 92-99). Dubuque, IA: Kendall-Hunt.

Williams, J. E. (1984). Secondary victimization: Confronting public attitudes about rape. *Victimology: An International Journal, 9,* 66-81.

Williams, J. E., & Holmes, K. A. (1981). *The second assault: Rape and public attitudes.* Westport, CT: Greenwood.

Willis, C. E. (1991). *Sex and question order effects on rape culpability attributions.* Unpublished paper, Kansas State University.

Willis, C. E., & Wrightsman, L. S. (1990). *The influence of relationship intimacy and victim eye contact patterns on rape responsibility attributions.* Unpublished manuscript, Kansas State University.

Wilson, J. Q., & Herrnstein, R. (1985). *Crime and human nature.* New York: Simon & Schuster.

Wirtz, P. W., & Harrell, A. V. (1986, August). *Rape, fear, and threatening life events.* Paper presented at the meetings of the American Psychological Association, Washington, DC.

Wohlers, A. J. (1982, August). *Blaming the victim: A sex-specific or more general phenomenon?* Paper presented at the meetings of the American Psychological Association, Washington, DC.

Wyatt, G. E., Notgrass, C. M., & Newcomb, M. (1990). Internal and external mediators of women's rape experiences. *Psychology of Women Quarterly, 14,* 153-176.

Wyatt, M., & Gold, S. (1978). The rape system: Old roles and new times. *Catholic University Law Review,* pp. 696-700.

Wyer, R. S., Jr., Bodenhausen, G. V., & Gorman, T. F. (1985). Cognitive mediators of reactions to rape. *Journal of Personality and Social Psychology, 48,* 324-338.

Zuckerman, M. (1979). Attribution of success and failure revisited, or: The motivational bias is alive and well in attribution theory. *Journal of Personality, 47,* 245-287.

Zuckerman, M., Gerbasi, K. C., Kravitz, R. I., & Wheeler, L. (1975). The belief in a just world and reactions to innocent victims. *JSAS Catalog of Selected Documents in Psychology, 5.*

Name Index

Subject Index

About the Authors

Julie A. Allison (Ph.D., University of Kansas, 1991) is Assistant Professor at Pittsburg State University, Pittsburg, KS. She has been involved in research in the area of rape and sexual aggression for the past 6 years, and has published papers on legal decisions in rape cases, as well as on judgments about rape victims. Her interests also include gender and psychology-and-law issues. She teaches courses in social psychology and offers workshops on various gender issues, including violence against women.

Lawrence S. Wrightsman (Ph.D., University of Minnesota, 1959) is Professor of Psychology at the University of Kansas, Lawrence. He has been doing research on legal processes for 15 years, and is director of the Kansas Jury Project. He is author or editor of six books relevant to the legal system, including *The Child Witness* (1991), *Psychology and the Legal System* (1991), *The American Jury on Trial* (1988), *In the Jury Box* (1987), *On the Witness Stand* (1987), and *The Psychology of Evidence and Trial Procedure* (1985). He has testified as an expert witness on the issue of the accuracy of eyewitness identification, and he has assisted defense attorneys in jury selection in various types of trials ranging from criminal murder cases to civil malpractice suits. He is a former President of the Society for the Psychological Study of Social Issues and of the Society of Personality and Social Psychology.

Lightning Source UK Ltd.
Milton Keynes UK
UKOW01f2039200917
309582UK00001B/145/P